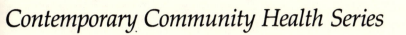

Contemporary Community Health Series

Instructional Counseling

Instructional Counseling

A Method for Counselors

Jack Martin and Bryan A. Hiebert

University of Pittsburgh Press

Published by the University of Pittsburgh Press,
Pittsburgh, Pa., 15260

Copyright © 1985, University of Pittsburgh Press

Feffer and Simons, Inc., London

Manufactured in the United States of America

Library of Congress Cataloging in Publication Data

Martin, Jack, 1950–
   Instructional counseling.

   (Contemporary community health series)
   Bibliography: p.
   Includes Index.
   1. Counseling.   I. Hiebert, Bryan A.   II. Title.
III. Series.
BF637.C6M365   1985   158'.3   84-19647
ISBN 0-8229-3506-6
ISBN 0-8229-5367-6 (pbk.)

Contents

Preface

TRADITIONAL THEORIES of counseling practice gradually are giving way to approaches that integrate existing knowledge and methods from a wide variety of social science and educational disciplines. Counseling in the eighties is in search of a comprehensive conceptual model under which to subsume and organize its diverse principles, practices, and evolving directions. Such a conceptualization must be able to (1) make sense of the limited amount of well-established, clinically relevant knowledge that currently exists in the field, (2) provide a basis for informed decision making and action by counseling practitioners, and (3) illuminate future areas in which empirical and theoretical work is likely to be productive and fruitful.

In the past, models of counseling have been cast within predominantly medical, sociological, psychological, or broad humanistic frames of reference. Developments in counseling practice typically have been tailored so as to respect classic divisions within these frames of reference. Such forced tailoring has had little positive impact upon the development of specific counseling practices per se. For example, counselors adopting methods associated with behavorial psychology often have described their undertakings more in order to preserve desired lines of demarcation between behavioral psychology and other "less-desirable" forms of psychological theory than to promote clear, direct descriptions of the methods themselves. Rogerian counselors similarly have provided descriptions and accounts of their practices that have been, perhaps inadvertently, edited in order to preserve the appearance of proper "connectedness" with nondirective, client-centered theory. The history of counseling is replete with instances in which concern with theoretical perspectives and arguments borrowed or assumed from larger disciplines has overridden straightforward, descriptive accounts of what counselors do and why they do it. The result of this exercise has been an increasing split between counseling practices and supportive theories. Numerous recent studies have demonstrated unequivocally that the actions of counselors bear little if any relationship to the theories they endorse and that attempts to rationalize practice in terms of theory are increasingly forced and artificial.

Instructional Counseling: A Method for Counselors describes a comprehensive, conceptual framework for counseling within which it is possible to relate specific counseling practices to a general model of instruction in a direct, nondogmatic manner. The instructional model adopted aligns counseling more with educational than with psychological theory. It functions as a subsumptive framework that allows counselors to articulate and to operationalize clearly what they do and why they do it. While most contemporary approaches to counseling can be conceptualized using the instructional methods and principles described in this book, the instructional framework adopted is most compatible with approaches to counseling that view the client's work in counseling as learning—learning different behaviors, cognitions, emotional reactions, attitudes, and perceptions.

The instructional model and the assumptions underlying it are described and discussed in the first chapter of the book. Chapter 2 shows how the specific instructional actions of a counselor can be determined and employed in relation to basic requirements for desired client learning. Chapters 3 through 6 illustrate specific instructional counseling strategies that can be employed to assist client learning in the areas of problem solving/decision making, skill acquisition, personal coping, and self-management. Chapter 7 explains how the instructional framework can be used to assist counselors in the development and use of flexible but rigorous eclectic strategies matched to individual clients, their situations, and their concerns. Chapter 8 is devoted to the evaluation of instructional counseling programs, and chapter 9 discusses counselor training, ethics, and professional issues as these are articulated within the instructional counseling framework. While it is possible to use the book in other ways, it is best read from beginning to end in the order in which it is presented. This ensures that important concepts and principles will be acquired as they are needed to comprehend the unfolding narrative. However, at the risk of some slight conceptual confusion, it is possible (assuming that the first two chapters are read first) for readers to skip ahead to a chapter that deals with an area of counseling content that is currently of particular interest to them. For example, a counselor searching for information about client self-management may read chapters 1 and 2 and then skip ahead to chapter 6 before reading the intervening chapters.

Instructional Counseling is intended to provide counselors and counselor-educators with a conceptual framework within which it is possible to relate counseling practice to relevant theory in a direct manner. By combining this advantage with a very specific account of a wide variety of instructional skills and strategies that can be used by counselors to promote desired client learning, the authors aim at equipping counselors with a concrete basis for effective and purposeful decision making and action in their work with clients. The instructional framework developed in the book views the client in counseling as a learner of new attitudes, perceptions, thoughts, behaviors, and feelings. It therefore should be of particular interest to counselors working with clients whose capacities to learn are not impaired in major ways by extreme pathologies or physical handicaps. The text is concerned with counseling, not with clinical psychology or psychiatry.

The intended primary use of the book is as a textbook for senior undergraduate and graduate students studying counseling theories and methods or acquiring counseling skills and strategies at the university/college level. However, the book also should be of particular interest and use to counselors working in educational, social service, vocational, pastoral, and business (personnel management) contexts.

Instructional Counseling

CHAPTER ONE

Counseling as Instruction

THE MAIN THEME of this book is that counseling is basically an instructional process. The role of the client in counseling is to learn the kinds of skills, attitudes, behaviors, cognitions, emotional responses, and perceptions that will facilitate the kind of change the client desires. The basic task of the counselor is to assist the client to learn. In this sense, the role of the counselor is one of instructor. It is this observation that gives rise to instructional counseling. In this chapter, a basic foundation for viewing counseling as instruction is presented. The rationale underlying instructional counseling is elaborated and an instructional model for counseling is described. Thus, chapter 1 provides a basic orientation to instructional counseling and gives a theoretical framework from which to view counseling as a process whose purpose is to produce client learning.

Rationale for Instructional Counseling

Few counselors would argue with the dictum that the purpose of counseling is to promote client change. Various theoretical orientations place more or less relative emphasis on the various modalities across which change occurs (e.g., phenomenologists emphasize perceptual change and changes to self-structures, behaviorists emphasize overt and covert behavior change, cognitivists emphasize changes in cognitive structure or patterns of self-dialogue, and so on) and pose different explanations in support of such changes. However, the general notion of change in one or more of these modalities remains the basic criterion that defines the counseling process. The clear implication is that the basic purpose of the client in counseling is to learn. When clients change their behaviors, perceptions, emotions, thoughts, and/ or attitudes, they have learned. Recent advances in counseling theory and practice have emphasized the client's role in learning a variety of personally functional behaviors, cognitions, perceptions, attitudes, and feelings (Cormier and Cormier 1979; Kanfer and Goldstein 1975; Krumboltz and Thoresen 1976; Meichenbaum 1977). The process of learning skills and strategies in areas such as decision making, problem solving, social interaction and assertion, self-control, anxiety and stress management, and career and vocational planning may be seen as a generic process that typifies contemporary counseling practice. In all of these areas, the role of the client increasingly is becoming defined as that of learner. However, the role of the counselor and the process of counseling itself have received less attention in the professional literature. It is our contention that when people describe client learning as occurring during counseling, and when they attribute client changes to counseling interventions, they are describing an instructional process—hence the name *instructional counseling*.

Instructional counseling is purposeful activity on the part of a counselor (instructor) that results in client learning changes that are consistent with intended counseling goals or outcomes (Hiebert, Martin, and Marx 1981). This definition has three components. First, there is a *structural* component. The counselor engages in some activity intended to produce client change. These are the counseling skills and strategies that form the basic professional repertoires of most counselors. Second, there is an *intentional* component. Counselor activity is purposeful. Instructional counselors enter the counseling interaction intending to use specified skills and strategies because of the effects these actions are likely to have on clients. Third, there is a *functional* component. In order for instruction to have taken place, learning (client change) must follow. In discussing the impact of instructional counseling, it is important to look beyond whether or not client change has occurred (client change must be evident if real instruction has taken place) to a consideration of variables such as the speed at which change was produced, the endurance of the change, and the quality and number of ongoing effects in the client's life (e.g., generalization, transfer). The important point is that client change *must* occur if it is to be said that instruction has taken place.

It follows that if the process of counseling is instructional and if the role of the client in this instructional process is that of learner, the role of the counselor should be that of instructor. When we counsel, we instruct (Christensen 1976; Ellis 1977). To make such a statement is likely to arouse nostalgic pangs of negative affect surrounding aversive, boring, or laborious interactions with former grade school teachers. In this regard it must be understood clearly that the term *instruction*, as employed within the framework of instructional counseling, represents an active, creative effort on the part of counselors that effectively facilitates learning outcomes desired by clients. The term in this context bears absolutely no relationship to the authoritarian, rigid connotations that many people have come to associate with the teaching encounters of their youths. There are many kinds of instruction that vary in degree of client self-direction or freedom, degree of counselor involvement and direction, the nature of the instructional (counseling) strategies enacted, the learning foci toward which instruction is directed, and the settings and interpersonal contexts within which instruction occurs. Instruction, in an operational sense, simply means purposeful activity that results in learning. When we talk about counseling as instruction, we are talking about purposeful interactions of any kind between a counselor and a client that result in client learning changes.

An Instructional Counseling Model

The instructional counseling process normally contains, as would any instructional process, five essential elements (see Anderson and Faust, 1974; Dick and Carey 1978; Martin 1983; Popham and Baker 1970): (1) *general goals* toward which learning is directed, (2) *preassessment* of current client capabilities and characteristics in relation to these general goals, (3) *objectives* that transform general goals into specific statements of personal learning outcomes suggested by preassessment data,

(4) *instructional* activities aimed at facilitating changes toward the objectives, and (5) *evaluation* of changes in relation to goals and objectives (see figure 1:1). Whether or not these five instructional elements occur explicitly, consciously, or sequentially, and regardless of the language used to describe them, they normally are present in counseling that attempts to engender client learning. It is this realization that allows the instructional model in figure 1:1 to act as a subsumptive framework for counseling theory and practice when client learning is desired and when client learning capacities are not impaired severely.

GENERAL GOALS

Counseling goals are general statements of intended client learning. These goals are determined by the client and clarified with the counselor's assistance. They might be represented by statements such as: the general goal is to "feel better," "experience less anxiety," "feel more self-confident or more self-accepting," or "encounter fewer hassles when dealing with your children." The final form in which counseling goals are expressed typically reflects both the client's presenting problem and the counselor's theoretical orientation. The nature of the presenting problem of the client will affect the general content and direction of subsequent counseling interactions. The counselor's worldview, that is, the extent to which particular beliefs and theories are held by the counselor, will influence the types of client needs that are perceived and the general areas in which the counselor is prepared to work. Counseling goals are usually derived after an initial interview but may be revised or modified at various points throughout the counseling process. They map out the general area in which intervention will occur and determine the nature of the information the counselor will gather in subsequent sessions.

PREASSESSMENT

After the general area for intervention has been identified, the instructional counselor, with the client's assistance, begins to gather information that will assist in planning the specific course

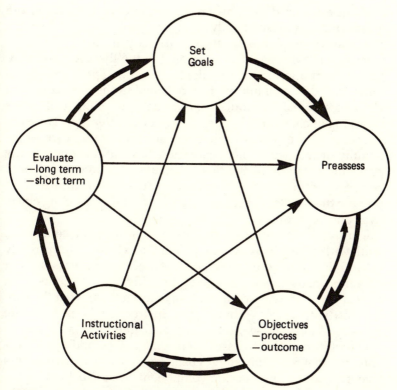

Figure 1:1. An instructional counseling model

of counseling. This information gathering is referred to as the preassessment phase of counseling. The purpose of the prefix "pre" is to distinguish this assessment from both the ongoing assessment of counselor effectiveness that occurs throughout the counseling interchange and the formal evaluation of counseling that occurs during the latter stages of counseling. The purpose of the preassessment is twofold: (1) to determine the *entering behavior* of the client and (2) to assist in the formulation of specific counseling objectives and procedures. In this context, the expression *client entering behavior* refers to client strengths and weaknesses in affective, behavioral, or cognitive domains. The preassessment phase may include such things as a formal history taking, administration of standardized tests, acquisition of client-monitored baseline data, collection of information from a referring physician, family, or work supervisor, and so on. The relative emphasis on these various procedures to assess entering behavior will vary according to the theoretical orientation of the counselor and the client's presenting problem. Sometimes the additional information obtained in the preassessment will necessitate a reformulation of initial counseling goals, thus enlarging or changing the general area of intervention. The basic purposes of the preassessment remain the same, however; to identify the particular client characteristics that contribute to the problem, to determine the client attributes that potentially could be recruited in enacting a counseling plan, and ultimately to prepare the way for the formulation of specific counseling objectives and procedures.

During the preassessment phase, instructional counselors work with clients to determine where their clients "are currently at" in relation to counseling goals. An effective preassessment prevents counselors from wasting time in teaching clients what they already know or in attempting to teach them what they are not ready to learn without prior instruction in prerequisite areas. *Task analysis* (see, for example, Gagné 1977) is an invaluable tool during the preassessment phase. By working with clients to analyze counseling goals (such as "experience less anxiety") into more specific component tasks (such as "learn techniques of deep muscle relaxation," "use relaxation techniques at the initial signs of anxiety," "learn to recognize anxiety-eliciting situations," "accurately monitor earliest signs of anxiety," etc.), instructional counselors set the stage for a careful consideration of clients' entering behavior (as determined by the use of many of the information-gathering techniques mentioned earlier in this section) in relation to each of these component tasks. Task analysis, together with the ensuing evaluation of client entering behavior, leads to the formulation of specific counseling objectives and procedures.

OBJECTIVES

Now that both counselor and client know "where the client is" in relation to counseling goals, specific counseling objectives may be formulated. Usually, counseling objectives are statements as to who will do what, to what extent, and under what conditions (Gottman and Leiblum 1974). Objectives describe what the client will be able to do or think or feel at various stages of counseling and at the end of the formal counseling intervention. It is reasonable and useful for clients to know the probable end results of counseling before embarking on any given intervention. Counseling objectives describe these outcomes in *client-centered* terms.

To be useful in informing and motivating subsequent counseling activities, objectives should be operationalized in *specific performance terms* (e.g., "I *will practice* my deep muscle relaxation exercises"). Oftentimes objectives can be made more concrete and useful with the addition of criteria that specify standards for the client performances contained in objectives (e.g., "I will practice my deep muscle relaxation exercises *at two twenty-minute practice sessions each day*"). When counseling objectives are stated in specific, concrete ways, and when they are based upon precise information about what clients currently can do in relation to counseling goals (a result of good preassessment procedures), they prepare the way for instructional/learning activities that are purposeful and efficient.

Depending upon the results of preassessment procedures, it is common for a single counseling goal to lead to the formulation of as many as ten or twenty specific objectives. While it is not possible (and, in fact, would be counterproductive) to formulate objectives for each miniscule step in counseling, it is important that the major tasks confronting clients be specified and communicated through the establishment of specific counseling objectives.

INSTRUCTIONAL ACTIVITIES

The expression *instructional activities* refers to the actual things that the counselor and client do together during counseling. In determining which instructional activities to use, the counselor asks, "Given what we want to accomplish, what program or group of activities will be appropriate?" Some frequently used counseling strategies, along with the instructional skills they require, are detailed in chapters 2 through 6. Right now, it is sufficient to note that instructional activities are determined only after definite objectives have been set. This ensures that counseling procedures and counselor behaviors will be purposeful and directed to the attainment of counseling goals.

EVALUATION

Often the evaluation of counseling is seen as something that occurs at the end of a series of counseling interactions. Although this type of "end-of-treatment" evaluation is certainly important, it is equally important to evaluate the effects of counseling on an ongoing basis (Gottman and Leiblum 1974). In instructional counseling, intentional, structural, and functional elements are inextricably linked across, and within, the counseling sessions/activities that comprise the counseling intervention. It is the counselor's responsibility to determine if intended outcomes are achieved at each step of the overall counseling program. All evaluation in instructional counseling must relate back to specific counseling objectives. It is only when evaluation relates directly to counseling objectives that the direct effects of counselor behavior can be determined.

Evaluation procedures and techniques are as numerous and varied as counseling goals and objectives. Some of the most frequently employed and useful methods of evaluating the effects of instructional counseling are presented, discussed, and illustrated in chapter 8 of this book.

What Is Different About Instructional Counseling?

The notion of counseling as instruction does not originate here, nor does the observation that the field of instructional psychology has much to offer the counselor (cf. Carkhuff and Berenson 1976; Krumboltz and Thoresen 1976). What is unique about instructional counseling is its use of an instructional perspective as a subsumptive framework from which to view counseling, counselor effectiveness, and counselor training. Katz and Ivey

(1977) refer to the "counselor-as-teacher"; however, in their discussion the label is used primarily to distinguish between a one-to-one remedial counselor role and a group-oriented, developmental or preventative counselor role. West (1977) discusses the possibility of viewing the counselor as a teacher but does not integrate this concept with an elaborated instructional model. Osborne (1978) emphasizes the importance of instructional psychology for counselors; however, he confines his remarks to "what you should know about instruction to help you do a more effective job" rather than elaborating the utility of viewing counseling as instruction per se. We contend that the counselor is, first and foremost, an instructor who should possess all of the conceptual, organizational, and practical skills that define an expert instructor.

Counseling traditionally has been viewed as an interactive (helping) process. In this view, counseling effectiveness is related either to counselor characteristics or to how well the counselor orchestrates the counseling experience. Thus, a "good" counselor is one who possesses a certain type of information base (e.g., knowledge of referral sources, group processes, psychodynamics, personality theory, human development, and so forth) and who demonstrates an ability to perform certain types of counseling activities (e.g., conduct initial interviews, reflect empathically, confront inconsistency, plan interventions, demonstrate genuineness and understanding, etc.). In this framework, the usual methods for assessing the adequacy of a counselor's knowledge base and the execution of counseling functions involve determining whether the counselor's explanations are clear to some observer and whether his or her performance of counseling actions compares favorably with some optimal (often subjective) criterion for adequate performance. While a sound knowledge base and the ability to perform counseling actions are important elements of counseling effectiveness, they do not, by themselves, define effective counseling. Effective counseling depends, in the final analysis, upon whether or not the counselor's use of knowledge and skills mattered—that is, whether or not the client changed. It is the three-way emphasis upon counselor *intention*, the use of counseling skills in instruction-learning interactions (counseling *process* or *structure*), and client change (counseling *product* or *function*) that characterizes instructional counseling.

When thus envisioned, instructional counseling is a subsumptive framework applicable across a wide variety of theoretical orientations. It theoretically is possible to perform Rogerian, Adlerian, or behavioral counseling interventions within an instructional counseling framework. Transactional analysis, reality therapy, and other schools of counseling similarly may be informed by instructional concepts and procedures. To the extent that the client in counseling may be viewed as a learner, the framework of instructional counseling may be employed. It is interesting to note at this point that "good" counselors (i.e., counselors whose clients change) invariably can identify what they are doing, why they are doing it, and the predicted and actual effects of their behavior on clients. It often takes some persistent probing and clarification to produce a clearly articulated picture of what they are doing and why; but typically, good counselors can identify these factors. Instructional counseling brings the three factors of structure, intention, and function into focus and gives counselors a framework within which they can engage in more purposeful planning and talk more meaningfully about what they do. The specific way in which this can be accomplished is made explicit in the following chapters of this book.

The implications of adopting a subsumptive instructional framework for counseling are extensive:

1. Counselors can conceptualize counseling as an instructional process and acquire explicit skills in the broad instructional areas of assisting clients to formulate instructionally useful goals and objectives for counseling intervention, pre-assessing current client repertoires (behaviors, feelings, cognitions, attitudes, perceptions, beliefs, etc.) in relation to general statements of desired learning outcomes contained in counseling goals, planning and executing (with the client's full involvement) instructional activities likely to lead to client learning consistent with counseling objectives, and evaluating learning progress in relation to counseling objectives. In practice, this instructional process may be made explicit, and the attempt, may be made to help the client understand and

acquire skills in using the generic instructional process itself. Like any good instruction, the overall goal is to teach the client how to teach himself/herself in a self-directed manner (Rogers, 1969). If counselors understand the basic process of instruction and learn to teach this process to their clients in an open, honest fashion, they may increase their effectiveness in relation to this long-term generic goal. In this sense, the general goal of all instructional counseling is client self-instruction.

2. Counselors knowledgeable about basic principles of learning and instruction can operationalize these principles through their counseling interactions. Instructional counseling requires that counselors know how to make instruction meaningful, how to provide both opportunities for client activity (practice) in the learning areas being addressed and valid and useful instructional feedback to client activity, and how to organize and sequence counseling activities in instructionally valid ways.

3. Counselors can acquire extensive repertoires of discrete counseling skills in the three basic teaching areas (cf. Gage and Berliner, 1979) of *structuring* instruction (e.g., giving overviews, stating objectives, using set induction, giving examples, maximizing the physical arrangement of the counseling setting, modeling or demonstrating, summarizing and reviewing counseling activities, focusing by means of rhetorical questions, stating clear transitions from one activity to another, using verbal markers of importance), *soliciting* client activity (e.g., asking probing questions, prompting client responses, redirecting questions from one client to another, controlling the pace of instruction, giving clear directions, using post-question wait time), and *reacting* to client activity (e.g., giving informational feedback, reflecting meaning and affect, describing inconsistencies, maintaining active listening postures, suggesting alternatives, giving descriptive praise). Counselors can learn about the typical instructional effects produced by these numerous counseling skills and how to select and sequence such skills to produce counseling strategies appropriate to the learning needs of individual clients in relation to specific problems and difficulties (e.g., job search techniques, decision-making strategies, anxiety-control procedures, cognitive restructuring, participant modeling, cognitive stress inoculation).

4. By combining a thorough knowledge of instructional/learning principles and processes with a full repertoire of instructional skills and strategies, instructional counselors are in a unique position as professional *decision makers*. They are able to comprehend basic requirements for specific client learning and to select and execute specific instructional skills that will facilitate the learning changes clients desire.

5. Finally, instructional counselors systematically can evaluate their own counseling effectiveness through combining a careful evaluation of client learning changes with an ongoing analysis of their own counseling performances of basic instructional skills and strategies. As instructors, counselors continuously must be concerned with an evaluation of their instructional actions from the functional perspective of "What are the learning outcomes associated with my counseling actions, and are these consistent with client learning objectives?" Effective counseling (instruction) is not a matter of "good form" alone but is defined in a functional manner in relation to client learning outcomes (Dunkin and Biddle 1974).

Chapter Summary

When clients in counseling are seen primarily as learners, it becomes appropriate to view counseling as an instructional process and to view the counselor's role in this process as that of instructor. Instructional counseling contains intentional, structural, and functional elements that may be portrayed accurately through an analysis of the components of the general instructional framework depicted in figure 1:1. This framework can function as a broad, subsumptive network under which it is possible to house a broad range of counseling approaches and methods.

When the instructional actions typically associated with the elements in figure 1:1 are examined (cf. Dick and Carey 1978, Gagné 1977), it becomes clear that counseling effectiveness can be determined by the degree to which a counselor's actions succeed in facilitating client change as specified in counseling goals and objectives. As instructors, counselors conduct initial interviews that help clients formulate general learning goals. These goals may be used as a basis for reliable, valid, and purposeful preassessments of currently relevant feelings, beliefs, behaviors, and perceptions of clients. The data furnished by preassessments may then be used to translate broad counseling goals into objectives containing statements of specific learning outcomes, including some indication of the performance criteria and conditions associated with the demonstration of such outcomes (Mager 1962). Carefully orchestrated instructional activities provide meaningful opportunities for clients to engage in active practice appropriate for the acquisition of the learning performances (e.g., covert coping statements, systematic problem-solving skills and strategies, specific social interaction skills, cognitive imaginal representations, perception-checking procedures) described in counseling objectives. Finally, as instructors, counselors engage in careful evaluations of client learning (increments in cognitive, behavioral, or affective repertoires) to determine whether or not counseling goals and objectives have been attained (Martin, Hiebert, and Marx 1981). In all of this, counselors and clients work together toward the overall goal of client self-instruction. In successful instructional counseling, the client determines (with the counselor's assistance and support) counseling goals and through ongoing, interactive work with the counselor comes to internalize the process of instruction itself, thus ensuring generalization and transfer of client growth beyond the confines of the specific context and content associated with the counseling intervention. In both these ways, instructional counseling is a client-centered instructional-learning system.

REFERENCES

Anderson, R. C., and Faust, C. W. 1974. *Educational Psychology: The Science of Instruction and Learning.* New York: Dodd, Mead.
Carkhuff, R. R., and Berenson, B. G. 1976. *Teaching as Treatment.* Amherst, Mass.: Human Resource Development Press.
Christensen, C. 1976. Editorial. *Canadian Counsellor* 10: 45–49.

Cormier, W. H., and Cormier, S. C. 1979. *Interviewing Strategies for Helpers*. Monterey: Brook/Cole.

Dick, W., and Carey, L. 1978. *The Systematic Design of Instruction*. Glenview: Scott, Foresman.

Dunkin, M. J., and Biddle, B. J. 1974. *The Study of Teaching*. New York: Holt, Rinehart & Winston.

Ellis, A. Skill training in counselling and psychotherapy 1977. *Canadian Counsellor* 12: 30–35.

Gage, N. L., and Berliner, D. C. 1979. *Educational Psychology* (2d ed.). Chicago: Rand McNally.

Gagné, R. M. 1977. *Conditions of Learning* (3d ed.). New York: Holt, Rinehart & Winston.

Gottman, J. M., and Leiblum, S. R. 1974. *How to Do Psychotherapy and How to Evaluate It: A Manual for Beginners*. New York: Holt, Rinehart & Winston.

Hiebert, B. A., Martin, J., and Marx, R. W. 1981. Instructional counselling: The counsellor as teacher. *Canadian Counsellor* 15: 107–14.

Kanfer, F. H., and Goldstein, A. P. (Eds.). 1975. *Helping People Change*. New York: Pergamon.

Katz, J. H., and Ivey, A. E. 1977. Developing the counsellor as teacher: A systematic program. *Canadian Counsellor*, 11: 176–81.

Krumboltz, J. D. and Thoresen, C. E. 1976. *Counseling Methods*. New York: Holt, Rinehart & Winston.

Mager, R. F. *Preparing Instructional Objectives*. 1962. Belmont, Calif.: Fearon.

Martin, J. *Mastering Instruction*. 1983. Boston: Allyn and Bacon.

————, Hiebert, B. A., and Marx, R. W. Instructional supervision in counselor training. 1981. *Counselor Education and Supervision* 20: 193–202.

Meichenbaum, D. H. 1977. *Cognitive Behavior Modification: An Integrative Approach*. New York: Plenum.

Osborne, J. W. 1978. Instructional psychology for school counsellors. *Canadian Counsellor* 12: 117–22.

Popham, W. J., and Baker, E. L. 1970. *Systematic Instruction*. Englewood Cliffs, N. J.: Prentice-Hall.

Rogers, C. *Freedom to Learn*. 1969. Columbus: Charles E. Merrill.

West. L. W. 1977. Teaching: The substance of counselling. *Canadian Counsellor* 12: 3–4.

CHAPTER TWO

Learning Conditions And Instructional Actions

WHEN COUNSELING is conceptualized as an instructional process, it is clear that the client's role in counseling is that of *learner* and that the counselor's role is that of *instructor*. Instructional counselors must possess a good understanding of the conditions necessary for client learning and of the instructional actions they can employ to ensure that these conditions are present in their counseling practice. In this chapter three major conditions necessary for client learning are discussed. This discussion is succeeded by the presentation of an extensive taxonomy of instructional actions that may be used in various combinations to ensure that the three major learning conditions are engaged actively in counseling practice. The taxonomy of instructional actions embodies three major levels of action—counseling *skills*, counseling *strategies*, and counseling *styles*. Within each action level, constituent skills, strategies, or styles are defined; their purpose or functions are clearly indicated; and examples from hypothetical counseling sessions are provided to illustrate their applications in active counseling contexts. The chapter concludes with a brief summary of central ideas and themes.

The main purpose of chapter 2 is to assist the reader to recognize a wide variety of possible instructional actions that may be selected purposefully in relation to counseling objectives and employed within active counseling practice to promote relevant client learning in relation to those objectives. The initial information about necessary conditions for client learning is presented so that the effects of various instructional counseling actions may be understood in relation to the client learning requirements that are fulfilled by the various counseling actions described. The most important message of the chapter is that what an instructional counselor does is determined by the learning requirements of the client as specified in the goals and objectives of counseling. The purpose of instructional counseling is to help clients learn. The purpose of any instructional counseling action is to supply some element or condition that makes possible relevant client learning.

Learning Conditions

There are three major conditions necessary for client learning. Quite simply, whatever is to be learned must be specified in a meaningful way; the behavior, thought, or affect to be learned must be practiced actively by the client; and this client activity or practice must result in instructional feedback that promotes client learning of the practiced behavior, thought, or affect. In this first section of chapter 2, each of these major learning conditions is discussed in some detail from the client's point of view.

MEANINGFUL SPECIFICATION

In general, we all learn more efficiently when what is to be learned is meaningful to us (Anderson 1980; Smith 1975; Underwood and Swartz 1960). Meaningfulness refers to the number and quality of the associations or connections that a client (learner) can make between what is to be learned and what he/she already knows. Meaningfulness bridges the gap between existing information from past experience and novel information from current experience. It helps to assimilate and accommodate new knowledge and skills into existing knowledge structures and skill repertoires (Anderson 1980; Smith 1975).

Meaningfulness is an individual thing. What is extremely meaningful for one client given his/her unique combination of past experience and current perception may not be at all meaningful to another client given a different combination of experience and perception. It is further true that a counselor's associational networks may be very different from a client's associational networks. While a counselor may attach meaning to the social stresses of a cocktail party by associating such events with professional conferences and job interviews, a client may find a stress-management scenario based on such social events to be completely meaningless if his/her own stress reactions are associated with entirely different experiences. It becomes the counselor's job to structure the activities and context of counseling sessions so that clients are able to make associations and connections between what they already know and can do as a result of their experiences and what is to be learned in counseling.

The more a counselor knows about a client's current levels of skills, knowledge, and capabilities that are in any way relevant to the learning performances contained in instructional goals (see chapter 1: preassessment), the more likely it is that the counselor will be able to make counseling activities meaningful by casting them in the context of the client's experiences and life situations. There are many ways to inject meaning into instructional counseling activities. While the specific structuring skills that a counselor can employ to promote meaningfulness are explored later in this chapter, the following points are indications of the kinds of counseling procedures that may increase meaningful specification of required learning from a client's point of view.

1. Clients, like other learners, tend to attach more meaning to instructional activities whose *purposes or objectives* are clear to them (Gagné 1977, Mager 1962; Martin 1983; Popham and Baker 1970). When clients understand why they are being asked to do and say certain things and how these activities are intended to increase the likelihood that they will learn in relation to counseling goals, they are more likely, and better able, to act efficiently and productively within their learning roles. Like travelers, learners attach more meaning to an undertaking if they know where they are going and why they are going there. Unspecified, meaningless experience is no better than no experience at all. In Lawrence Peter's words, "Experience can be the worst teacher—it gives the test before explaining the lesson" (Peters 1979).

2. Clients are more likely to find counseling meaningful if the language and *language structures and idioms* used by the counselor are sufficiently congruent with their own language norms so as to increase the likelihood of comprehension and clear

communication. Instructions, responses, directions, and suggestions that are couched in language unfamiliar to the client are unlikely to be effective since they lack meaning for the client to whom they are directed.

3. Clients are likely to find *examples and illustrations* used to convey information about behaviors, thoughts, and emotional reactions more meaningful if such examples and illustrations relate to their personal experience, interests, and/or activities outside the counseling situation. If new information relevant to client learning can be advanced within the general context of familiar information (Ausubel 1968), client learning will be enhanced. Clients tend to find examples and illustrations taken from their day-to-day activities and experiences very useful in this regard.

4. If examples and illustrations for new learning are not readily available from a client's past and current experiences, clients may benefit from demonstrations or experiences that are created within the counseling situation itself. Such *created or induced experiences* have the advantage of being observed firsthand by both counselor and client. Inducing common experiences during counseling may be done in a wide variety of ways. Conducting role plays or simulations, viewing films, actively practicing and coaching new skills, and jointly creating visual images are but a few commonly used counseling techniques for creating common experiences for clients and counselors. Modeling new skills, behaviors, thought patterns, and emotional reactions for the client can be a very effective means of creating here-and-now, observational experiences for clients that add significant meaning to verbal descriptions and instructions (Bandura 1969, 1977).

5. Meaningful specification of what is to be learned in counseling may be increased by making connections or associations with client experiences outside the counseling situation and by creating commonly shared experiences within the counseling session itself. Meaningfulness also may be increased if clients perceive associations and connections among various elements both within a single counseling session and across a number of counseling sessions. There are many things a counselor can do to convey this kind of *organization* to the client. Each counseling

session should be planned and conducted so that it has an obvious beginning and end and so that what goes on between these points moves smoothly from one activity to another or from one issue to another. Further, meaningfulness for clients also is enhanced if it is clear how each counseling session relates to the immediately preceding and succeeding sessions as well as to the overall counseling plan or program. Perceived organization is of great utility to prospective learners (Bower 1970; Calfee 1981).

Meaningful specification of what is to be learned in counseling is a major condition that must be satisfied before successful client learning progress can be expected to occur. Clearly associating and matching instructional counseling procedures and activities with counseling objectives, client language, client personal experiences, and induced here-and-now experiences, as well as a clear organization both within and between individual counseling sessions, can help to increase the likelihood that instructional counseling will be meaningful to clients. Many of the structuring skills described later in this chapter help an instructional counselor ensure that his/her clients benefit from the principle of meaningful specification.

PRACTICE (ACTIVITY)

Practice opportunities must also be present in counseling situations that promote learning. If instruction in counseling is to be effective, clients must be given the opportunity of engaging in activity that gives them practice in the skills, behaviors, cognitions, or emotional reactions specified in counseling goals and objectives. It cannot be assumed that new learning will occur in the absence of such practice (Kanfer and Goldstein 1980). In arranging for active client practice, instructional counselors should be aware of the following client learning reactions to specific practice elements.

1. Clients tend to learn more readily if the practice opportunities available in counseling are *appropriate* to the kinds of learning specified in counseling objectives (Popham and Baker 1970). If, for example, a counseling objective for an unassertive client is to acquire specific communication skills that can be used

to promote reasoned exchanges of viewpoints with others, a good deal of counseling time should be devoted to the actual practice or rehearsal of such communication skills (Lazarus 1966; Martin 1983). Sitting around talking about behavior, cognitions, or affective reactions to be learned is not sufficient to ensure that actual learning of new skills in these areas will occur. A good deal of time in instructional counseling must be devoted to appropriate practice of the learning performances described in counseling objectives.

2. Related to the preceding point is the notion that the *domain* within which practice is to occur should be communicated clearly to the client. Instructional counseling is concerned with change in three domains: (a) behavioral, (b) cognitive, and (c) affective. Client learning always takes place in one or more of these domains. Depending upon the nature of client problems and goals, active practice within some domains will be more appropriate than practice within other domains. For example, some phobic clients have been able to overcome their avoidance of feared objects while still suffering from worry and cognitive anxiety in the presence of these objects (Kanter and Goldfried 1979). In such cases it is clear that the kind of learning necessary for the client to undertake lies in the cognitive and affective domains, not in the behavorial domain. This being so, practice time may be directed to the rehearsal of cognitive self-statements incompatible with worry or to self-induced relaxation incompatible with negative emotional arousal (e.g., Meichenbaum 1977), as opposed to practice of approach behaviors per se.

3. Clients, like anyone else, tend to learn more efficiently and positively if complex performances to be learned are broken down into *graduated sequences* of subperformances that may be approached one step at a time. Rather than expecting socially unskilled clients suddenly to practice a broad gamut of sophisticated social behaviors in a cocktail party setting, the instructional counselor may arrange a series of smaller-scale practice opportunities. Over time, a number of basic social skills gradually are built up that eventually culminate in complex, real-life practice assignments, during which a number of social skills are integrated for joint practice (Liberman et al. 1975). *Graduated*

practice makes use of proximal subgoals through which clients can proceed toward overall counseling objectives with minimal setbacks and maximal gains in confidence and perceived self-efficacy (Bandura and Schunk, 1980).

4. While client practice in instructional counseling should be graduated, it also must be realistic. *Realistic practice* refers to the notion that before counseling is concluded, the client must be practicing his/her new skills and learnings in the context of his/her everyday life situations. Clients don't need just to be able to perform learned actions in the counselor's office; they need to perform them where they will be of some use in resolving ongoing difficulties and concerns. For example, newly learned rational thought patterns must transfer from counselor-dominated situations to home and work situations in which the client is faced with others acting in less rational ways. If such cognitive learning does not transfer in this way, it is of little use to the client. The best way to ensure transfer of learning is to arrange for realistic practice (Travers 1977).

Clients in counseling tend to learn more efficiently and significantly if practice opportunities are appropriate with respect to counseling objectives and if the domains within which practice is to occur are clearly specified. It also helps if practice is graduated from simple to more complex forms and if practice eventually occurs in realistic situations. Instructional counselors acting within their instructional roles attempt to facilitate client learning by arranging practice opportunities that possess these essential characteristics.

FEEDBACK

The third condition essential for client learning follows quite naturally from the first two conditions, If clients can be engaged in meaningful practice, it is possible to arrange instructionally useful feedback in response to such client practice. Feedback has two basic functions: (1) it gives clients *information* about what they have done (information they can use in formulating future actions), and (2) it *motivates* clients to continue to expend energy and effort to learn required behaviors, cognitions, and/or affective responses. To be optimally effective in performing these two vital instructional functions, instructional feedback should possess certain essential qualities.

1. Clients are assisted in learning if feedback is given to them *immediately* upon, or as close as possible to, the completion of a practice interval. Feedback tends to lose its ability to convey pertinent information and motivation as the temporal gap between practice and receipt of feedback widens (Martin 1983).

2. Clients also are helped to learn when the feedback they receive is *specific* to the actual performance being practiced. Feedback should be focused on the specific elements of behavior, cognition, or affective reactions that the client was attempting to practice. Vague, nonfocused feedback is practically useless as an aid to learning (Martin 1983).

3. Instructional counselors should attempt to limit the feedback they give about client performances during practice to a descriptive account of what occurred. *Descriptive feedback* simply informs clients of what they did and how it related to what they were trying to do. It does not offer inferences about *why* clients did what they did or evaluate how good or bad the performance was. Descriptive feedback simply provides clients with complete and accurate information about what they did.

4. Generally speaking, clients learn most efficiently from feedback that is *positive* and *encouraging*. If the purpose of instructional counseling were to point out every mistake a client makes and to teach the client to be equally vigilant in this regard, criticism and specification of errors would be important feedback elements. Obviously, this is not the goal of feedback in instructional counseling. In order to motivate clients to continue practicing, and to give them information about those things they are doing that are very effective, instructional counselors should take great care to focus on positive descriptions of the things a client does that are in line with counseling goals and objectives. Unproductive client behavior most often can be ignored or dealt with by suggesting alternatives for action (see point 5 below) without any loss in the informational value of instructional feedback (Martin 1983).

5. When the client obviously requires further clarification or demonstration of the performances he/she is attempting to practice and learn, this can be accomplished without criticizing or focusing on currently unproductive client practice perform-

ances. In such instances, it is sufficient for the counselor briefly to summarize any productive elements in the client's practice performance and then to move on to set the stage for another practice trial. During this specification for subsequent practice, the instructional counselor can *suggest and model alternatives* for productive action with which the client is currently unfamiliar or about which he/she lacks adequate information.

6. Clients generally find feedback that *recognizes* their *affective reactions* to practice performances to be supportive and encouraging. Instructional counselors can take good instructional advantage of recognizing and reflecting client affective reactions to practice trials. Giving the client a sense that some of the difficulties, trepidations, and self-doubts associated with the acquisition of new skills and reactions are appreciated and understood can be particularly reassuring and productive in promoting continued client practice.

Feedback that is immediate, specific, descriptive and positive and that contains information for alternative actions and recognizes client affect is likely to be effective in promoting positive client learning. Taken together, the three basic learning conditions of meaningful specification, active practice, and feedback, if incorporated into instructional counseling programs in the ways suggested in this section, can help to ensure that clients will have full advantage of solid learning opportunities in counseling. The specific actions that instructional counselors can use to ensure that these basic learning conditions are present are the subject for the remainder of this chapter.

Instructional Actions

The actions of instructional counselors may be considered at three distinct levels (see figure 2:1). The taxonomy of instructional counseling actions presented here borrows heavily from recent work in instructional psychology, particularly in the analysis of instruction (Bellack et al. 1966; Clark et al. 1979; Gage and Berliner 1979). Each level in the taxonomy is overviewed briefly and then discussed in greater detail.

Instructional counseling skills are relatively brief, discrete

COUNSELING STYLE

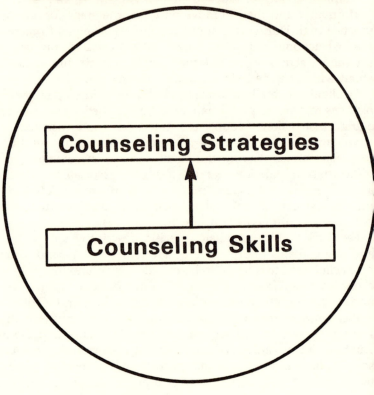

Figure 2:1. *Levels of counseling action*

aspects of counselor behavior that can be described readily and then practiced and acquired by almost any counselor who chooses to engage seriously in skill acquisition. As such, counseling skills make up the basic repertoire of the professional counselor. Just as the tennis player possesses a variety of discrete tennis skills, such as forehand groundstroke, backhand, volley, lob, and serve, so the instructional counselor possesses a variety of discrete skills, such as reflecting affect, stating counseling objectives, giving informational feedback, summarizing, and probing.

Instructional counseling strategies are arrangements or se quences of counseling skills that are grouped together for the accomplishment of a specific counseling purpose. The tennis player, faced with an opponent playing a strong net game, may adopt a playing strategy consisting of hard, deep serves, deep groundstrokes, lobs, and passing shots for the purpose of keeping the opponent from the net. Similarly, a counselor may adopt and arrange a variety of discrete counseling skills to form an instructional strategy well matched to the specific learning needs of a particular client.

Instructional counseling styles add the personal stamp of each counselor to the skilled performances described by counseling skills and strategies. A counseling style can be defined as the sum total of all the characteristics, mannerisms, and unique personal qualities of an individual counselor that are communicated to clients in a variety of subtle, idiosyncratic ways. Just as the tennis player can select a repertoire of skills and strategies that are likely to function effectively given his/her physical stature, strength, and quickness, so the instructional counselor can select a repertoire of skills and strategies that fit and/or extend his/her overall counseling style.

In the remainder of this chapter, an extensive taxonomy of possible instructional skills, strategies, and styles for instructional counselors is presented. In studying this taxonomy, the reader is encouraged to use the numerous definitions and examples provided as aids to visualize the exact way in which each of the skills, strategy sequences, or stylistic elements might operate in actual counseling situations.

INSTRUCTIONAL COUNSELING SKILLS

As brief, discrete instances of counselor behavior, instructional counseling skills are numerous and varied. It would be almost impossible to describe every possible skill that an effective instructional counselor might employ. Fortunately, it is possible to group counseling skills into three major areas of action (Hiebert, Martin, and Marx 1981) that are related functionally to the three major conditions necessary for client learning discussed earlier in this chapter (see figure 2:2). *Structuring skills* are used to ensure meaningful specification of counseling processes

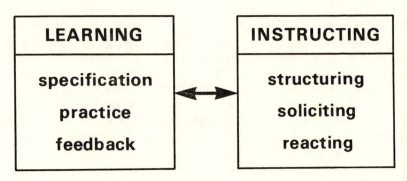

Figure 2:2. Conditions for learning and instructional skills

and procedures, *soliciting skills* are used to promote appropriate client practice in relation to counseling goals and objectives, and *reacting skills* are employed to provide useful instructional feedback about practice performances. When counseling is viewed as an instructional process, it is possible to begin the construction of a comprehensive taxonomy of counseling actions with the specification and categorization of discrete counseling skills in the generic instructional areas of structuring, soliciting, and reacting.

Each of the skill descriptions that follow contains a formal definition of the skill's *structure* (what the counselor actually does) and its *function* (what the client will tend to do or gain, and what the counselor will tend to do or gain, when the skill is used appropriately). In most cases, an illustration or example of how the skill might be used in a hypothetical instructional counseling situation accompanies the formal skill definition. Both skill structures and functions are defined because effective instructional counseling depends heavily upon the purposeful employment of counseling skills for the attainment of specific, moment-to-moment instructional ends. Counseling skills do not occur in vacuums. They are used because they tend to have a predictable effect upon client learning. Instructional counselors, to be effective, must know what skills are appropriate for what immediate counseling purposes and must be able to employ counseling skills in ways that acheive these purposes. Understanding both the structure and function of a skill helps a counselor to employ the skill within the purposeful framework of instruction.

In what follows, a number of frequently employed counseling skills are categorized in relation to the functions (structuring, soliciting, or reacting) that the skills most commonly perform. Since some skills commonly serve more than one function, this classification of skills as to prevailing functions is, at times, rather arbitrary. For example, a skill such as "describing discrepancies" (see below), which is used to react to perceived inconsistencies in client communications, may give useful feedback to the client (reacting function) but also may be used to solicit further clarification from the client (soliciting function). In such cases, skills have been placed in a single area of function so as to avoid redundancy, but both functions are noted in the description of the skill.

Structuring Skills

The skills in this area are used to provide an organized, meaningful context for client learning. The examples used in the following skill descriptions are taken from a variety of hypothetical individual and group counseling situations.

Giving overviews. An overview is a short presentation at the beginning of a counseling session that helps the client(s) to comprehend the overall structure of the forthcoming session and to develop realistic expectations of the session. An overview outlines the major issues and activities for the forthcoming counseling session. Overviews may be oral, written (handouts, chalkboard presentations, or overhead transparency displays), or a combination of these. A permanent medium like a handout can be kept by clients for future reference.

> Well, let's see if we can start today's session by reviewing the anxiety hierarchies we constructed last time. After we do this, I'd like to see if you can isolate some of the specific statements you make to yourself in anxiety situations. As we discuss these statements, perhaps we can move on to a consideration of how these statements affect you emotionally and then see if there are other, and more productive statements you can discover that might counteract some of the more self-defeating thoughts you experience.

Stating objectives or goals. This skill enables the counselor to clarify further the purpose of counseling sessions by telling clients what they should be able to do after the session that they couldn't do before the session. The focus may be on acquiring information, developing and applying a skill or strategy, altering a perception or attitude, or whatever. The communication of objectives may be oral or written on a chalkboard or handout.

> O.K., simply put, by the time we wrap things up today, you should all be able to (1) identify the anxiety-eliciting self-statements you make in fearful situations and (2) discover some initial ways of stopping these self-defeating statements and replacing them with effective coping communications.

Stating transitions. Using this skill, the counselor alerts clients to a change in the focus of the session's content or process by stating that what was happening is now over and identifying what is about to occur next.

> Now that I've finished my little introduction about what we'll be doing today, let's break into small groups of three and continue practicing the active listening skills we discussed last time.

Summarizing. This skill helps clients to recall and organize events in a session by providing a brief review of the major themes and actions that have occurred to date. Such summaries often come at the end of a session but may be inserted at key transition points throughout a session.

> Well, it looks as if we've discovered at least a few things about the ways in which we often present ourselves to other people that result in less than optimally satisfying encounters. George has talked eloquently about difficulties associated with eye contact and physical closeness, and Sally has alerted us to the importance of listening carefully to others in addition to talking sensibly ourselves.

Using markers of importance. This skill helps clients to attend carefully to important or crucial elements in a counseling ses sion. Using a word or phrase to stress the significance of a fact, concept, or process; changing vocal intonations and pitch to highlight a crucial understanding; or writing down key commitments and decisions are all ways of using markers of importance.

> Now remember, it is *absolutely critical* that you practice these skills whenever you find yourselves in the social situations we have discussed.

Using set induction. The counselor provides a common experience in the here-and-now by presenting a scenario, an example from common knowledge, a film, a role play, and so on. Set induction helps clients to focus meaningfully upon specific elements associated with the counseling process.

> Imagine that you are at the fair and a friend asks you to go on the Ferris wheel with him/her. At first you refuse, but when it becomes clear to you that this is really important to your friend, you agree. As you buy your tickets and stand in line waiting for your turn, you notice that your hands are sweating, your heart is pounding, and you are looking around frantically for a way to escape.

Using rhetorical questions. Using this skill, the counselor asks a question to which a client is not expected to respond so as to highlight a significant aspect of the session. These questions usually are embedded in a longer statement.

> So it seems clear that when we get angry, we often panic in response to the anger, and this in turn makes us even more angry. How can we possibly break out of this vicious circle? That is the major concern for today's session.

Modeling or demonstrating. With this skill the counselor becomes involved in the performance of an action in a slow, deliberate manner while verbally referencing crucial aspects of the action so as to make it clear to observing clients. There are many variations of modeling—some brief, some extended (as in role plays and simulations). The counselor, while modeling, does whatever he/she can to assist clients in replicating the critical components of a modeled action, whether it is a way of acting, a method of talking, a nonverbal posture, or a facial expression.

> As I sit and listen to you, notice that I am relaxed with my hands loosely in my lap, both feet on the floor, eyes open and alert, body leaning slightly forward.

Employing physical arrangements. This skill enables the counselor to place clients, self, and any materials in a special arrangement that allows, and perhaps encourages, a desired kind of communication. A good example might be to arrange chairs in a circle without any table or other prop in the middle, if it is important for the session that everyone have the opportunity of seeing fully, attending to, and speaking directly to anyone else in a counseling group.

Giving examples and illustrations. The counselor makes counseling content meaningful for the client by providing examples that establish links with familiar or common experiences.

> The kind of attitude I am talking about here is similar to the way in which a professional athlete might view a forthcoming game with a strong opponent. When you played football . . .

Soliciting Skills

The skills in this second major skill area are used to elicit appropriate client learning practice (activity) in relation to counseling goals and objectives. Some commonly employed soliciting skills are illustrated in what follows. Once again, examples are taken from a variety of individual and group counseling situations.

Probing. The counselor asks an open-ended question or makes a statement that encourages verbal activity and elaboration. Counselors most often should avoid using closed questions to which clients can simply say "yes" or "no." Such client responses convey little useful information. Probing questions and statements should not lead the client by containing hints as to the anticipated response.

What are some of the things you do when you first get up in the morning?

versus

Can you tell me what you do when you first get up in the morning?

or

I'd like you to tell me more about your reactions to that situation.

versus

Did that situation really bother you, then?

Prompting. Using this skill the counselor asks a question or makes a statement that follows an incomplete or inaccurate client response. The counselor asks the client to justify or elaborate upon the first answer and assists the client in forming the second response by providing a hint or clue about a possible type of response.

You're saying that somehow what you think about failure creates your anxiety. Now, recall our discussion of common irrational thoughts and see if you can tell us which of these really is creating your problem.

Redirecting (promoting peer involvement). The counselor asks the same question of two or more clients in succession to encourage participants to respond to each other's opinions or statements. Redirecting encourages client-to-client interaction and assists clients in engaging in the often therapeutic task of assisting each other.

Bill doesn't think his anger is unjustified, given the behavior of his boss. What is your opinion about this, Nancy? . . . What can you add to Nancy's statement, Peter?

Calling for demonstration. The counselor provides opportunities for clients to demonstrate that they actively are thinking, working, or problem solving by asking for evidence of these processes.

Last time, we agreed that we should each make a list of

all the things we like about ourselves. Let's see how some of you did. Can you share part of your list with us, Joe?

Giving clear instructions or directions (initiating action). This skill translates into the giving of specific, succinct, and non-ambiguous directions for client learning activity. Giving clear instructions prevents clients from becoming confused and increases the likelihood of productive client involvement in the instruction-learning process.

> Write down ten things that you like about your job.
> versus
> Record some things about your job that you think you like.

Pacing. By asking fewer or more questions within a given period of time, a counselor can control the speed with which information and ideas are brought into the session. Pacing also includes controlling the level of affect generated in the session so as to keep it congruent with current individual and group insights and coping capacities.

Using post-question wait time. The counselor using this skill pauses three or more seconds after directing a question to an individual or to a group as a whole so as to give potential respondents the opportunity to formulate a reply. This also indicates to clients that you respect and value their inputs, thus increasing the future likelihood of active client involvement.

> What are some specific self-statements that accompany the anxiety? [pause for 3 seconds] Peter?

Cueing cognitive practice. The counselor provides a structured opportunity for cognitive rehearsal on the part of the client.

> Think about all the things you do when you first get up. Take two minutes to reflect on your actions.

Using group altering cues. The counselor makes statements or performs actions that let group members know that they are expected to attend carefully to what is going on.

> Remember, even though I'm working specifically with Jim at this moment, Jim's situation is similar enough to the

rest of our difficulties that we all can learn something from this interchange.

Reacting Skills

The skills in this final major skill area are used to provide instructionally useful feedback and motivation to clients with respect to their learning progress. While the following list of reacting skills is probably incomplete, it does illustrate some of the reacting skills most frequently employed in instructional counseling.

Nonverbal listening (attending). The counselor uses the following elements of body position to convey to the client that he/she is concerned about, and attempting to understand, what the client is saying.

S Sitting *squarely*, facing the client, with a confident posture, not slouching.
O *Open* arms to the side of the body rather than in front, avoiding closed postures such as folding arms over the chest or crossing legs away from the client.
L *Leaning* slightly forward to convey interest.
E Maintaining *eye contact*, but keeping a comfortable balance between no eye contact and being "locked in."
R Relaxing so that the client is helped to relax, too.

Paraphrasing verbal content. The counselor rephrases the content portion of the client's communication. Paraphrasing verbal content demonstrates to the client that the counselor has heard and understood what the client has said. It also permits the client to further elaborate his/her communication should he/she judge the counselor's parapharse to be somewhat incomplete or inaccurate.

> Client: "I can't handle things now. When my wife was alive, I could talk to her and we could plan together. All these things to do, and no one to help me."

> Counselor: "Since your wife's death, all of the responsibilities and decisions to be made are totally on your shoulders."

Reflecting meaning. The counselor using this skill rephrases the meaning portion of the client's communication and makes a very slight, tentative inference about something the client seems to imply but actually does not say. Using this skill encourages the client to explore the topic further and thus allows the counselor to check his/her perceptions, or to receive clarification, about what the client is getting at.

> You really don't know how things are going to turn out for you without your wife.

Reflecting affect. The counselor makes a statement that portrays the feeling portion of the client's communication. This helps to convey empathic understanding and helps to build a relationship of trust and support between client and counselor. The skill also may be used to defuse negative emotions that the client is experiencing. Like reflecting meaning, reflections of affect most often should be tentative and gradual rather than sudden and threatening.

> You're overwhelmed by all the things that you need to do, and you're feeling pretty scared about your ability to hold things together now that your wife's gone.

Promoting ownership (personalization). This skill is used in response to client statements that do not recognize any personal involvement in life situations. The skill helps clients to comprehend their own roles in the events that affect them. Promoting ownership is a reflective skill that rephrases a client statement and adds an element of active client involvement and responsibility where it was previously absent.

> Client: "She's always at me. She goes on and on until she makes me go completely wild."

> Counselor: "When she nags you get more and more worked up, until you get yourself completely out of control."

Describing discrepancies (confronting). In response to a perceived discrepancy in the client's behaviors, thoughts, and/or feelings, the counselor promotes client awareness of, or attention to, such discrepancies without overly threatening the client. This skill also can be used to solicit further clarification from the client.

> On the one hand you're saying you're not nervous, but on the other hand you tell me that your stomach was so "flip-floppy" you couldn't eat before the concert. (*Pause* to give the client time to absorb the description and to respond to it.)

Expressing counselor reactions with "I" messages. This skill enables the counselor to communicate his/her own reactions in a clear nonambiguous fashion. Through the use of the pronoun "I," and the avoidance of generalized language, the counselor makes it clear that this is his/her own reaction and not a sweeping statement about the judgments or evaluations of people in general. This skill also can be used to solicit reactions to the substance of the counselor statement.

> I don't like it when you break an agreement we have.
> versus
> Nobody enjoys it when you break an agreement.
> or
> You're really stupid to behave like that.

Giving descriptive praise. The counselor motivates client learning by expressing that a client action was valuable. The counselor describes the effectiveness of a client action and emphasizes the personal aspect of the action.

> You were able, in this role play, to control your anger and redirect that energy into a calmly delivered but forceful assertive response. Notice how effective this behavior was in comparison with a wild, hostile outburst.

Giving informational feedback. The counselor with this skill provides feedback to client learning performances through a straightforward description of what the client did and what the consequences of the client's actions were. Interpretations and value judgments are removed as much as possible. This skill is particularly useful for giving feedback to unsuccessful client learning performance.

O.K., I saw you adopt an attending posture in which your body was learning slightly forward, but your eyes were not looking at Mary while you were talking. That created the impression that you were ill at ease.

Suggesting alternatives. In response to ineffective client actions, the counselor suggests alternatives for action in a clear, direct manner without evaluating or judging previous client actions.

I'd like to see you try that again, with your hands at your sides, resting lightly at midpoint between you knees and your thighs.

Post-response wait time. The counselor pauses three or more seconds after a client finishes a statement so as to demonstrate that he/she has listened carefully and is considering the answer, suggestion, or expression of feeling.

Summary

Instructional counseling skills are brief, discrete aspects of counselor behavior whose structure (the elements of counselor behavior that make up the skill) and function (the consequences for client learning and counselor instruction that follow from the appropriate use of the skill) can be described readily. Knowing how to perform a variety of counseling skills and how to use these skills intentionally to acheive moment-by-moment instructional purposes in relation to client learning objectives helps instructional counselors to operate effectively within the instructional context that typifies counseling. Through the use of structuring skills, the client is helped to perceive the meaning and purpose of counseling events and procedures. Through the use of soliciting skills, the client is helped to practice actively the various thoughts, behaviors, and emotional reactions that will lead to resolving, or coping with, current or ongoing problems and concerns. Through the use of reacting skills, the client receives instructional feedback useful for the facilitation of learning in relation to counseling goals and objectives. Once counselors have acquired a sound set of basic counseling skills in each of the areas of structuring, soliciting, and reacting, they are in a position to engage clients in the active instruction-learning process that typifies instructional counseling.

The next level of activity in the taxonomy of instructional counseling actions (see figure 2:1) is concerned with the sequencing and organization of a variety of counseling skills into smoothly functioning counseling strategies for the achievement of longer-term client learning objectives.

INSTRUCTIONAL COUNSELING STRATEGIES

Instructional counseling strategies are sequences of skills that are arranged purposefully for the accomplishment of particular counseling goals. As such, strategies fall between the level of discrete techniques (skills) and the level of personal counselor style. Understanding how to and being able to, combine a variety of skilled performances into a counseling strategy that is appropriate to the learning needs and counseling objectives of a particular client are perhaps the most important aspects of instructional counseling. Many counselors have recognized that it is impossible for any given counseling strategy to be applied successfully to all client problems under all circumstances (e.g., Goldfried 1980). As Paul (1967, 111) has noted, the basic question for counselors is "*What* treatment, by *whom*, is most effective for *this* individual with *that* specific problem, and under *which* set of circumstances?"

Possessing a wide repertoire of counseling skills permits an instructional counselor to experiment systematically with different skill combinations for different instructional purposes as determined by clients with different learning needs under differing circumstances. There is a potentially limitless number of counseling strategies. Some, such as systematic desensitization, participant modeling, assertion training, cognitive stress inoculation, and role playing, are familiar to many counselors. The approach to instructional counseling advocated in this book is built upon four basic counseling strategies—(1) *decision making/ problem solving*, (2) *skill training*, (3) *personal coping*, and (4) *self-management*. These strategies are related to four major client concerns (see figure 2.3).

The four basic instructional-counseling strategies will be dis-

Decision making ⟷ "What do I need to do "

Skill training ⟷ "How can I learn to do it "

Personal coping ⟷ "How can I reduce anxiety/stress
associated with doing it "

Self-management ⟷ "How can I keep doing it "

Figure 2:3 Counseling strategies and client concerns

cussed and illustrated at considerable length in the following chapters. This part of the present chapter briefly extends the taxonomy of instructional-counseling actions through a simple listing of the four basic strategies together with an indication of the general goals toward which they may be mobilized.

Decision Making/Problem Solving

This multipurpose strategy helps clients to formulate alternatives for action, select an alternative to be acted upon, and to implement the chosen course of action. It is a strategy that has broad applications but that is particularly useful to clients who are attempting to learn how to generate alternative action plans and/or to decide among such alternatives. The strategy addresses the client concern "What do I want to do?"

Skill Training

This strategy has the general purpose of assisting clients in their attempts to learn new skills or actions in a wide variety of domains—psychomotor, social-interpersonal, academic, cognitive, and affective. Since many client-learning difficulties are associated in one way or another with skill deficits and inappropriate or incomplete skill use (Krumboltz and Thoresen, 1976), this strategy has a wide application within the overall framework of instructional counseling. It addresses the, client concern "Now that I know what to do, how can I learn to do it?"

Personal Coping

This strategy helps clients learn to manage the variety of stresses and anxieties attendant upon living within their chosen life contexts. There are, as will be seen in chapter 5, a great many techniques currently available for anxiety/stress management. The personal coping strategy within the framework of instructional counseling is a broad-based instructional strategy that incorporates many of the more powerful aspects of these separate techniques or methods. It addresses the client concern "Now that I know what to do and how to do it, how can I overcome my anxiety associated with doing it?"

Self-Management

This strategy is concerned primarily with helping clients to manage their own learning, that is, helping them maintain and extend learning that has occurred in counseling and initiate and conduct new learning in the absence of formal counseling relationships. Put simply, the self-management strategy in instructional counseling helps clients to become their own counselors—to manage their own instruction and learning in an effective, independent manner. It addresses the client concern "Now that I know what to do, how to do it, and am no longer anxious about it, how can I continue to do what I want to do?"

Summary

As indicated at the beginning of this brief section on instructional strategies, there is a great number of counseling strategies that have been described in the professional literature dealing with counseling and therapy. There are many more strategies that can be taken from methods of instruction studied by instructional psychologists (e.g., Gage and Berliner 1979; Martin 1983). Finally, a limitless number of novel strategies or purposeful skill sequences can be tailored specifically and employed effectively in response to individual client situations and concerns. The four basic strategies of instructional counseling that form the basis for much of this book are, however, particularly versatile and appropriate to an amazingly wide range of client learning goals. As will be seen, each of these strategies may be employed separately, or they may be combined in various ways within the overall framework of the five-step instructional counseling model presented in chapter 1. Whenever any strategy is employed within instructional counseling, it must attend specifically to each of the instructional elements contained in this basic five-step model. Counseling goals always should be stated clearly, a sound preassessment of current client capabilities in relation to these goals should be undertaken, specific counseling objectives must then be constructed, active instruction and learning must follow, and the results of such learning-instruction exchanges always must be evaluated in terms of demonstrable client progress in relation to counseling goals and objectives.

INSTRUCTIONAL COUNSELING STYLES

The third level of counseling activity in the instructional counseling taxonomy (see figure 2:1) is the level of counseling styles. Counseling styles are reflections of the personal characteristics, mannerisms, and idiosyncrasies of individual counselors. While they may be altered and developed through the extended practice of skills and strategies, counseling styles are not easy to modify or acquire. Different counselors will use the same skills and strategies in slightly different ways because of their own individual styles. In one sense, it can be said that a counselor can learn all kinds of skills and strategies but must learn to work with his/her own counseling style as more of a "given." As already indicated, styles gradually can be affected by the acquisition and incorporation of new skills and strategies (indeed, this is probably one of the only ways in which to affect styles), but stylistic variables also color significantly the manner in which each counselor employs specific skills and strategies.

It should be understood clearly that counseling styles, within the instructional counseling paradigm, do *not* refer to positional bias or belief in favor of one theoretical or applied approach to counseling over all others. While counseling styles may influence counselors' beliefs or biases with respect to theoretical and applied positions, stylistic variables cut across, and through, such distinctions. Behavioral counselors are no more likely to share a particular style than developmental or cognitively oriented counselors. Major schools or positions within counseling demonstrate differing skill and strategy perferences and may advocate certain stylistic dimensions as being of greater or lesser theoretical importance. Nonetheless, there is probably as much stylistic difference among counselors who adhere to a particular position as there is among counselors of varying theoretical and positional orientations (Goldfried 1980).

Some of the more common dimensions of counseling style that have been examined and discussed in the general literature of counseling include counselor attractiveness, warmth, involvement, genuineness, understanding, congruence, trustworthiness, authenticity, and empathy (when considered beyond the operational skill level). Again, different theories of counseling may focus on one or more of such stylistic variables as being of particular importance (e.g., existential counselors are particularly concerned with the counseling implications of authenticity). However, a counselor does not possess these style dimensions, let alone communicate them to his/her clients, because he/she happens to favor a particular approach to counseling. Styles are the products of individual, experiential (developmental/learning) histories, not of contemporary theoretical preferences.

Because of the idiosyncratic character of styles, the effects of different counseling styles are difficult to assess. While a great deal of research has attempted to associated different counseling-style variables with counseling effectiveness and client change, this research has been largely unsuccessful in consistently linking such style variables to client change (e.g., Krumboltz, Becker-Haven, and Burnett 1979). Clients appear to change in direct response to the skills and strategies employed in counseling. To the extent that a counselor's style influences the degree to which he/she effectively employs different skills and strategies, counselors should be aware of their personal styles and should work to match their development of skill/ strategy repertoires with the gradual evolution of their own counseling styles.

There are five stylistic variables that are particularly relevant to instructional counseling—(1) purposefulness, (2) openness (honesty), (3) respectfulness, (4) industry, and (5) accountability. If the basic skills and strategies for instructing clients in a wide variety of cognitive, behavioral, and affective change programs can be employed within counseling relationships typified by these five dimensions, the likelihood of effective instruction is enhanced.

Purposefulness

This stylistic dimension refers to the degree to which a counselor is organized in a goal-oriented manner. Specifically, a purposeful counselor is one who employs particular skills or strategies with the full intention that they will be useful in promoting client changes congruent with those specified in counseling goals and objectives. As such, purposefulness is a dimension of counselor style that is directly relevant to working within the basic goal-referenced instructional counseling framework outlined in chapter 1.

Openness (Honesty)

This stylistic variable may be considered as the degree to which counselors openly can share counseling procedures, processes, and their own intentions with clients. In order to ensure that client learning opportunities are enhanced, counseling situations should be meaningful for clients. Counselors can enhance meaningfulness if they are willing and able to articulate clearly counseling procedures and their own intentions to clients. Such openness helps clients learn in relation to specific counseling goals but also may help them learn something about the processes of learning and instruction that will help them to resolve future difficulties and concerns without formal counseling assistance (Rogers 1969).

Respectfulness

Respectfulness refers to the willingness of counselors to treat clients with equality in matters of basic rights and privileges and to respect the potential learning capabilities that all clients possess. Clients are first and foremost learners; and, since resolving and/or coping with life's situations and problems is a matter of learning necessary skills and techniques, all clients are potentially capable of handling their own affairs. Respectfulness stems from the observation that in this basic business of learning skills and techniques that enable people to exert some control over their own lives, counselors and clients, as human beings, are involved in an identical process. The only relevant difference between counselors and clients is that in relation to the specific life problems currently experienced by clients, counselors possess knowledge about some basic instructional skills and strategies that can help clients learn to manage these areas of their lives.

Industry

Industry references the strength of the working commitment that counselors are willing to extend to clients. The facilitation of client learning typically requires the expenditure of focused, organized time and energy on the part of a counselor. Not all client learning needs may be met in the classic forty-five-to-fifty-five minute counseling hour. At times, counselors must be prepared to work with clients and significant others in clients' lives in domestic, vocational, and leisure environments at irregular time intervals. This is not to say that counselors should not protect their own private time. The point is that counselors must be willing to organize their professional practice so that sufficient time and energy are available for the instructional work that needs to be done to promote desired client learning changes.

Accountability

The final stylistic variable refers to the degree to which counselors can accept responsibility for client learning progress. In the final analysis, it is the client who learns or does not learn; however, each counselor must be willing to accept the fact that client learning progress is a strong indication of his/her own effectiveness as an instructor. There are certain client-learning problems that inevitably may be outside the instructional capabilities or resources of a counselor and that thus are associated with little client change in counseling. In analyzing such cases, a counselor should be able to recognize his/her own limitations and avoid unwarranted blaming of the client for lack of counseling progress. At the same time, counselors must learn not to heap unwarranted blame upon themselves because they are incapable of facilitating optimal change for all clients under all instructional circumstances.

Summary
The foregoing stylistic dimensions or attitudes may be made manifest to clients in a wide variety of idiosyncratic ways. There is no single way of being industrious, respectful, honest, accountable, or purposeful. Each counselor will enact these style dimensions in slightly different ways. While recognizing the inevitability of such individual differences, it is nonetheless necessary for instructional counselors to act in basic accordance with the commitments and benefits contained within these stylistic dimensions. The basic instructional counseling paradigm demands that counselors operate as instructors who make every reasonable effort to accommodate, within their counseling efforts, the basic conditions for client learning described at the outset of this chapter. It is difficult to imagine effective instruction, in this context, without some incorporation of the dimensions of purposefulness, openness, respectfulness, industry, and accountability.

Chapter Summary

When counseling is conceptualized as an instructional process, special attention must be given to the conditions under which clients learn and to the instructional actions of counselors that satisfy these conditions. In this chapter three necessary conditions for client learning were discussed—meaningful specification, practice, and feedback. These learning conditions were then related to specific sets of counseling skills—structuring, soliciting, and reacting—that can be used by counselors during counseling interactions to satisfy the three client learning conditions. Counseling skills, strategies, and styles were described as three levels of instructional activity that counselors can employ purposefully to facilitate client learning.

REFERENCES

Anderson, J. R. 1980. *Cognitive Psychology and Its Implications*. San Francisco: W. H. Freeman.

Ausubel, D. P. 1968. *Educational Psychology: A Cognitive View*. New York: Holt, Rinehart & Winston.

Bandura, A. 1969. *Principles of Behavior Modification*. Englewood Cliffs, N.J.: Prentice-Hall.

————. 1977. *Social Learning Theory*. Englewood Cliffs, N.J.: Prentice-Hall.

————, and Schunck, D. H. 1980. Cultivating competence, self-efficacy, and intrinsic interest through proximal self-motivation. Unpublished manuscript, Sanford University.

Bellack, A. A., Kliebard, H. M., Hyman, R. T., and Smith, F. L. 1966. *The Language of the Classroom*. New York: Teachers College Press.

Bower, G. H. 1970. Organizational factors in memory. *Journal of Cognitive Psychology* 1: 18–46.

Calfee, R. 1981. Cognitive psychology and educational practice. In: D. C. Berliner (ed), *Review of Research in Education* (vol. 9). Washington, D.C.: American Educational Research Association.

Clark, C. M., Gage, N. L., Marx, R. W., Peterson, P.L., Stayrook, N. G., and Winne, P. H. 1979. A factorial experiment on teacher structuring, soliciting, and reacting. *Journal of Educational Psychology* 71: 534–552.

Gage, N. L., and Berliner, D. C. 1979. *Educational Psychology* (2d ed.). Chicago: Rand McNally.

Gagné, R. M. 1977. *Conditions of Learning* (3d ed.). New York: Holt, Rinehart & Winston.

Goldfried, M. R. 1980. Toward the delineation of therapeutic change principles. *American Psychologist* 35: 991–99.

Hiebert, B. A., Martin, J., and Marx, R. W. 1981. Instructional counselling: The counsellor as teacher. *Canadian Counsellor* 15: 107–14.

Kanfer, F. H., and Goldstein, A. P. 1980 *Helping People Change: A Textbook of Methods* (2d ed.). New York: Pergamon.

Kanter, N. J., and Goldfried, M. R. 1979. Relative effectiveness of rational restructuring and self-control desensitization in the reduction of interpersonal anxiety. *Behavior Therapy* 10: 472–90.

Krumboltz, J. D., Becker-Haven, J. F., and Burnett, K. F. 1979.

Counseling Psychology. In: M. R. Rosenzweig and L. W. Porter (eds.), *Annual Review of Psychology* 30: 555–602.

_____, and Thoresen, C. E. (eds.). *Counseling Methods*. New York: Holt, Rinehart & Winston.

Lazarus, A. A. 1966. Behavior rehearsal vs. non-directive therapy vs. advice in effecting behavior change. *Behavior Research and Therapy* 4: 209–12.

Liberman, R. P., King, L. W., DeRisi, W. J., and McCann, M. 1975. *Personal Effectiveness: Guiding People to Assert Themselves and Improve Their Social Skills*. Champaign, Ill.: Research Press.

Mager, R. F. 1962. *Preparing Instructional Objectives*. Belmont, Calif.: Fearon.

Martin, J. 1983. *Mastering Instruction*. Boston: Allyn and Bacon.

Meichenbaum, D. 1977. *Cognitive-Behavior Modification: An Intergrative Approach*. New York: Plenum.

Paul, G. L. 1967. Strategy of outcome research in psychotherapy. *Journal of Consulting Psychology* 1: 109–19.

Peter, L. 1979. *Peter's People and Their Marvelous Ideas*. New York: Morrow.

Popham, W. J. and Baker, E. L. 1970. *Systematic Instruction*. Englewood Cliffs, N.J.: Prentice-Hall.

Rogers, C. R. 1969. *Freedom to Learn*. Columbus: Charles E. Merrill.

Smith, F. 1975. *Comprehension and Learning: A Conceptual Framework for Teachers*. New York: Holt, Rinehart & Winston.

Travers, R. M. W. 1977. *Essentials of Learning* (4th ed.). New York: MacMillan.

Underwood, B. J., and Swartz, R. W. 1960. *Meaningfulness and Verbal Learning*. Philadelphia: Lippincott.

CHAPTER THREE

Decision Making and Problem Solving

DECISION MAKING and problem solving are inextricably associated with counseling. A great deal of counseling is directed at assisting clients to make and act upon decisions that are aimed at resolving existing problems. Because of the close, and necessary, relationships among the making of decisions, the enactment of actions associated with these decisions, and the resolution of problems, many writers and counselors use the expressions *problem solving* and *decision making* interchangeably (e.g., Krumboltz and Thoresen 1976) or view decision making as merely a subset of problem solving (e.g., D'Zurilla and Goldfried 1971). The conceptual framework adopted in this chapter is that decision making and problem solving can be considered as a single, multistage process involving a closely integrated series of cognitive and behavioral steps.

A problem exists when a client desires change but (for whatever reason) is incapable of changing. The domain in which change is desired may be affective, behavioral, cognitive, or some combination of these modalities. Clients who want to feel better but are not able to, clients who wish to perform more productively but can't, clients who want to stop ruminating about problems at work but find themselves constantly thinking about their job situations—all of these people are experiencing problems. Problem solving is a pervasive process in which each of us frequently engages as we go about our daily affairs. When our usual decision-making and problem-solving skills or strategies break down or fail to function in a particular situation, we may benefit from instructional assistance that attempts to help us generalize our existing skills to these new situations or that helps us to acquire new sets of skills that might be effective where old skills have failed us. Effective problem solving and decision making are essential aspects of successful living.

In this chapter, a variety of decision-making and problem-solving theories are examined, some of the empirical findings relevant to problem solving are summarized, and a general approach to problem solving/decision making is developed in accordance with the five-step instructional counseling model presented in chapter 1. The chapter concludes with a detailed illustration of the application of this instructional approach within a hypothetical counseling context.

Theories of Decision Making and Problem Solving

Theories of problem solving and decision making have been extremely popular throughout the twentieth century. While it would be impossible to review all of these theories in this chapter, a brief description of some of the earliest formal theories (Dewey 1933; Gagné 1959; Wallas 1926) helps to place some of the more recent counseling theories of problem solving (D'Zurilla and Goldfried 1971; Urban and Ford 1971) and decision making (Greenwald 1973; Krumboltz 1966) in a broader ideational context.

EARLY STAGE THEORIES

Influenced by the German physicist Helmholtz and the French mathematician Poincaré, *Wallas* (1926) put forward one of the earliest stage theories of problem solving in his metaphysical treatise, *The Art of Thought*. While it is not a well-operationalized theory (because of its reliance upon unconscious and unobservable processes), Wallas's model contains four distinct phases—(1) *preparation*, (2) *incubation*, (3) *illumination*, and (4) *verification*.

Very briefly, the preparation stage consists of a period of time during which a problem is investigated "in all directions." In the incubation stage the unconscious mind of the problem solver "picks away" at the problem while the problem solver is engaged in other activities. The third stage consists of a subjective experience of sudden inspiration or illumination during which a possible viable solution occurs to the otherwise-engaged problem solver. During the verification stage the problem solver implements the proposed solution in a manner intended to test the real-life adequacy of the inspiration.

While much of Wallas's theory is decidedly metaphysical (attempting descriptions of the subjective experiences of problem solving) and is thus impossible to operationalize at a perscriptive level, it does indicate a general pattern of analysis, open-ended reflection, consideration, and testing. This general pattern is given much greater operational, conceptual clarity in the writings of John Dewey (1933).

Dewey proposed a five-phase model of reflective thought that has probably had more pervasive influence on contemporary notions about problem solving than any other early work. Dewey's five stages are: (1) *suggestion*, (2) *intellectualization*, (3) *hypothesis formation*, (4) *reasoning*, and (5) *testing*. The initial phase involves the recognition of a problem situation and a conscious decision to work to resolve it. The second phase, intellectualization, involves a detailed examination and definition of all aspects of the problem. (This phase is assisted by an active decision on the part of the problem solver to suspend action until "all the facts are in.") The hypothesis-formation stage combines the general suggestion for action from stage one with the reflective information acquired during stage two to produce a hypothesis for action that seems in line with the problem situation as defined. The reasoning stage attempts to determine the logical consequences of adopting the action hypothesis. Finally, the testing phase involves the deliberate arrangement of conditions as implied by the action hypothesis to see whether or not the results theoretically indicated by the earlier phases of the model actually occur.

Gagné (1959) places Dewey's five-step process within the framework of *classic decision theory*, that is based on particular models, sometimes statistical, of behavior. These models are built upon various permutations of the concepts of "value" and "probability," together with a broad assortment of functional rules and assumptions. The theory dates from the eighteenth century, when Pascal and other French mathematicians were employed by court gamblers to distinguish between "fair" and "unfair" bets. Gagné's five steps are: (1) *reception* of the stimulus situation, (2) *concept formation*, (3) *determination of action*, (4) *decision making* (in the narrow sense of "choosing"), and (5) *verification*. During phase one, the problem solver is motivated to achieve a definable goal. In phase two, a conception of the problem situation is achieved through the employment of cognitive rules that dictate which parts of the stimulus situation will receive attention. Phase three involves the generation of a list of action alternatives (some conservative, others risky). In phase four, the problem solver selects the alternative for action that has the highest probability of desired utility; and in phase five, the problem solver implements and evaluates the attempted solution in terms of the feedback yielded by its implementation (was it functional, inadequate, etc.?). Gagné's reliance upon classic decision theory is indicated by his use of processes such as listing alternatives and estimating the probabilities that alternatives will accomplish intended or valued outcomes (see Bross 1953 for a closely related model).

CONTEMPORARY THEORIES

While Gagné's theory of problem solving is slightly more prescriptive than the descriptive theories of Wallas and Dewey, most early theorists of problem solving (with the historical exceptions of the prescriptions for gambling given by Pascal and others) were more interested in describing problem-solving phenomena than in assisting individuals to adopt strategies that would make them better problem solvers. The work of D'Zurilla and Goldfried (1971) and Urban and Ford (1971), departs from this descriptive tradition and denotes the first formal recognition of the relevance of the general literature on problem solving to counseling per se.

D'Zurilla and Goldfried (1971) define problem solving as "a behavioral process, whether overt or cognitive in nature, which (a) makes available a variety of potentially effective response alternatives for dealing with the problematic situation and (b) increases the probability of selecting the most effective response from among these various alternatives" (p. 108). The D'Zurilla and Goldfried counseling approach consists of five stages, which encompass the general problem-solving processes indicated by Dewey, Gagné, and others.

1. *General Orientation*—In this stage, the client is helped to develop a functional attitude toward problems and their resolutions. The client comes to understand that problems are a normal part of living and that one can learn to deal with them in effective ways.

2. *Problem Definition*—After orienting to problem solving in general, the client is helped to define operationally all aspects of the problem situation, to separate relevant from irrelevant aspects of the the situation, and to identify primary goals for problem resolution.

3. *Generation of Alternatives*—As in Gagné's model, the client next generates a variety of alternatives for action. D'Zurilla and Goldfried employ a wide range of stimulation and brainstorming techniques to assist the client in this regard.

4. *Decision Making*—Alternatives are weighed (in relation to their probability of accomplishing primary goals without unwanted side effects) and prioritized, and the best available alternative is selected.

5. *Verification*—Feedback from implementing the selected alternative is evaluated in relation to desired goals; if the selected alternative has proved unsatisfactory, a recycling of the problem-solving process is undertaken.

The D'Zurilla and Goldfried model constitutes a definite "blueprint" for prescriptive counseling. The general purposes for employing this approach with a client are to assist the client in resolving a current problem and to help the client acquire a general problem-solving strategy that may be employed to resolve other problems as they occur.

Urban and Ford's (1971) system of problem solving in counseling is very similar to that proposed by D'Zurilla and Goldfried. This similarity is obvious from a quick scan of the descriptive labels for the Urban and Ford problem-solving steps: (1) *identification* of the problem, (2) *analysis* of the problem, (3) *selection* of goals, (4) *implementation* of the problem solution, and (5) subsequent *evaluation*. Urban and Ford appear to place slightly greater emphasis than D'Zurilla and Goldfried upon the formulation of goals and the precise methods to be used in implementing the problem solution.

Two additional approaches to problem solving and decision making in counseling and psychotherapy have been proposed by Krumboltz (Krumboltz 1966; Krumboltz and Baker 1973; Krumboltz and Thoresen 1964) and Greenwald (1973). Unlike D'Zurilla and Goldfried (1971) and Urban and Ford (1971), who tend to subordinate decision making to problem solving in their overall conception of these processes, these authors place a strong emphasis on decision making as an overarching process for resolving problems and life concerns. (Recall that the current chapter considers problem solving and decision making as a single, multistage process.)

Krumboltz's eight stages of adaptive decision making are: (1) *generating a list of all possible courses of action*, (2) *gathering relevant information about each feasible alternative course of action*, (3) *estimating the probability of success for each alternative on the bases of the experience of others and projections of current trends*, (4) *considering the personal values that may be enhanced or diminished under each course of action*, (5) *deliberating and weighing the facts, probable outcomes, and values for each course of action*, (6) *eliminating from consideration the least favorable courses of action*, (7) *formulating a tentative plan of action subject to new developments and opportunities*, and (8) *generalizing the decision-making process to future problems*. As should be obvious from these labels, Krumboltz's views on decision making are closely congruent with prescriptions from classical decision theory and define a process similar to that defined by the contemporary problem-solving approaches just reviewed.

A relatively recent approach to psychotherapy and counseling that makes extensive use of decision making is the *direct decision therapy* advocated by *Greenwald* (1973). While it arises from reflections on his own life and the lives of his clients and is unaffected by any formal study of decision theory or problem solving, Greenwald's approach shows the now-familiar pattern of analysis/conceptualization, open-ended reflection and generation of alternatives, and selection and implementation evaluation of a single "best" alternative that typifies almost all of the models reviewed. Specifically, Greenwald's therapy involves (1) *conceptualization* of a problem in concrete terms, (2) *examination of past decisions* relevant to the problem and its creation, (3) *identification of advantages and disadvantages* associated with the current situation, (4) *generation of alternatives*, and (5) *selection and implementation of one alternative*.

While many theories of problem solving and decision making have been formulated, almost all of them show a characteristic pattern, indicating that the major stages in effective problem solving are generally agreed upon and understood. The next section of this chapter examines the empirical evidence that is currently available in support of many of the crucial prescriptive actions contained in contemporary counseling approaches to decision making and problem solving.

Empirical Studies of Decision Making and Problem Solving

Research findings relevant to counseling for problem solving and decision making come from a wide variety of sources, including (1) *descriptive studies* of the characteristics of good and poor problem solvers, (2) *training studies* that attempt to impart problem-solving/decision-making skills to trainees, and (3) *counseling outcome studies* that evaluate the clinical effects produced by decision-making counseling.

DESCRIPTIVE STUDIES

Perhaps the most important, and certainly the most widely cited, investigation of the characteristics of good and poor problem solvers was conducted by *Bloom and Broder* (1950). Among other things, Bloom and Broder found that less successful problem solvers tend to be impulsive, impatient, and quick to give up if they do not find immediate solutions to their problems. On the other hand, more effective problem solvers are better able to define problem situations in concrete terms than are their less successful counterparts, who flail about in abstractions. The main implications arising from the Bloom and Broder study are that poor problem solvers are incapable of defining problem situations in concrete terms and tend not to generate alternative problem solutions.

The inability of poor problem solvers to formulate solution options has led to the development of a variety of training procedures that attempt to teach the specific skill of generating alternatives. *Maltzman*'s (1960) *originality training* and the *brainstorming* techniques presented by *Clark* (1958) and *Osborn* (1963) are among the better-developed approaches in this area. Maltzman's originality-training approach consists of the systematic reinforcement of novel, uncommon responses in controlled situations wherein participants are instructed to "be original" and not "to censure" spontaneous reactions. The Maltzman technique has been tested empirically on numerous occasions (e.g., Caron, Unger, and Parloff 1963; Penney and McCann 1962) and has received very favorable evaluations concerning its effectiveness in increasing participants' abilities to generate solutions.

The brainstorming approaches of Clark (1958) and Osborn (1963) initially were developed for use in industrial settings and typically are employed in group contexts. During brainstorming sessions, participants are instructed and encouraged to avoid criticism, to "freewheel" (not to censure any ideas no matter how unusual, bizarre, or "offbeat"), to foster quantity of output (as many different ideas as possible), and to make constructive suggestions for improving each other's ideas. Once again, the efficacy of various brainstorming rules in helping people generate solutions is well supported by empirical studies (e.g., Bayless 1967; Davis and Manske 1966; Parnes 1967). Anecdotal evidence concerning the efficacy of brainstorming is also impressive (for example, Sylvania Electric's popular flashcube resulted from a brainstorming session—Horan 1979).

TRAINING AND OUTCOME STUDIES

Additional support for the consensus problem-solving/decision-making steps of defining situations and generating alternatives, together with support for the notions of setting problem-solving goals and selecting one alternative through a process of consequential thinking (e.g., "What might happen if I implemented this alternative?") comes from a variety of training studies. These studies document the effects of comprehensive training programs, such as the *ICPS* ("interpersonal cognitive problem solving") *skills training* approach developed by Spivack, Platt, and Shure (1976).

While direct tests of the clinical effectiveness of the specific counseling approaches to decision making and problem solving reviewed in the preceding theoretical section of this chapter are not numerous, a few such studies do exist. Feldman (1976) successfully employed an explicit counseling strategy for decision making in the treatment of alcoholics. Russell (1977) incorporated the Krumboltz model of decision-making counseling to good effect in a program to provide delinquent youths with skills needed to resolve problems of choice. Still other studies (Evans and Cody 1969; Smith and Evans 1973) have shown positive results for decision-making strategies, derived largely from Bross (1953), in analog studies with college and public school subjects.

Taken together, most of the training and outcome studies that have been undertaken to date tend to provide empirical support for the existence and importance of many of the basic steps in problem-solving and decision-making models for counseling (e.g., Spivack, Platt, and Shure 1976). They also indicate that the skills associated with steps such as defining problem situations, setting goals, generating alternatives, and selecting one "best" alternative may be trained successfully and once acquired by trainees may be employed to resolve and/or to cope with a variety of problem situations. (For an in-depth review of literature on decision making and problem solving, the interested reader is directed to Horan 1979.)

Decision Making and Problem Solving in Instructional Counseling

The model for problem solving/decision making presented in this chapter makes use of many of the processes and techniques just reviewed, within the operational context of the general model for instructional counseling presented in chapter 1. Each of the steps (*goals, preassessment, objectives, activities,* and *evaluation*) is detailed and described as it is employed in problem-solving/decision-making counseling. Following descriptions and discussions of the specific processes of learning and instruction that define each of these steps, specific instructional skills (see chapter 2) that instructional counselors use in executing these steps will be analyzed and illustrated within the context of a hypothetical case study.

THE STEPS

Goals

The initial goal-setting step involves: (1) a determination of what the client wishes to accomplish as a result of participating in counseling, (2) a general orientation to instructional counseling, and (3) a specific orientation to problem solving/decision making within an instructional counseling framework. In the initial meeting(s) with the client, the instructional counselor employs a variety of reacting skills to encourage the client to describe the general concerns or difficulties that have resulted in his/her decision to seek assistance through counseling. As these presenting concerns are discussed, the counselor gradually leads the client to a consideration of what she/he wishes to accomplish as a result of participating in counseling. To ensure that the general goal statement or statements that result from such consideration are client centered and amenable to subsequent evaluation (see chapter 1), the counselor helps the client to state general goals, that is, what she/he would like to be able to do, think, and/or feel after engaging in counseling that she/he is not presently able to do, think, and/or feel (e.g., "I'd like to make up my mind about what I want to do—raise kids or pursue my career; and then to commit myself to the choice I've made so that I can be a success at it"). At this stage, it is not necessary that the client's goal(s) be specifically operationalized, logically consistent with a full range of options, or totally rational. What is necessary is that goals be specific enough to indicate the general counseling strategy or strategies that are best suited for facilitating the general direction of change desired by the client.

Once general goals have been clarified (a process that may take as little as fifteen minutes or as long as five or six full counseling sessions), the instructional counselor orients the client to the general model of instruction and learning described in chapter 1, giving specific emphasis to the roles and performance expectations of the counselor as teacher (instructor) and the client as learner. Counseling is described as a process in which clients (with the assistance, resources, and encouragement of the counselor) determine exactly what they wish to do, work and practice hard to acquire the skills that will permit them to attain these goals, and learn to evaluate their own learning progress in relation to their goals and objectives. Care is taken to express these notions in terms that will be comprehended readily by individual clients and to discuss any client misconceptions, concerns, or questions at length. Before terminating this process of general orientation, the counselor describes the various responsibilities and commitments that she or he will make in working with the client and clarifies the responsibilities and commitments that will be expected from the client. At this stage, informed consent forms and/or contracts that explicitly describe the general process of instructional counseling, indicate the general goal(s) to which counseling will be directed, and detail the responsibilities and commitments of both client (and guardians in the case of minors) and counselor are jointly prepared and signed (see Hare-Mustin et al. 1979).

To this point, the goal-setting phase of problem-solving/decision-making counseling is identical to the general goal-setting process that typifies any kind of instructional counseling. However, once general goals have been determined and a general orientation to instructional counseling has occurred, the goal-setting phase (on the assumption that the general goals identified are clearly indicative of counseling in problem solving or decision making) becomes more specific with respect to decision making/problem solving per se. The instructional counselor now focuses upon the specific assumptions and orientations that underlie problem solving within an instructional counseling framework. Clients are informed that problems are a normal part of living, that everyone experiences them from time to time, and that people who resolve and/or cope with problems successfully have learned skills that enable them to do this. Clients also are told that they too can learn such skills and that the general purpose of counseling is to teach clients problem-solving/decision-making skills that they can use to attain the general goals they have set. The instructional counselor uses a variety of means to convey these messages, including direct verbal explanation; illustrations and examples from the client's own experience, from fiction, from public media, etc.; the assignment of readings (bibliotherapy); and testimonials from others. By the end of the goal-setting phase, client and counselor have determined general counseling goals. The client now has become familiar with the general method of instructional counseling and has acquired a specific set of cognitive assumptions and expectations about solving problems. The client has been prepared to participate actively as a learner in a process of instruction aimed at accomplishing his/her goals.

Preassessment

In the preassessment phase of problem-solving counseling, client problems and problem situations are conceptualized in concrete detail, current and past responses of the client to these situations are specified, and existing client capabilities are assessed in relation to general problem-solving skills required to resolve or cope with the problem as specified.

So that both counselor and client share a clear, concrete understanding of the problem that the client is experiencing, the situations in which the problem occurs and the exact nature of client reactions to these situations are probed rigorously. Clients work, with the counselor's assistance, to describe *when* the problem arises, *where* it arises, *how long* it lasts, what *others* in the situation do, and what the client *thinks*, *does*, and *feels* in these situations. Current and past attempts by the client to resolve or cope with the problem are explored in detail, as is the nature of the results achieved. Particular attention is paid to client actions, thoughts, and emotions *prior to*, *during*, and *following upon* intense problem experiences. In this way, the instructional counselor works with the client to produce a detailed conceptua map of the current problem situation as it encompasses the client. Again, a variety of methods may be employed, including focused discussion, cognitive techniques of asking clients to "play back films in their heads" and to describe what they see (Meichenbaum 1977), out-of-office discussions with others involved in the problem, role-plays and simulations of problem scenarios, and so on.

Once the problem has been operationalized concretely and the client's current behavioral, cognitive, and affective status in relation to the problem has been ascertained, the instructional counselor and client learner work to determine the existing capabilities of the client in relation to known skills of problem solving and decision making. Such skills include the client's abilities to define problem situations concretely, to generate alternatives, to select a single alternative through a process of consequential thinking, to take specific steps to implement the selected alternative, and to evaluate the success or lack of success of the enacted alternative in relation to the overall goal of problem solving. As indicated in chapter 1, such skills are derived from a process of task analysis in which the instructional counselor and client analyze the various tasks that must be executed effectively before the generic goal of successful problem solving can be attained. With some knowledge of these tasks (gained from cognitive analysis on the part of the counselor, from a careful reading of the professional literature on problem solving and decision making, and from specific knowledge of the particular problem situation just defined), the counselor and client then attempt to evaluate the client's current abilities to perform each relevant task step. In addition to using client self-judgments in making determinations of client "entry" (current) capabilities, instructional counselors can test or assess relevant client skills by presenting simulated problem situations and asking clients to generate alternatives, predict the likely consequences of engaging in various alternatives, select a single alternative that best satisfies anticipated action criteria, and so on.

At the conclusion of the preassessment phase, both counselor and client should have a concrete conception of the problem situation and the client's current reactions to it. They also should have a reasonably reliable and valid indication of the client's current capabilities (*entering behavior*) in relation to the various skills needed to execute the series of tasks that result in successful problem solving. All of this information is invaluable in formulating specific instructional objectives that will guide subsequent counseling/learning activities.

Objectives

The third phase of instructional counseling is concerned with the translation of the general counseling goals formulated in step one into specific statements of desired client performance. In problem-solving counseling, specific counseling objectives are framed that specify the precise course of action to be undertaken by the client in resolving his/her problem situation. Most often, several such objectives will be necessary to convey the number of things that clients will do or be able to do at various stages and at the end of the overall counseling process.

Any problem-solving process that involves the initiation of client action must be preceded logically by a determination or a decision as to exactly what this action will be. The objectives stage of problem-solving counseling (within an instructional counseling framework) is concerned with both the determination of client action and the framing of client action in terms of attainable counseling objectives. To determine the best alternatives for client action, the instructional counselor and client first work together (assisted by their joint knowledge of current client capabilities as determined in the preassessment phase) to brainstorm a wide variety of alternatives for action. Clients are encouraged "not to censure" possible alternatives and "to be creative" in their suggestions. Such an open-ended generation of alternatives may be assisted by instructions such as "imagine what others might do," "imagine what you'd like to do regardless of what you think you can do," and so on.

Once a variety of alternative courses of action have been recorded, the instructional counselor urges the client to consider each alternative in turn in relation to the likely consequences that would accrue to self and others, both in the short and long term, as a result of implementing the alternative being considered. If the client has limited skills to perform such speculation, the counselor must assist the client in acquiring consequential thinking abilities. This may involve modeling the process of consequential thinking for the client, teaching the client to differentiate between short-term and long-term results, and/or assisting the client in considering perspectives other than his/ her own.

When the various alternatives have been weighed and considered in relation to the consequences they might produce, the client is asked to prioritize the alternatives in some systematic fashion. One good way of doing this is to use a procedure of "matched comparisons" in which every possible alternative is compared with every other alternative and given a numerical value of 1 each time the client judges it to be the superior alternative in any given pair of alternatives. When this process has been completed, numerical totals for each alternative may be determined and the alternatives listed in sequence from "most desirable" to "least desirable."

Careful discussion is given to the "most desirable" alternative to determine its feasibility relative to the current status of the problem situation and the current and potential capabilities of the client to engage the alternative (a process that might result in discarding the first or first few choices from the prioritized list). An alternative for action is then agreed upon and framed in a client-centered objective (e.g., "I will arrange a one-year leave of absence to devote myself to full-time parenting, after which I will return to my present career and my wife and I will hire a live-in nanny to care for our son").

Where such objectives are complex and long term, the instructional counselor helps the client to break down the objective into a series of more proximal objectives that are likely to culminate in the longer-term objective (e.g., "I will discuss my desires thoroughly with my wife and work out specific financial and practical arrangements with her"; "I will discuss my plans with my current boss and work out the details and conditions of a leave of absence"; etc.). When a series of specific objectives is formulated in relation to a chosen alternative for action, the objectives phase of problem-solving/decision-making counseling is concluded.

Activities

The actual implementation of activities associated with the various counseling objectives is now undertaken. Client and counselor negotiate a specific sequence of client and counselor actions that likely will result in the accomplishment of the goals. Actions to be undertaken are charted on a general time line, decisions are made as to who is responsible for doing what, specific time deadlines are determined for each action, and means of evaluating progress are planned. This latter undertaking sets the stage for final evaluation of the counseling program and integrates evaluation components into the active instruction/ learning phase of counseling. Throughout the activities phase, periodic meetings are held in which client and counselor report the execution of assigned tasks, the counselor provides feedback and encouragement to the client (constantly reinforcing the efforts of the client to work systematically at resolving the problem), and the counselor and client clarify the next set of actions to be executed and the mutual commitments involved. As the activities phase evolves, the instructional counselor gradually places more and more responsibility on the client for organizing and conducting such meetings and devotes a portion of each session to a discussion of problem-solving skills and processes in general. In this way, the client is helped to acquire a problem-solving process that can be generalized to other situations or concerns as these arise in the natural course of living.

Evaluation

By the time the activities phase of counseling is terminated, the client has taken effective control of all the major aspects of the counseling program. When this occurs, client and counselor meet to review the program, to discuss progress to date, and to arrange periodic follow-up contacts. Many evaluation components already have been integrated into the overall counseling process at the activities phase (many instructional counselors and their clients create graphic displays of goal achievement and/or relevant skill improvement). Consequently, the final evaluation phase of instructional counseling is primarily a time for revisiting instructional goals and objectives, reviewing the process of problem solving itself, and assessing accomplishments in relation to initial goals and objectives. Some system by which the client periodically reports subsequent progress in the present and/or other problem areas typically is negotiated for purposes of future encouragement and support. Such an arrangement also is useful in attaining longer-term information that can help the instructional counselor evaluate the overall effectiveness of the counseling program. (Note that the foregoing problem-solving/decision-making process has no fixed time line. All steps may be accomplished in one or two sessions, or they may require numerous sessions over several months. The instructional counselor moves only as quickly as the client is able to grasp and master the essential skills and processes that define each step in the counseling sequence.)

THE INSTRUCTIONAL SKILLS USED

One of the primary advantages of viewing counseling as an instructional enterprise is that such a framework helps a counselor to determine the exact skills needed to facilitate the learning and instructional processes that define counseling interventions such as the problem-solving/decision-making program just described. In order to *specify* counseling processes and procedures to clients in ways they will find *meaningful*, in order to arrange for appropriate client *practice* of the learning performances specified in counseling objectives and goals, and in order to provide the all-important ingredient of effective *instructional feedback* to client learning efforts, instructional counselors make extensive use of the various structuring, soliciting, and reacting skills described in chapter 2. The specific skills that allow the instructional counselor to promote the various client learning processes essential to effective problem-solving/decision-making counseling are described and illustrated in this section. The following discussion of skills is organized according to the five phases of problem-solving counseling discussed in the previous section of this chapter. A wide variety of skills can be employed in different combinations and sequences to accomplish a single counseling objective.

The emphasis in this section is upon noting and illustrating those skills that the authors view as being most essential in

facilitating the client learning activities and instructional processes associated with each phase of the instructional counseling process for problem solving/decision making. For each of the
five major instructional steps that define this process, "key"
skills are listed, described, and illustrated by examples taken
from a hypothetical problem-solving situation. Each of the skills
referenced may be used numerous times in different manners,
but only a single illustration will be given. The purposes of this
section are (1) to indicate the exact counseling skills that are most
important to the facilitation of an effective problem-solving/
decision-making process, (2) to illustrate their use by including
segments from a constructed counseling transcript, and (3) to
indicate the purposeful way in which counseling skills can be
selected and employed to encourage predictable client learning
in the context of a well-structured instructional environment.
(Remember that the client in the following illustrations is a well-
educated professional in his early thirties. The exact way in
which counseling skills are employed and the words used to
convey them must always be tailored to individual clients.)

Goals

Major Counseling Skills	Illustrated Use
Nonverbal Listening (Attending)	S Sitting squarely, facing client O Open posture L Leaning slightly forward E Eye contact R Relaxed
Paraphrasing Content	"So, you really want to make a decision about how best to spend your time and energy."
Reflecting Meaning	"And it's particularly difficult to come to any resolution when you really

Major Counseling Skills	Illustrated Use
	want to do both things— even though you only have time to do one job really well."
Reflecting Affect	"Always changing your mind creates a very frustrating, annoying feeling."
Summarizing	"The situation you've described is indeed perplexing. At this point, you are really uncertain as to what you want to do with respect to raising a family. Both you and your wife have careers that you enjoy, and the nature of your wife's career makes it impossible for her to interrupt it in order to stay at home with your son. Yet both of you feel very strongly about the desirability of parents spending a great deal of time with their children."
Stating Goals	"Your overall goal might be stated as 'I want to make up my mind about what I want to do—raise kids or pursue my career; and then to commit myself to the choice I've made so that I can do it successfully.' "

Major Counseling Skills	Illustrated Use
Giving Overviews	"Now that we both have a common idea about what you want to achieve as a result of our work together, I'd like to give you a clear idea about the general approach I think we should take, the various stages in this approach, and the specific kinds of things we probably will do together. Basically, your task will be to achieve your goal—to make up your mind about what you want to do and to do it. My task will be to teach you ways in which you can reach your goal and to help you acquire the kinds of skills and abilities that are useful in resolving such situations. Problem solving is a very natural process. Everyone has problems and needs to make decisions and undertake actions that will help to resolve, or cope with, problems. The skills required to do this can be learned, and we can work together to help you acquire these skills."
Using Markers of Importance	"Yes, that's *absolutely critical.* There's no magic solution.

Major Counseling Skills	Illustrated Use
	Only well-planned, consistent effort will get you where you want to be."
Stating Transitions	"Well, when we meet again, we'll try to take stock of exactly where things stand right now, and we'll begin to focus on your current abilities in relation to the problem-solving/decision-making skills necessary to resolve your situation."

Preassessment

Major Counseling Skills	Illustrated Use
Using Set Induction	"I'd like you to think very carefully about the last time you really felt upset about the current conflict between child rearing and your job. Try to imagine the exact situation you were in. What are you thinking, what are you feeling, what are you doing, what things are you saying to yourself?"
Probing	"What do you do when you start feeling like that?" "I'd like you to tell me what you've done in the past to try to resolve this problem."

Major Counseling Skills	Illustrated Use
(Paraphrasing Content, Reflecting Meaning, and Reflecting Affect also are used extensively at the Preassessment Phase of problem solving/decision making.)	
Calling for Demonstration	"Last time we met, I asked you to make a list of all the things you've done to attempt to resolve this predicament. May I see the list you've constructed?"
Summarizing	"Let's stop now and review what we've done and what we've found out. We now have a clear, concrete picture of what the exact dimensions of the problem are and of how you typically react to the problem situation. And while you have every capability of systematically charting alternatives for action, you really have never approached the problem in this way."

Objectives

Major Counseling Skills	Illustrated Use
Giving Clear Instructions and Using Set Induction	"I'd like you to think of anything that might be done in this situation. What are all the possible actions? Don't worry about how feasible or realistic they are. Just speak about any idea that enters your head—no matter how silly or crazy it seems. There's lots of time to censure later. Right now, just be creative."
Prompting	"What might you do if you weren't worried about anyone else? You hinted at this in your last idea when you said that you've always wanted to . . ."
Giving Descriptive Praise	"O.K., great. You've produced a list of over twenty-five possible courses of action."
Modeling	"Now, notice in this demonstration of what we're calling consequential thinking how careful I'm being to consider each and every alternative in terms of its short- and long-term consequences both for myself and for the other people involved."

Major Counseling Skills	Illustrated Use
(Paraphrasing Content, Reflecting Meaning, Reflecting Affect, Probing, and Summarizing are used extensively at this stage to help clients clarify their reactions to each action alternative and to select a single "best" solution.)	
Stating Objectives	"Your specific objectives in relation to your selected course of action will be 'to arrange a one-year leave of absence to devote yourself to full-time parenting, after which time you will return to your career and will hire a live-in nanny to care for your son.' "

Activities

Major Counseling Skills	Illustrated Use
Stating Transitions	"Now that we have a very specific indication of the various concrete tasks that need to be accomplished so that you can achieve your selected action objective,. let's see if we can determine the order in which these steps will be accomplished,

Major Counseling Skills	Illustrated Use
	when each step will be completed, and what specific responsibilities we will each have in ensuring that everything gets done as we've planned."
Using Markers of Importance	"The really crucial point is that we've agreed to accept these responsibilities as *firm commitments*."
Expressing Counselor Reactions with "I" Messages	"I want to know what you did and how that relates to our coordinated plan of action."
Promoting Ownership	"But even though things were a bit different from what we'd imagined they would be, the fact remains that you made a commitment and that you did not keep that commitment."
Probing (used here to initiate further action)	"What are you going to do now so that we can keep our plan on target?"
Descriptive Praise	"You've really kept up your end of our arrangements. You must feel pretty proud of your ability to control your own situation."

Evaluation

Major Counseling Skills	Illustrated Use
Summarizing	"We've now reached the end of our action plan, and you've managed to take all of the steps you needed to take to reach your overall goal. A leave of absence has been arranged in a way that will allow you to return to your present career in a year's time. Your wife has agreed to arrange her work week so that you will have time together with and without the little boy. You have begun to make further arrangements for securing a nanny. In short, you're now in a position to enjoy a year with your son without sacrificing any of your major career aspirations."
Giving Informational Feedback	"With respect to the general skills of problem solving that you've been practicing in relation to this situation, think you've developed a good, sound ability to generate alternatives, state useful objectives, and make specific action plans. Your skill at evaluating your actions in relation to your objectives also has improved

Major Counseling Skills	Illustrated Use
	a great deal. You still balk a bit at keeping careful records of your actions so that you can evaluate them in a more objective manner. This is something that could create difficulties for you if you let it slip too much."
Stating Transitions	"So, we've agreed that you're on your own now and that there is no need for any further meetings on a regular basis. You'll give me a follow-up call each Monday for the next two months to let me know how things are going, but our formal contract is ended as of now."

Decision Making/Problem Solving in Multifaceted Instructional Counseling

The foregoing sections describing the instructional skills and process steps associated with decision making/problem solving within an instructional counseling framework have treated problem solving as an instructional learning activity appropriate for the attainment of client goals that indicate a specific problem-solving focus. Oftentimes client concerns, difficulties, and desires may be broader or more numerous than those that may be dealt with effectively through problem solving/decision making alone. In addition to determining and mounting courses of action associated with generic decision-making/problem-solving questions (such as "What do I want to do?" and "How can I do what I want to do?"), many clients will require remediation of specific skill deficits ("How can I learn to do what I want to do?"); assistance in coping with anxieties, fears, and stress associated with acting ("How can I relax while I'm learning to do this?"); and/or assistance in managing their own lives in generally enhancing directions ("How can I continue to do what I want to do?"). Consequently, while almost all instructional counseling situations necessitate some work in problem solving/decision making, other instructional counseling strategies often will be required in association with problem-solving/decision-making steps (e.g., skill training, personal coping, and/or self-management).

Whatever multifaceted counseling approach (combination of strategies) may be necessary for the attainment of counseling goals in specific situations for particular clients, many elements of the problem-solving/decision-making strategy described in this chapter are particularly useful during the goal-setting, pre-assessment, and objective-setting phases of multifaceted instructional counseling. In fact, the very nature of instructional counseling, commencing as it does with the determination of goals and specific objectives in relation to existing client capabilities and counseling methods, demands a great deal of initial attention to the generic decision-making question "What do I want to do?"

Chapter Summary

Lawrence Peter's (1979) principle of management by objectives states that if you don't know where you are going, you will end up somewhere else. This chapter on decision making and problem solving within an instructional counseling framework has discussed a systematic, five-step process of learning and instruction that may be employed to help clients decide where they are going and to assist them in planning and executing action sequences that will get them there. The chapter began with a survey of decision-making/problem-solving theories and relevant empirical findings. Many of the consensual notions and processes arising from this survey were interwoven with the general model of instructional counseling to produce the basic problem-solving/decision-making model that was discussed. To assist readers in conceptualizing the most important instructional actions that counselors must develop and use in order to facilitate client learning of basic problem-solving/decision-making processes, an extensive illustration of many of the specific skills used by instructional counselors when instructing with a problem-solving/decision-making focus was provided. The chapter concluded with a brief consideration of problem solving/decision making within multifaceted instructional counseling.

It should be stated once again that the overall objective of instructional counseling is to enable the client to get along without the counselor. With respect to decision making/problem solving, the instructional counseling process is not complete until the client has demonstrated an ability to generalize the problem-solving process itself to problem areas in his/her life other than that specific problem area that provided the concrete opportunity for the client's initial acquisition of problem-solving skills. The instructional counselor aims at imparting the basic strategy of problem solving/decision making to the client so that the client is able to engage in self-instruction independent of formal counseling intervention. One of the major advantages to be gained from conceptualizing counseling as instruction is that this conceptualization helps to clarify the major objective of assisting clients in carrying on self-directed learning that is relevant to successful living through the inculcation of the process of self-instruction. Instructional counselors provide external models of the kind of instructional strategies and actions that client learners can acquire as a result of their participation in instructional counseling.

REFERENCES

Bayless, O. L. 1967. An alternative pattern for problem-solving discussions. *Journal of Communication* 17: 188–97.

Bloom, B. S., and Broder, L. J. 1950. *Problem-Solving Processes of College Students.* Chicago: University of Chicago Press.

Bross, I. D. J. 1953. *Design for Decision: An Introduction to Statistical Decision-Making.* New York: Macmillan.

Caron, A. J., Unger, S. M., and Parloff, M. B. 1963. A test of Maltzman's theory of originality training. *Journal of Verbal Learning and Verbal Behavior* 1: 436–42.

Clark, C. H. 1958. *Brainstorming.* New York: Doubleday.

Davis, G. A., and Manske, M. E. 1966. An instructional method of increasing originality. *Psychonomic Science* 6: 73–74.

Dewey, J. 1933. *How We Think.* Boston: Heath.

D'Zurilla, T. J., and Goldfried, M. R. 1971. Problem-solving and behavior modification. *Journal of Abnormal Psychology* 78: 107–26.

Evans, J. R., and Cody, J. J. 1969. Transfer of decision-making skills learned in a counseling-like setting to similar and dissimilar situations. *Journal of Counseling Psychology* 16: 427–32.

Feldman, B. A. 1976. An investigation of a decision-based counseling paradigm for use with alcoholics. Unpublished master's thesis, Pennsylvania State University.

Gagné, R. M. 1959. Problem solving and thinking. *Annual Review of Psychology* 10: 147–72.

Greenwald, H. 1973. *Direct Decision Therapy.* San Diego: Edits.

Hare-Mustin, R. T., Marecek, J., Kaplan, A. G., and Liss-Levinson, N. 1979. Rights of clients, responsibilities of therapists. *American Psychologist* 34: 3–16.

Horan, J. J. 1979. *Counseling for Effective Decision-Making: A Cognitive-Behavioral Perspective.* North Scituate, Mass.: Duxbury.

Krumboltz, J. D. 1966. *Stating the Goals of Counseling.* California Counseling and Guidance Association Monograph No. 1.

————, and Baker, R. D. 1973. Behavioral counseling for vocational decisions. *In*: H. Borrow (ed.), *Career Guidance for a New Age.* Boston: Houghton Mifflin.

Krumboltz, J. D., and Thoresen, C. E. 1964. The effect of behavioral counseling in group and individual settings on information seeking behavior. *Journal of Counseling Psychology* 11: 324–33.

————, and ———— (Eds.) 1976. *Counseling Methods.* New York: Holt, Rinehart & Winston.

Maltzman, I. 1960. On the training of originality. *Psychological Review* 67: 229, 242.

Meichenbaum, D. H. 1977. *Cognitive-Behavior Modification: An Integrative Approach.* New York: Plenum.

Osborn, A. F., 1963. *Applied Imagination: Principles and Procedures of Creative Problem Solving.* New York: Scribner's.

Parnes, S. J. 1967. *Creative Behavior Guidebook.* New York: Scribner's.

Penney, R. K., and McCann, B. 1962. Application of originality training to the mentally retarded. *Psychological Reports,* 11: 347–51.

Peter, L. J. 1979. *Peter's People and Their Marvelous Ideas.* New York: Morrow.

Russell, M. L. 1977. *A Program of Clinical Research Development: Developing Decision-Making Skills in Children.* Paper presented at the annual meeting of the American Educational Research Association, New York.

Smith, R. D., and Evans, J. R. 1973. Comparison of experimental group guidance and individual counseling as facilitators of vocational development. *Journal of Counseling Psychology* 20: 202–08.

Spivack, G., Platt, J. J., and Shure, M. B. 1976. *The Problem-Solving Approach to Adjustment.* San Francisco: Jossey-Bass.

Urban, H. B., and Ford, D. H. 1971. Some historical and conceptual perspectives on psychotherapy and behavior change. *In*: A. E. Bergin and S. L. Garfield (eds.), *Handbook of Psychotherapy and Behavior Change: An Empirical Analysis.* New York: Wiley.

Wallas, G. 1926. *The Art of Thought.* New York: Harcourt, Brace & Company.

CHAPTER FOUR

Skill Training

SKILL TRAINING, like decision making/problem solving, is one of the most frequently employed instructional counseling strategies. A host of client difficulties are associated wholly or in part with skill deficits in areas as far ranging as interpersonal communication, assertion, planning, time management, parenting, academic/vocational achievement, leisure/recreational activities, and money management. Almost any human activity can be analyzed in terms of constituent skills (both behavioral and cognitive), the satisfactory performances of which are fundamentally prerequisite to the successful execution of the overall activity (Engelmann and Carnine 1982). Playing tennis requires the acquisition of behavioral skills such as groundstrokes, lobs, volleys, and serves, as well as cognitive skills/strategies such as knowledge of scoring procedures and court rules, perception of court positions, and conceptualization of playing strategies. Public speaking requires the acquisition of behavioral skills such as clear enunciation, pacing, coordination of hand gestures and postures with spoken words, and using cue cards, as well as cognitive skills/strategies such as organization of material, perception of audience reactions, and conceptualization of meaningful illustrations and examples. Such skill analyses of complex human activities are particularly useful for counseling purposes. A wide variety of instructional procedures can be used by counselors to help clients acquire the cognitive and behavioral skills basic to the accomplishment of specific client objectives and goals.

Three empirically valid premises have resulted in recent rapid growth in instructional counseling strategies for skill training. First, it is possible to isolate component skills contributing to complex human accomplishments. Second, it is possible to teach these skills to clients who have not yet learned them. Finally, once such skills are learned they may be combined to result in effective client execution of the overall performances to which they contribute. In this chapter, theories of learning and instruction, together with empirical research studies that support these three tenets and that suggest specific counseling methods that apply such premises to areas of client concern, are reviewed and summarized. A general approach to skill training is then described and illustrated in accordance with the basic five-step instructional counseling model (see chapter 1). The chapter concludes with a discussion of ways in which skill training may be combined and associated with other counseling strategies in mulifaceted instructional counseling interventions.

Instructional information relevant to skill training may not have advanced to the utopian state of affairs in which it is essentially possible for anyone to learn to do anything. However, it is no longer the case that specialized accomplishments need to be viewed as the relatively exclusive preserves of gifted or naturally endowed fortunates. The strategy for skill training described in this chapter can assist counselors in helping clients to learn skills. The possession and use of these skills can assist clients in resolving or coping with current difficulties and concerns in many areas of contemporary living.

Theories of Skill Training

Theoretical perspectives on skill training are nested within the major theories of learning and instruction that have been advanced in this century. The current section looks briefly at each of these theories and at the specific skill-training methods that have been developed in association with them. The theoretical perspectives to be surveyed include operant-learning theory, social-learning theory, cognitive-learning theory, cognitive-behavioral theory, and instructional-psychological theories relevant to skill acquisition and training.

OPERANT-LEARNING THEORY

Originated in the seminal work of B. F. Skinner (1953, 1969), operant-learning theory views learning as synonymous with behavior change. Through careful empirical and descriptive analyses of the major determinants of behavior change, a succession of operant theorists and researchers has articulated a number of basic processes that describe and predict increases or decreases in behavior frequency and/or alterations in the essential topography of behavior. All of these basic operant processes are described in terms of contingent relationships among behaviors and their antecedant and consequent environments (i.e., specific behaviors and the events that precede them and follow upon them). Within specific, observable stimulus settings, behaviors operate on the environment to produce certain additions to, or deletions from, that environment. When behavior increases (in its future rate of emission) as a result of such consequences, it is said to be *reinforced*. When it decreases, it is said to be *punished* or *extinguished*. (Operant extinction differs from operant punishment in that extinction involves no environmental changes as a consequence of behavior.)

When basic operant-learning principles such as reinforcement, punishment, and extinction are combined with other operant concepts such as *shaping* (gradually changing behavior by reinforcing a succession of minute changes until a major behavior change has occurred) and *reinforcement scheduling* (varying the ratio of reinforcers to behaviors or the time intervals across which reinforcers are available to produce different behavior effects), it is possible to produce systematic changes in a wide variety of human behaviors. Hundreds of research reports and textbooks have been written since the mid-1950s that describe such operant change methods (e.g., Kazdin 1975; Sulzer-Azaroff and Mayer 1977; Williams 1973). The application of operant-learning principles to the purposeful alteration of human behaviors in natural home, school, social, and work environments is commonly referred to as *behavior modification* or *contingency management*.

Behavior modification approaches to skill training typically involve the following steps: (1) *desired skills are carefully defined and targeted* as training goals, (2) *existing skills or behaviors are monitored* to determine existing skill repertories and emission frequencies (*baselines*), (3) a specific operant *change strategy is determined* (usually some combination of positive reinforcement for desired skill emissions and extinction of responses incompatible with the skills being trained), (4) the operant *change strategy is implemented*, and (5) the *effects of the change strategy are evaluated* by ongoing systematic recording of the frequencies of targeted skills (cf. Martin 1981).

SOCIAL-LEARNING THEORY

Social-learning theory (Bandura 1977) combines operant-learning principles with principles of observational and cognitive learning to explain the acquisition and performance of behaviors. Acquisition is defined as changes in the cognitive representations and symbolic organizations of behavior. Such changes occur inside the head of the learner usually as a result of simple, focused observation of the behavior of another (a *model*). Actual performance of learned (acquired) behaviors continues to be governed predominantly by operant principles.

The great advantage of social-learning theory, when compared with pure operant theory, is that it indicates a variety of observational modeling strategies that can be used to facilitate quick, initial acquisition of behavorial skills. Modeling becomes a primary vehicle for initial skill training. This is particularly true if a model's performance of a skill to be learned results in reinforcement to the model. Such *modeling with vicarious reinforcement* provides essential information to the learner (*observer*) about the component parts of the skill to be learned and also motivates the learner to perform the skill himself/herself.

The application of sound learning theory to skill training has resulted in a number of specific training methods that have been employed widely in clinical, counseling, and educational contexts (cf. Perry and Furukawa 1980). Among the most frequently employed social learning methods are *participant modeling* and *behavioral rehearsal*. In these methods the following phases typically occur: (1) *desired skills are repeatedly modeled*, preferably by different models who demonstrate progressively more sophisticated skill use; (2) *learners are guided to perform the skills themselves* under favorable, nonstressful conditions (often these are simulated conditions in which the counselor provides ongoing verbal reassurance and coaching); and (3) *newly acquired skills are transfered to natural situations* in ways that guarantee that they will result in reinforcing experiences of success (Bandura 1976).

COGNITIVE-LEARNING THEORY

Many recent advances in cognitive-learning theory are relevant to skill training. In cognitive terms, learning is best understood as changes in cognitive structures that underlie overt behavioral changes (Neisser 1976). To facilitate desired changes in cognitive structure that will be consistent with subsequent successful skill performances, skills to be learned must be presented in meaningful contexts, and cognitive attributions and/or expectancies must be created that will be supportive of subsequent skill performances (see Winne 1983).

In cognitive counseling interventions, clients are encouraged to view skills as behaviors that can be learned and, once learned, can be self-controlled and employed with success. Such cognitive counseling may include disputation of nonsupportive attributions (e.g., Ellis 1962) and/or the creation of positive enhancing cognitive expectancies (Bandura 1977; Meichenbaum 1977). Clients are helped to attribute their skill performances to their own efforts and perseverance and to acquire confidence in their own abilities to perform skills competently and effectively. Such cognitive interventions depend heavily upon verbal persuasion, argument, and encouragement. In actual practice, cognitive approaches to the modification of attribution and expectancy structures are most often combined with behavioral-change methods derived from operant- and social-learning theory.

COGNITIVE-BEHAVIORAL THEORY

The past few years have witnessed a growing rapprochement between cognitive and behavioral (operant) theories of learning

While social learning theory has long advocated both cognitive and behavioral influences and processes, the new cognitive-behavioral theories (e.g., Meichenbaum 1977; Stone 1980) have created an eclectic blend of theoretical principles and viewpoints that permit practitioners in the area of skill training to employ multifaceted training interventions that focus on changing both cognitions (in the form of self-statements or -thoughts) and accompanying behaviors. Such training programs take advantage of reciprocal influences among cognitions, behaviors, and external situations (cf. Bandura 1978).

Two of the best examples of cognitive-behavioral strategies relevant to skill training are *self-instruction* (Meichenbaum 1977) and *self-reinforcement* (e.g., Watson and Tharp 1977; Thoresen and Mahoney 1974). Self-instruction combines methods of verbal instruction, modeling, and behavior modification. Steps in the use of self-instruction for skill acquisition include: (1) *the performance of the skill by a model who talks to himself out loud* while performing the skill (the model's talk takes the form of specific self-instructions about performing the skill—e.g., "Remember to look straight ahead and focus on the road"), (2) *performance of the skill by the learner under the direction of the model's instructions,* (3) *performance of the skill by the learner, who instructs him/herself out loud,* (4) *performance of the skill by the learner, who guides performance via private speech* (Meichenbaum and Goodman 1971).

Self-reinforcement is a cognitive-behavorial strategy that parallels the essential steps of operant behavior modification, with the important difference that in self-reinforcement the learner is taught to perform each of these steps with a minimum of external assistance. Specific steps in self-reinforcement are: (1) *self-prescription* of skill goals and standards, (2) *self-monitoring* of skill performances, (3) *self-evaluation* of skill performances in relation to standards and goals, and (4) *self-reward* of performances that meet or exceed performance standards (Martin 1980).

INSTRUCTIONAL PSYCHOLOGY

While instructional psychology is not a learning theory per se, it is a disciplinary focus that makes extensive use of theories of learning. The primary function of the discipline of instructional psychology is to generate information about what kinds of instruction reliably produce what kinds of learning. Even though instructional psychology is a relatively new area of theory and research, its concern with learning outcomes associated with specific instructional variables has resulted in an impressive array of information of potential use to skill trainers.

While the models of skill training developed by instructional psychologists (e.g. Joyce 1979; Martin 1983) are aimed primarily at training in teaching skills, the training steps that comprise these models should be generalizable to most forms of skill training. Specifically, these steps are: (1) *verbal descriptions and explanation* of skills, (2) *modeling and/or demonstration of skills*, (3) *skill practice in simulated settings*, (4) *structured, focused feedback to the skill practice*, and (5) *coaching for application of skills in natural settings*.

Empirical Studies of Skill Training

A number of common elements or phases are evident in a careful analysis of the skill-training strategies and models briefly reviewed in the foregoing section. Verbal specifications of skills to be learned; modeling of skills; active, graduated practice of skills by learners; feedback and reinforcement of skill practice and progress; and graduated transfer of skills to natural environments and to direct learner control are training elements that achieve some degree of noteworthy consensus across most of the theories examined. This section examines a few of the training and outcome studies that have been reported in support of all or many of these training elements. Many of the studies and conclusions cited cut across basic conceptual distinctions among learning theories, and no attempt will be made to categorize the studies reviewed in relation to theoretical constructs per se.

The basic skill-training components of verbal instruction, modeling/demonstration, active skill practice (rehearsal), and feedback to skill practice (through counselor coaching, videotape, and/or peer reaction) have been employed successfully to assist a wide variety of individuals to acquire skills in an equally wide variety of performance areas. In most of these studies, client acquisition of the skills taught also has resulted in empirically demonstrable decrements in client difficulties and concerns.

Bennet and Maley (1973) used a combination of verbal instruction, practice, and feedback to teach chronic psychiatric patients a series of basic interpersonal behaviors. Eisler, Hersen, and Miller (1974), also working with psychiatric patients, employed a similar skill training approach to help their clients acquire basic assertion skills that, once acquired, generalized to real-life situations.

Skills training programs which contain basic elements of description, modeling, rehearsal, and feedback also have been used with a variety of nonhospitalized clients. Eisler, Miller, Hersen, and Alford (1974) assisted married couples in acquiring discussion skills to resolve interpersonal conflicts. Eisler (1976) also has used skill training to help clients acquire assertive responses necessary for successful vocational performances. Goldstein and Sorcher (1973) applied the skill training methods of modeling, practice, reinforcement, and transfer training to business-management training with good results. Basic skill training programs have been utilized effectively to promote positive dating behaviors and heterosexual interactions (Newman 1969; Twentyman and McFall 1975). Goldstein and Goodhart (1973) and Wallace, Marx, and Martin (1981) provide empirical results that support the use of instruction, modeling, rehearsal, and feedback methods in assisting hospital nursing staff to acquire basic skills of empathic responding and social approval. McFall and Lillesand (1971) added a cognitive practice component to this basic skill-training strategy to teach college students to refuse unreasonable requests from solicitors of merchandise.

Skill training also has been demonstrated to be effective with young children. Using a systematic training regime consisting of instructions, modeling, behavioral rehearsal, and feedback, Bornstein, Bellack, and Hersen (1977) trained withdrawn elementary school children to increase their eye contact, loudness of speech, speech duration, and requests for behavior change in others. Oden and Asher (1977) used a similar training program, but without a systematic modeling component, to help socially isolated children learn a number of basic skills for forming friendships.

A final study that gives a strong indication of the far-reaching instructional implications for skill training is provided by Brooks and Richardson (1980), who used assertion skills training to help alleviate the duodenal ulcer symptoms of a number of male adults. This study, in particular, draws attention to the fact that skill training is a very pervasive counseling strategy that is employed extensively in almost any counseling situation. Whether a client wishes to change behavior, cognition, or emotional reaction, such changes usually necessitate some action on the client's part. When potentially effective actions currently are absent from a client's action repertoire, some kind of skill training is inevitably required. More will be said about the use of skill-training procedures in multifaceted instructional counseling toward the end of this chapter.

The empirical studies reviewed so far have provided an indication of the extensive range of client concerns and difficulties for which skill training may be employed as an appropriate instructional strategy. Hundreds of similar studies are reviewed extensively by Curran (1977), Heimberg et al. (1977), and Twentyman and Zimmering (1979).

One of the questions that remains unanswered in the empirical literature on skill training concerns the relative contributions to skill acquisition of each component of basic skill-training programs such as those employed in the foregoing studies. Several studies exist that show that modeling and instruction are more effective than either modeling or instruction alone in specifying skills to be learned by clients (e.g., Hersen et al. 1973). Other studies show that the addition of feedback and/or practice components significantly enhances the skill-acquisition effects of modeling and/or verbal instruction (e.g., Maston et al. 1980; Nelson, Gibson, and Cutting 1973). Finally, there is some indication that both rehearsal (practice) and coaching (feedback) make significant additive contributions to improved skill performances (McFall and Twentyman 1973).

To date, results of component analyses studies that attempt

to determine the relative contributions of various skill-training components to overall training effects are only suggestive. However, it makes logical sense to include both modeling/demonstration and practice/rehearsal methods in instructional counseling programs for skill training. As Phillips and Bierman (1981) point out, verbal skill descriptions and modeling provide a cognitive representation of the desired skill, while practice (rehearsal) and feedback provide opportunities for successive behavorial change. All these elements are undoubtedly necessary from the viewpoints of contemporary cognitive-behavorial and instructional-psychological theories. Finally, there is beginning to be some evidence that indicates that the addition of specific self-instruction components to the basic instruction, modeling, practice, and feedback sequence may help to ensure generalization (to new situations) and maintenance (over time) of skill training effects (Rehm et al. 1979; Snyder and White 1979).

Skill Training in Instructional Counseling

Skill training within an instructional counseling framework incorporates the basic components of verbal instruction, modeling/demonstration, practice (rehearsal), feedback (coaching), and transfer training that are common to most skill-training models. By systematically organizing these components within the five-step program of goals, preassessment, objectives, activities, and evaluation, instructional counselors can create a powerful change strategy for assisting clients in engaging in planned, purposeful skill acquisition relevant to their current difficulties and concerns. Such skill training may be used to teach clients to be more assertive, to interact more positively and effectively with children, to manage their own time, and to learn a wide variety of skills associated with successful daily living. The illustrative examples included in the succeeding descriptions of skill training steps and instructional skills are based, in part, upon an instructional counseling program for chronic academic underachievers described by Martin, Marx, and Martin (1980).

THE STEPS

Goals

The initial goal-setting step in any form of instructional counseling involves: (1) a determination of what the client wishes to accomplish as a result of participating in counseling, (2) a general orientation to the basic processes and assumptions of an instructional counseling approach, and (3) a specific orientation to the instructional counseling strategy or strategies that appear to be most relevant to the client's wishes and desires for change. The first and second of these elements remain essentially unvaried across any instructional counseling strategy. Through the intelligent, purposeful use of a variety of basic reacting and probing skills, the instructional counselor listens carefully to the clients concerns and assists the client in considering and stating what she/he wishes to accomplish as a result of participating in counseling. Once a general goal statement has been achieved (stated in proper client-centered and performance terms), the instructional counselor explains the basic processes and assumptions of instructional counseling in general, together with the kinds of commitments and responsibilities associated with the roles of "counselor as instructor" and "client as learner."

It is only when a client's overall goal statement clearly indicates the necessity of specific skill acquisition that the goal-setting step moves to a skill-training focus per se (e.g., "I want to get better grades at school so that I can graduate and get a decent job."). When goals are negotiated that demand that the client learn new skills and/or refine existing skill levels, the goal-setting step also includes a specific orientation to skill training. The instructional counselor emphasizes that successful accomplishments always involve the ability to perform relevant skills in an effective manner; that skills can be clearly specified, practiced, and learned; that such learning involves considerable effort and commitment; and that the instructional counseling process can help the client to learn skills that will help him/her achieve the overall goal that has been agreed upon. Considerable time is often spent at this stage in gently disputing mistaken client ideas such as "only gifted people can do this," "I'm just not good at this and never will be," and so on. Demystifying counseling so that the client clearly understands that skill acquisition is a process that can be dealt with through basic learning activities as opposed to some kind of "magical" personality insight or effortless, quasi-hypnotic transmogrification also can be important at the goal-setting step of skill training.

Preassessment

The preassessment phase of skill training in instructional counseling includes: (1) a detailed *operationalization of current client performances* (behaviors, cognitions, and emotional reactions) in relevant skill areas and situations, (2) a *determination*, through a sound task analysis, *of the specific skills required* to achieve the overall counseling goal, and (3) a *consideration of current client capabilities in relation to required skills.*

Concrete operationalization of current client performances and relevant skill situations (i.e., those specific contexts within which difficulties arise because of skill deficits or inappropriate skill selections) involves extensive specification of situational elements through client responses to specific questions of "what," "where," "when," and "who." Exacting descriptions of client behaviors, thoughts, and emotions prior to, during, and following upon relevant skill situations are accumulated. Preassessment techniques such as role playing, imaginal simulation (giving clients specific instructions and cues to imagine recent skill situations and their responses to them), interviews with others associated with or active in relevant skill situations, and direct counselor observation and systematic recording of current client performances in skill situations all may be employed. Information from these sources should be added to information from conversations between client and counselor to help ensure the collection of reliable and valid preassessment data.

Once current client skills and relevant skill situations have been determined, a task analysis of the overall counseling goal (e.g., "to get better grades at school") should be undertaken, with the client's full involvement, to determine all of the skills and subskills relevant to the overall goal. Using the task analysis methods referenced in chapter 1, counselor and client work together to determine all of the things that are done by individuals who currently are meeting goals similar to the client's goal. In the illustrative case of school achievement, such general skills as reading for comprehension, taking notes systematically, using memory enhancement methods and effective examination-writing methods, planning study times and schedules, writing reports, completing assignments and participating effectively in class might be identified. Each of these skills will in turn depend upon still smaller subskills. For example, planning might involve writing assignment due dates in a pocket calendar as soon as these are given, questioning teachers about due dates if these aren't clear, setting aside a portion of each day for study and assignment work, breaking down large assignments into smaller bits that can be sequenced over time, dividing study time across the various subjects to be studied, making study schedules, rewarding oneself for completing assignments, withholding rewards until planned work is completed, and so forth. Such task analyses can provide a clear indication of relevant skills against which to match the client's current skill performances.

When current client skill levels and capabilities are considered in relation to a "map" of all (or most) of the required skills achieved through task analysis methods, both client and counselor come to understand where the client currently is in relation to the specific skills needed to accomplish his/her overall goal.

Objectives
Framing specific instructional objectives for skill training is a fairly easy process if a good, sound preassessment has been undertaken. At this stage, client and counselor review the results of the preassessment and decide upon the specific skills they will work toward acquiring and/or improving. Specific learning objectives are written that relate to these specific skills (i.e., "I will maintain a positive listening posture—sitting squarely and openly, leaning slightly forward, maintaining eye contact—when teachers are speaking," "I will develop a systematic method for taking notes on points that teachers emphasize as important," etc.). Instructional counselors discuss each objective with clients to ensure that the skills described and the

commitments implied are understood clearly by, and are acceptable to, the clients. A very good way to do this and at the same time to help ensure that clients are involved actively in the instructional counseling process is to teach clients the basic skill of writing specific instructional objectives. After a few demonstrations and joint efforts, clients usually can transform pre-assessment information into instructional objectives for specific skill acquisition without a great deal of counselor assistance. Remember that a very important objective for all instructional counseling is to help clients acquire skills in instructing themselves (in directing their own learning) without the assistance of a counselor.

Activities
The actual instructional/learning activities phase of skill training consists of repetitive interactions between counselor and client during which each of the skills to be acquired in relation to the instructional objectives is verbally specified, modeled or demonstrated, rehearsed by the client, coached, and transferred to natural, real-life situations. To ensure that this active skill-acquisition phase operates as efficiently as possible, the instructional counselor and client first sequence all of the skills to be improved or acquired in a logical manner. This ensures that skills that are prerequisite to the attainment of other skills will be learned in advance of more complex behaviors or skill combinations. Once this has been done, skill-training activities begin by focusing on the first skill or skills in this acquisition sequence.

Initial specification and explanation of skills to be acquired are supplemented by extensive modeling, demonstration, and discussion of skill performances. While much of this specification can be done through counselor modeling and verbal descriptions, it also may be helpful to arrange for direct observations of skilled performers in natural situations and/or via videotape or film. The purpose of such initial specification (both verbal and through modeling/demonstration) is to ensure that the client has a clear cognitive understanding of the skills to be learned and is motivated to practice them. It must be clear to the client what the skills are and how their acquisition will assist him/her in meeting overall counseling goals.

Once clients understand and are motivated to perform targeted skills, the instructional counselor arranges opportunities for graduated and appropriate practice of the skills by the client. Such practice initially may take the form of structured role plays in the counselor's office under the direct verbal guidance of the counselor. Gradually, however, it will evolve into unguided practice attempts by the client alone in natural situations that require efficient use of the skills being acquired. As the client negotiates this increasingly more natural and client-controlled practice sequence, the counselor provides a continuous flow of immediate, specific, and descriptive feedback to the client's skill performances. Client successes are reinforced and descriptively praised, while client difficulties are specifically discussed and suggestions and encouragement for further practice are supplied. Systematic records are kept that document the client's progress with respect to each of the targeted skills. As practice moves to progressively more natural environments so as to ensure transfer of skill training to relevant skill situations in the client's life, meetings may be arranged with significant others active in these environments (e.g., parents, teachers, children, spouses, employers, supervisors, etc.) The cooperation and assistance of these people is often essential to successful skill training.

By the end of the instructional-activities phase of skill training, the client should be performing all of the targeted skills in natural skill environments with no obvious, moment-to-moment assistance from the instructional counselor. In short, the client should be capable of independent skill performances and should have taken over most of the responsibility for monitoring, evaluating, and rewarding his/her own skill-development program.

Evaluation

As in all instructional counseling, an ongoing evaluation of the effects of skill training (that is monitoring and assessing client performances in relation to counseling goals and objectives) is built into the counseling activities phase through a system of observing and recording client progress in skill development across each of the targeted skill areas. Such record keeping may make use of graphing methods in which numerical scores representing the client's skill performances, as rated or observed by the counselor and/or significant others in relevant skill situations, are plotted against an ongoing time line. Record keeping also may involve systematic monitoring of the products of efficient skill use (e.g., completion of homework assignments, course grades, etc.) or monitoring of skill practice time commitments (e.g., study hours). The client should be taught to monitor his/her own skill acquisition progress, using these and other methods. As counseling progresses, client evaluations (monitoring records) can be compared to similar evaluations by others (e.g., counselor, teacher, parents). This helps to guarantee the development of the client's ability to monitor and evaluate personal skill performances in reliable and valid ways.

When significant progress has been made with respect to the documented acquisition of all targeted skills and the client is demonstrating a good ability to monitor and evaluate personal skill acquisition and development, counseling goals and objectives should be revisited to determine the extent to which they have been met. When all objectives have been met (remembering that some of these undoubtedly will have been altered, revised, or excluded by explicit, mutual agreement as counseling has progressed), the counselor and client negotiate a process of follow-up reporting. Usually, the client takes responsibility for informing the counselor of future developments at regular intervals over a period of six to twelve months. At this stage, formal instructional counseling for skill acquisition is terminated.

THE INSTRUCTIONAL SKILLS USED

The specific instructional skills that instructional counselors can use to assist clients in moving through the five steps of skill acquisition elaborated in the preceding section are drawn from the taxonomy of structuring, soliciting, and reacting skills initially described and illustrated in chapter 2. The most important skills employed, together with the general sequence in which they are used, may be illustrated through a fine-grained analysis of "key" counselor statements associated with an instructional counseling program for training chronic academic underachievers in basic academic survival skills (cf. Martin, Marx, and Martin 1980). While skills other than those illustrated may be employed effectively at the various counseling phases depicted, the skills selected are basic to any skill-training program. As was the case in chapter 3, the purposes of this section are (1) to indicate the exact counseling skills that are most important to facilitation of an effective skill training process, (2) to illustrate the use of these skills by including modified segments from hypothetical counseling transcripts, and (3) to indicate the purposeful way in which counseling skills can be selected and employed to encourage predictable client learning in the context of a well-structured instructional environment. In what follows, the hypothetical client in receipt of the counseling skills described is a sixteen-year-old boy in the tenth grade. The entire counseling program from which the brief skill illustrations are excerpted covers many counselor-client interactions over a four-month period.

Goals

Major Counseling Skills	Illustrated Use
Reflecting Meaning and Affect	"You really want to get a decent job, and you know that you will need to get through school to do this. The frustration and anger you feel don't really come from not liking school but from not being able to do well in your school courses—well enough to make sure that you'll get through grade twelve eventually."
Summarizing	"Let me see if I've managed to understand the situation

Major Counseling Skills	Illustrated Use
	you've talked about. You currently are failing three of the grade ten courses you are taking this semester. If this continues, you probably will be asked to leave school. If, however, you can show some signs of improvement, the school principal is prepared to let you push on, even though you may still fail one or two courses this semester. You really want to show some improvement because staying in school is very important to your plans to get a good job in the future."
Stating Goals	"At this stage, your major goal is to show some improvement in the grades you are getting this semester. Our job together is to teach you how to do this."
Giving an Overview	"Before I can help you to improve your course work, we need to see exactly what you are doing right now and then try to determine what specific things you could do that would help you do better in school. From there on, it will be a

Major Counseling Skills	Illustrated Use
	matter of hard work in which you will practice these things over and over until you are able to do them well enough to have them make a difference in your grades."
Giving Examples and Illustrations	"For example, if one of the things we discover is that you are having difficulty concentrating in class, we'll need to work together to figure out some things you could do to help yourself concentrate on what the teacher is saying. Once we've figured out what things you could do to concentrate better, we'll work together to help you learn how to do these things. Then you'll try doing them in class, and we'll keep track of your grades and class participation (with your teachers' help) to see if doing these things makes any positive difference."
Stating Transitions	"O.K., now that you know a bit about what we'll be doing when we work together, I'd like to ask you several questions about what you are doing right

Major Counseling Skills	Illustrated Use
	now to improve your school work."

Preassessment

Major Counseling Skills	Illustrated Use
Using Set Induction	"Let's start first thing in the morning when you get up to go to school. Think about everything you do from the time your feet hit the bedroom floor and describe your entire day to me. I'll ask you a few questions as you go along, but keep your thoughts focused on your actions during a typical school day from the time you wake up until the time you go to sleep at night."
Probing	"What do you do when the science teacher gives instructions for doing the laboratory experiment and writing it up?"
	"So the final buzzer sounds, and you are talking to some friends in the hallway. What do you do just before you leave the school? . . . What do you take home with you?"

Major Counseling Skills	Illustrated Use
Giving Clear Instructions	"I am going to give you a list of many different things people can do that might help them study more effectively. Read each point aloud once, then once to yourself, think about it for a bit, and then tell me whether or not you think you do it."
Prompting	"So, what other things could you do to make sure that you haven't missed any assignments teachers have given? . . . Remember our discussion about not being afraid to ask teachers questions?"
Calling for Demonstration	"Show me how you would solve this problem. As you work at it, talk out loud about what you are doing at each step."
Summarizing and Stating Transitions	"Well, this has taken a long time, but we now have a list of things you can learn to do that should result in better school work. These are all things you currently are not doing, but we've agreed they might be good things to try. Take a careful look at these items, and let's see if you can make some

Major Counseling Skills	Illustrated Use
	specific commitments to work hard at learning to perform these different skills."

Objectives

Major Counseling Skills	Illustrated Use
Stating Objectives, Modeling, and Giving Examples	"One of the first objectives we can work toward might be stated as 'you will develop a plan for taking notes on important points that come up in class and will use this method to record important information in each class period.' Notice that this objective states exactly what you will do. We might also consider how you will determine whether you've done this or not. For example, in this case you might check your notes with the teacher at the end of the class to see whether or not you noted all of the important points."
Giving Clear Instructions and Calling for Demonstration	"Let's return to the list of skills we developed. Select another skill related to

Major Counseling Skills	Illustrated Use
	paying attention during classroom periods and try to state it as an objective for you to achieve."
Summarizing and Stating Transitions	"Great, now we know precisely what skills you will be working on, the sequence in which you'll attack them, and some of the ways in which we can determine whether or nor you are using these skills effectively. (pause) Let's take the first skill objective and get started."

Activities

Major Counseling Skills	Illustrated Use
Giving Clear Directions and Using Markers of Importance	"It is important when reading a textbook to develop the skills of picking out main ideas in what you read and jotting these ideas down in a notebook as you go along. Then, when you need to study for an exam, you can use your textbook notes for quick and easy reviews of major textbook ideas."

Major Counseling Skills	Illustrated Use
Modeling	"Now, as I read this page from your textbook, notice how I ask myself questions about what I am reading and how I jot down the main points on the page."
Calling for Demonstration	"We've now worked on many of the specific skills you need to read textbooks effectively and to take useful notes while reading. Here are five pages from your social studies text. Let's see if you can use these skills when you read these pages."
Giving Descriptive Praise	"Good for you. In just fifteen minutes you read those five pages thoroughly, asked relevant questions to yourself as you went along, took down brief notes on important points, and, most important, when I asked you questions about what you'd read, you were able to answer all of them accurately."
Suggesting Alternatives	"I think we might be able to use your English teacher's idea here. As you write this next book report, try to make the kind of topic outline she suggested and see if that helps."

Major Counseling Skills	Illustrated Use
Summarizing and Stating Transitions	"So far we've covered reading, note taking, report writing, and classroom listening and participation skills. We're now going to move on to tackle the objectives we wrote that deal with preparing for examinations."
Giving Informational Feedback	"When you combine important notes on your textbook and from class into a master outline to use for study purposes as you just did, you sometimes find bits of information that contradict each other. One way of dealing with such inconsistencies is to jot them down and ask your teacher about them at the earliest opportunity, which is just what you did."

Evaluation

Major Counseling Skills	Illustrated Use
Expressing Counselor Reactions with "I" Messages and Descriptive Praise	"I'm pleased with the progress you've made. I've enjoyed working with you because you've worked so hard to help yourself learn

Major Counseling Skills	Illustrated Use
	the skills we've been focusing on."
Summarizing	"At this stage, you've achieved every one of the objectives you set, except for the objective about learning to cope with anxiety during exams, which we discarded once we found out that your anxiety was caused by poor exam preparation and that it disappeared when you were well prepared. You now have some very effective classroom-interaction, study, notetaking, reading, report-writing, remembering, planning, and exam-preparation and exam-writing skills. You've come a long way this semester, and your improved grades show it."
Stating Transitions	"Since we agree on our evaluation of your progress, and since all our main objectives have been met, it's now time for you to handle things pretty much on your own. If you run into any major difficulties, you always can talk to Ms. Pratt, Mr. Finch, or me about them. There's no

Major Counseling Skills	Illustrated Use
	need for any more regular meetings between you and me, but I would like you to call me each week on Friday afternoon just to let me know how you are doing. How does this sound to you?"

Skill Training in Multifaceted Instructional Counseling

The foregoing sections have dealt with skill training as an instructional activity appropriate for client goals that are associated almost exculsively with the remediation of skill deficits. Skill training also may be a component part of more elaborate, multifacted instructional counseling strategies. Indeed, the attainment of most counseling goals typically requires some attention to the development of specific skills. Even when counseling goals and processes are concerned predominantly with decision making (see chapter 3), skills such as "brainstorming" or "consequential thinking" may need to be acquired before the client can engage in desired decision-making steps. Once decisions are made with respect to the selection of a specific alternative for action, additional skill training may be needed to provide clients with the cognitive, behavorial, and/or affective tools necessary to implement the chosen "game plan." In short, whenever any counseling process reaches a stage where clients must address the generic question "How can I learn to do what I want to do?" some variety of skill training usually is indicated.

The two instructional counseling strategies that have been examined so far in this book—decision making/problem solving and skill training—may be combined for a variety of counseling purposes in which client learners must both determine what it is that they wish to do and then learn to do what they want to do. Subsequent strategies, discussed in chapters 5 and 6, will focus upon assisting clients in managing stress while they are learning and performing and in managing their own learning independent of direct, external counselor assistance. The section on multifacted instructional counseling at the end of chapter 6 provides a detailed description of how counseling strategies for problem solving/decision making, skill training, personal coping, and self-management may be combined to form a powerful, flexible general counseling strategy appropriate for a wide variety of client goals.

Chapter Summary

A review of major theories and empirical studies of skill acquisition revealed that the basic process of skill acquisition requires precise specification of the skill to be acquired through direct verbal description and modeling/demonstration; active and appropriate practice of the skill; and immediate, descriptive feedback to this skill practice. In addition, techniques of sequencing the acquisition of complex skills by arranging cumulative practice of progressively more complex skill components and gradual transfer of skill training to progressively more threatening real-life situations were seen to be indispensable instructional/learning processes with respect to skill training. To quote an ancient Chinese proverb, "The journey of a thousand miles begins with a single step."

The chapter proceeded to outline an instructional counseling strategy for skill training that incorporates the foregoing empirically supported skill-training components into a systematic, five-step instructional framework. Specific instructional skills used by counselors to promote the instructional/learning processes basic to this strategy were illustrated by a hypothetical counseling program from a sixteen-year-old boy receiving training in academic skills basic to success at school. Finally, the chapter concluded with a brief consideration of skill training in a multifacted instructional counseling context.

REFERENCES

Bandura, A. 1976. Effecting change through participant modeling. In J. D. Krumboltz and C. E. Thoresen (eds), *Counseling Methods*. New York: Holt, Rinehart & Winston.
————. 1977. *Social Learning Theory*. Englewood Cliffs, N.J.: Prentice-Hall.
————. 1978. The self system in reciprocal determinism. *American Psychologist* 33: 344–58.
Bennet, P. S., and Maley, R. G. 1973. Modification of interactive behaviors in chronic mental patients. *Journal of Applied Behavior Analysis* 6: 609–20.
Bornstien, M. R., Bellack, A. S., and Hersen, M. 1977. Social skills training for unassertive children: A multiple-baseline analysis. *Journal of Applied Behavior Analysis* 10:183–95.
Brooks, G. R., and Richardson, F. C., 1980. Emotional skills training: A treatment program for duodenal ulcer. *Behavior Therapy* 11: 198–207.
Curran, J. P. 1977. Skills training as an approach to the treatment of heterosexual social anxiety: A review. *Psychological Bulletin* 84: 140–57.
Eisler, R. M. 1976. Assertive training in the work situation. In: J. D. Krumboltz and C. E. Thoresen (eds), *Counseling Methods*. New York: Holt, Rinehart & Winston.
————, Herson, M., and Miller, P. M. 1974. Shaping components of assertive behavior with instructions and feedback. *American Journal of Psychiatry* 131: 1344–47.
————, Miller, P. M., Hersen, M., and Alford, H. 1974. Effects of Assertive training on marital interaction. *Archives of General Psychiatry* 30: 643–49.
Ellis, A. 1962. *Reason and Emotion in Psychotherapy*. New York: Lyle Stuart.
Engelmann, S., and Carnine, D. 1982. *Theory of Instruction: Principles and Applications*. New York: Irvington.
Goldstein, A. P., and Goodhart, A. 1973. The use of structured learning for empathy enhancement in paraprofessional psychotherapist training. *Journal of Community Psychology* 1: 168–73.
————, and Sorcher, M. 1973. Changing managerial behavior by applied learning techniques. *Training and Development Journal*, March. 1–24.
Heimberg, R. G., Montgomery, D., Madsen C. H, Jr., and Heim-

berg, J. S. 1977. Assertion training: A review of the literature. *Behavior Therapy* 8: 953–71.

Hersen, M., Eisler, R. M., Miller P. M., Johnson, M. B., and Pinkston, S. G. 1973. Effects of practice, instructions and modeling on components of assertion behavior. *Behavior Research and Therapy* 11: 443–51.

Joyce, B. 1979. In-service: New perspectives on an old term. In: M. Wideen, D. Hopkins, and I. Pye (eds.), *In-Service: A Means of Progress in Tough Times*. Burnaby, B. C.: Simon Fraser University.

Kazdin, A. E. 1975. *Behavior Modification in Applied Settings*. Homewood, Ill.: Dorsey Press.

Martin, J. 1980. External versus self-reinforcement: A review of methodological and theoretical issues. *Canadian Journal of Behavioural Science* 12: 111–25.

_____. 1981. *Models of Classroom Management*. Calgary: Detselig.

_____. 1983. *Mastering Instruction*. Boston: Allyn and Bacon.

_____, Marx, R. W., and Martin, W. 1980. Instructional counseling for chronic underachievers. *School Counselor* 28: 109–18.

Maston, J. L., Esveldt-Dawson, K., Andrasik, F., Ollendick, T. H., Petti, T., and Hersen, M. 1980. Direct, observational, and generalization effects of social skills training with emotionally disturbed children. *Behavior Therapy* 11: 522–31.

McFall, R. M., and Lillesand, D. B. 1971. Behavioral rehearsal with modeling and coaching in assertion training. *Journal of Abnormal Psychology* 77: 313–23.

_____, and Twentymen, C. T. 1973. Four experiments on the relative contributions of rehearsal, modeling, and coaching to assertion training. *Journal of Abnormal Psychology* 81: 199–218.

Meichenbaum, D. 1977. *Cognitive Behavior Modification: An Integrative Approach*. New York: Plenum.

_____, and Goodman, J. 1971. Training impulsive children to talk to themselves: A means of developing self-control. *Journal of Abnormal Psychology*, 77: 115–26.

Neisser, U. 1976. *Cognition and Reality: Principles and Implications of Cognitive Psychology*. San Francisco: Freeman.

Nelson R., Gibson, F., and Cutting, D. S. 1973. Videotaped modeling: The development of three appropriate responses in a mildly retarded child. *Mental Retardation* 11: 24–28.

Neuman, D. R. 1969. Using assertive training. In: J. D. Krumboltz and C. E. Thoresen (eds.), *Behavioral Counseling: Case Techniques*. New York: Holt, Rinehart & Winston.

Oden, S., and Asher, S. R. 1977. Coaching children in social skills for friendship making. *Child Development* 48: 495–506.

Perry, M.A., and Furukawa, M. J. 1980. Modeling methods. In: F. H. Kander and A. P. Goldstein (eds.), *Helping People Change: A Textbook of Methods* (2d ed.). New York: Pergamon.

Phillips, J. S., and Bierman, L. M. 1981. Clinical psychology: Individual methods. *Annual Review of Psychology* 32: 405–38.

Rehm, L. P., Fuchs, C. Z., Roth, D. M., Kornblith, S. J., and Romano, J. M. 1979. A comparison of self-control and assertion skills treatments of depression. *Behavior Therapy* 10: 429–42.

Skinner, B. F. 1953. *Science and Human Behavior.* New York: Macmillan.

————. 1969. *Contingencies of Reinforcement: A Theoretical Analysis.* New York: Appleton-Century-Crofts.

Synder, J. J., and White, M. J. 1979. The use of cognitive self-instruction in the treatment of behaviorally disturbed adolescents. *Behavior Therapy* 10: 227–35.

Stone, G. L. 1980. *A Cognitive-Behavioral Approach to Counseling Psychology: Implications for Practice, Research, and Training.* New York: Praeger.

Sulzer-Azaroff, B., and Myer, G. R. 1977. *Applying Behavior Analyses Procedures with Children and Youth.* New York: Holt, Rinehart & Winston.

Thoresen, C. E., and Mahoney, M. J. 1974. *Behavioral Self-Control.* New York: Holt, Rinehart & Winston.

Twentyman, C. T., and McFall, R. M. 1975. Behavioral training of social skills in shy males. *Journal of Consulting and Clinical Psychology* 43: 384–95.

————, and Zimmering, R. T. 1979. Behavioral training of social skills: A critical review. *Progress in Behavior Modification* 7: 321–400.

Wallace, G., Marx, R. W., and Martin, J. 1981. Training psychiatric nurses in social approval skills. *Canadian Journal of Behavioral Science.*

Watson, D. L., and Tharp, R. G. 1977. *Self-directed Behavior: Self-Modification for Personal Adjustment.* Monterey: Brooks/Cole.

Williams, J. L. 1973. *Operant Learning: Procedures for Changing Behavior* Monterey: Brooks/Cole.

Winne, P. H. 1983. Cognitive processing in the classroom. In: T. Husen and T. N. Postlethwaite (eds.), *International Encyclopedia of Education.* Oxford: Pergamon.

CHAPTER FIVE

Personal Coping

PERSONAL COPING strategies are aimed at reducing the anxiety and stress that clients experience. Clients frequently seek counseling for anxiety- and stress-related problems per se. In other cases, client anxiety may be a supplementary concern within a problem-solving or skill-acquisition intervention plan. In such cases, clients may have mapped out a course of action and may have acquired the skills necessary to implement the action plan, but they are thwarted in their attempts to use their skills by the anxiety they experience. Regardless of whether anxiety and stress are central problems or supplemental concerns, counseling intervention directed at increasing the client's personal coping skill is necessary if counseling is to be successful. In such cases, the primary client concern is not "What do I want to do?" or "How can I learn to do it?" but "How can I reduce the anxiety associated with doing it?"

In this chapter different approaches to personal coping are examined. Initially, several theories of anxiety will be overviewed with a view to determining common conceptual elements and the necessary factors to be addressed in personal coping intervention plans. Next, the research support for common personal coping strategies will be examined. Finally, an instructional approach to personal coping will be presented.

Theories of Anxiety and Personal Coping

While the notion of psychological stress is relatively new (Selye 1979), some common precursors (e.g., anxiety, arousal) have earlier roots in psychological literature. These words have acquired such a variety of meanings in professional circles and in common parlance that it becomes extremely important for writers to identify explicitly what they mean by such words as *anxiety* and *stress* (cf. Albrecht 1979; Mason 1980; Spielberger 1975; Wolpe 1970). To this end, a thumbnail sketch of the emergence of stress and anxiety as constructs will be provided in order that the reader might better understand the conceptual framework used in this chapter. The intent is not to provide a detailed review of the conceptual natures of anxiety and stress. Interested readers are referred to other excellent and more extensive reviews for that purpose (e.g., Barrios and Shigetomi 1979; Fischer 1970; Leavitt 1967; Spielberger and Sarason 1975; Kutash, Schlesenger and Associates 1980). It is our intent to provide only enough background for the reader to make an informed judgment with respect to Lazarus and Averill's (1972) plea that authors outline their notion of anxiety in order that readers might determine "whether anxiety as studied by one author has any relation to what is being studied by another" (p. 267). If personal coping strategies are used to reduce client anxiety, it is necessary to understand the "nature of the beast" before embarking on a plan of intervention.

ANXIETY: DEVELOPMENT OF THE CONSTRUCT

Early writers spoke of anxiety as a unidimensional motivating force that lay at the base of all emotional conflict (Freud 1959; Hall 1954; Jones 1953). The implication was that emotional conflict covaried with anxiety and that emotional trauma resulted when the level of anxiety became extreme. As research and thinking in the area of anxiety began to proliferate, related concepts also began to emerge. In 1955, Hebb summarized earlier work in the area of arousal and used the now-familiar inverted U-shaped curve to illustrate the relationship between arousal and performance (Buck 1976; Hebb 1955, 1972). Simply stated, human performance increases as arousal increases, until an optimal level of performance is reached, after which further increases in arousal result in decreasing performance. Further, the optimal level of arousal for maximum performance varies with task complexity. Generally speaking, as task complexity increases, optimum level of arousal is lower (Eysenck 1969). As increasing numbers of people began elaborating this notion, anxiety often was used synonymously with arousal, and the belief developed that performance covaried with anxiety in the same way that Hebb described the interaction of performance and arousal. As will be seen later, most current writers are careful to avoid this confusion.

Dollard and Miller (1950) were among the first writers to discuss the relationship between anxiety and fear. For Dollard and Miller, fear was a learned drive. When people repeatedly experience pain in certain situations, they learn to fear the resulting unpleasantness associated with that situation. When the source of the fear becomes vague (usually because of stimulus generalization), the person still "feels afraid," but cannot identify why. Dollard and Miller reserved the term anxiety to identify these latter situations. Other authors (Eysenck 1969; Hamilton 1969; Malmo 1972) elaborated on this notion to suggest that one primary characteristic of anxiety is "that the person afflicted reacts to ordinary life situations as though they were emergencies" (Malmo 1972, 976). Hamilton (1969) suggests that the reason for this overreaction is that the person's threshold becomes altered to the point that situations that are not intense enough to produce anxiety in a normal person give rise to considerable anxiety in an anxious person. Alexander (1972) further reports that because of the intensity of the response and the persistence (or prevalence) of the disturbed state, it takes longer for an anxious person to return to normal after being stimulated.

More recently, Wolpe (1958, 1969, 1973) has underscored the learned nature of anxiety reactions but has placed more emphasis on the learned behavioral characteristics of the anxiety response rather than on the drive-related characteristics. When only the physiological components of anxiety are considered, Wolpe sees little or no difference between fear and anxiety. However, fear can be distinguished from anxiety on the basis of *situational* and *behavioral* considerations. Initially, a dangerous or aversive situation may produce a state of excitation ("being worked up"). If a person's reaction to this situation is productive, the person's level of excitement returns to normal. If the person's reaction is not productive, the state of excitement is sustained. Furthermore, various aspects of the dangerous or aversive situation become associated with excitation and later may give rise to a similar state of excitation. Thus, the person may come to react to a normal situation as if it were extremely dangerous or aversive. If the situation is not truly dangerous or aversive, the person's reaction will be unproductive (usually some kind of avoidance response, where the amount of danger or aversion would not provoke most people to avoid the situation). Thus, anxiety, for Wolpe, is a learned response in which a person becomes excited and reacts to a normal situation as if it were an extremely dangerous or aversive situation.

Until the early 1970s most writers conceptualized anxiety as a unidimensional motivating force. People were thought to become either more or less anxious in differing situations, and a person's performance (behavior) was thought to change with the amount of anxiety experienced. Anxiety-producing situations were viewed as predictable in the individual case, and the individual's response to these situations, while habitual, always involved some sort of overreaction to an ordinary situation.

ANXIETY: MULTIFACETED ORIENTATIONS

In the early 1970s some writers began speaking of "other-than-arousal" components of anxiety. Valins (1970) manipulated sensory feedback so as falsely to indicate a state of physiological arousal and observed subsequent subject reactions. His observations demonstrated that the perception, not just the occurrence, of bodily change is an important determiner of emotional experience. Valins incorporated his own earlier work (1966) with that of Schacter (1966) to formulate a view of anxiety that gives cognitive appraisal mechanisms a central role. According to this position, perceived physiological changes give rise to subjective cues that are cognitively represented as feelings. These feelings in turn precipitate further cognitive activity geared toward attempting to identify the situation that elicits the perceived increase in arousal. When individuals experience a state of physiological arousal for which they have no immediate explanation, they will tend to scan the situation in which they are involved for cues as to why they are "worked up." The nature of their emotional experience will tend to depend on the environmental cues upon which they focus. Thus, the same perceived state of arousal could be labeled as joy, anger, fear, anxiety, or whatever, depending on the individual's perception of the situation. If a state of physiological arousal is experienced and no explanation as to the causal stimulus is immediately available, an individual likely will attach uncommon or inappropriate labels to environmental events in an attempt to explain the aroused condition. This is the manner in which bizarre or unadaptive behaviors, which are a part of most anxiety reactions, develop.

Lazarus and Averill (1972) expanded this argument. They claim that man is by nature an evaluative being who searches the environment for what is needed or desired and evaluates each input with respect to its relevance or significance (p. 242). This cognitively based appraisal process mediates the organism's reaction to environmental events; the emotional reaction is therefore the result of the cognitive appraisal rather than of the environmental event per se. For Lazarus and Averill, anxiety is the result of appraisal errors with respect to the consequences of future events, the degree of personal (ideational) threat in a situation, or the degree of ambiguity that a situation affords. Lazarus (1974) went on to say that all emotional experience (including anxiety) has three main components: (1) *a physiological component*, characterized by changes in arousal level; (2) *a subjective (cognitive) component*, involving the perception; labeling, and evaluation of the internal and external environmental situations; and (3) *a behavioral component*, having instrumental as well as expressive characteristics usually intended to reduce the arousal level. In an anxiety experience, a person perceives an arousal increase, evaluates the situation (i.e., anticipates consequences and evaluates the degree of personal and/or ideational threat, a process that is more or less difficult depending upon how ambiguous the situation is), and enacts some behavioral strategy intended to reduce the level of anxiety.

Meichenbaum (1972, 1975, 1976) has expanded this position. He suggests that the experience of anxiety has two main constituents: (1) *emotionality*, characterized by heightened arousal;

and (2) *worry*, characterized by self-denigrating thoughts and undue concern over performance. The resulting behavior is invariably impaired, because even though the heightened arousal could facilitate behavior, the attention demanded by the worry interferes drastically with performance. Further, Meichenbaum (1976) points out that a perceived arousal state that becomes labeled as anxiety is usually followed by feelings of personal inadequacy and denigrating self-verbalizations that increase anxiety level.

To illustrate the process, suppose Fred has studied hard in preparation for a statistics exam. Going into the exam, Fred is likely to perceive himself as being somewhat "worked up." (This is natural. A person's body typically gears up to meet the demands placed upon it.) Fred's perception of increased arousal (being worked up) will be followed by cognitive activity intended to answer the question "Why am I worked up?" If he decides that he has studied adequately, that he can recall the important information, that the exam likely will be fair, and that there likely will be enough time to finish the exam, then the arousal likely will be labeled eagerness, excitement (or some other positive label). His arousal will dissipate, or at least not increase further, and his performance on the exam will not be impaired. If, however, Fred decides that he did not study enough, and/or that he cannot recall effortlessly all the important information, and/or that the exam might have a lot of trick questions, and/or that the time allocation is likely to be too short, then the arousal likely will be labeled as anxiety. This perceived arousal, labeled as anxiety, likely will be accompanied by thoughts of personal inadequacy ("Oh, I know I'm not going to do very well") and self-denigration ("Why didn't you study more?" "Boy, Fred, you're sure going to blow it this time," "If I had studied more, or if I weren't so dumb, then I'd have a chance"). This kind of thinking usually increases arousal, which, in turn, makes the person more anxious ("Now I'm really getting worked up") and produces even more self-denigration ("You're always doing this to yourself. When are you going to smarten up?"). The negative thinking (what Meichenbaum calls worry) occupies an inordinate proportion of Fred's attention, and the combination of over-arousal and worry interferes drastically with Fred's performance on the exam. (Note that in this example, Fred was equally well prepared for the exam in both cases. It was his evaluation of his perceived increase in arousal that led to a different label for what was initially the same physiological state. If Fred had not prepared for the exam, then his appraisal in the second case might represent a more accurate description of the situation. If Fred were to seek out a counselor for his "exam anxiety," it is to be hoped that the counselor initially would recommend some study-skills training. If the exam anxiety persisted, some personal coping intervention to reduce Fred's anxiety, given that he was well prepared, would be appropriate.)

Since the early 1970s anxiety has been viewed increasingly as a multifaceted emotional phenomenon. Most writers acknowledge a physiological component in the experience of anxiety; that is, people become worked up. However, the authors referred to in this section would argue that it is the cognitive appraisal following a perceived increase in arousal that determines whether or not a particular reaction will be experienced as anxiety. Further, the overt and covert behavior following the perception of anxiety is typically maladaptive, serving to sustain or exacerbate the anxiety experience. Thus, while arousal may facilitate performance when the perceived arousal is positively labeled, if the arousal is experienced as anxiety, performance is inevitably impaired.

A CONTEMPORARY VIEWPOINT

Integration of differing theoretical conceptualizations of anxiety is difficult and seldom attempted (Fischer 1970). However, such integration is necessary if one wishes to achieve a conceptual basis that permits comparisons across theories (Spielberger 1975). Since instructional counseling is intended as a subsumptive framework capable of embracing many differing theoretical orientations, it becomes crucial to attempt such a synthesis. A frequent practice of writers who review research on anxiety is to point out areas of disagreement. Spanos and Barber (1974) have objected to this practice of emphasizing differences in theoretical orientation in cross-theoretical comparisons, saying that this practice fosters a distorted view of the research area, obscures areas of agreement, and often leads to polemical battles that have little practical value. With this in mind, we have attempted to extract conceptual commonalities and to weave them into a compatible conceptual framework.

Probably the most obvious point of agreement in the foregoing discussion is that virtually all theorists allow that anxiety is accompanied by an increase in physiological arousal (although most theorists would be careful not to equate anxiety and arousal). The increase in arousal is invariably followed by behavior intended to reduce the arousal level. This behavior is typically maladaptive (overt avoidance behavior or covert self-denigration) and tends to have a sustaining or even self-amplifying effect on emotional experience. The experience of anxiety typically follows the perception of an exaggerated degree of threat in an environmental situation. Thus, anxious people tend to overreact to what most people consider to be a normal situation. Anxiety is the appropriate label for a fearlike reaction to a situation that is not truly dangerous. (If the situation contains a high degree of objective threat, then fear is likely to be a more appropriate label for the person's emotional reaction, and the resulting behavior is likely to be adaptive [Eysenck 1969; Hamilton 1969; Lazarus 1974; Lazarus and Averill 1972; Malmo 1972; Meichenbaum 1972, 1975; Wolpe 1958, 1969].) The association between an environmental event and the experience of anxiety is usually strong, with the result that certain environmental stimuli predictably and repeatedly precipitate anxiety. The emotional experience of anxiety is generally held to be unpleasant, and reducing the intensity of an anxiety reaction is generally considered to be rewarding.

Thus, we would agree with Barrios and Shigetomi (1979), Lazarus (1974), and Meichenbaum (1972, 1975) that anxiety is a "complex multi-dimensional construct [involving] three separate but interacting response components (cognitive, motoric behavior, and physiological arousal)" (Barrios and Shigetomi 1979, 491) and that a person's anxiety reaction typically demonstrates the above characteristics.

RELATIONSHIP BETWEEN ANXIETY AND STRESS

Recently, there have been increasing reports of stress and stress-related problems in professional and lay reading materials. Stress has become a catchword for any number of emotional, behavioral, and medical reactions to environmental events, and only recently have there been pleas to "tighten-up" the way in which the word *stress* is used (cf. Albrecht 1979; Antonovsky 1980). Undoubtedly, the next few years will see a movement toward increased specificity in the conceptualization of stress and the interrelationship between stress and other emotional reactions like anxiety. In the initial pages of this chapter, the words *stress* and *anxiety* are used interchangeably; however, the use of only the word *anxiety* in the later part is intentional. Anxiety is a situation-specific reaction to some objectively non-threatening environmental event having the arousal, behavioral, and cognitive components mentioned in the preceding section. When anxiety becomes generalized to the degree that many environmental events trigger an anxious reaction, and a person's arousal level remains elevated for prolonged periods of time, such generalized, global reactions appropriately may be labeled as stress. In this way, anxiety reactions are seen as a subset of stress reactions. Teaching a person to cope more effectively with anxiety likely will prevent the occurrence of more general stress-related problems.

Training Models and Empirical Studies of Personal Coping

In the foregoing discussion of anxiety and personal coping, two major orientations were evident. The first thrust, emphasizing the arousal, behavioral, and situational aspects of an anxiety reaction, has given rise to *behavioral* treatment interventions. The second, multifaceted thrust, acknowledging the arousal, behavioral, and situational components but placing more emphasis on cognitive appraisal mechanisms and ongoing covert self-dialogue, has given rise to *cognitive* approaches to anxiety treatment. Some of the main treatment interventions from each approach and the empirical studies that support their use will be reviewed below. The intention is not to provide detailed instructions outlining the implementation of each strategy. Appropriate sources containing such detailed descriptions are indicated, but discussion is limited largely to a consideration of the empirical evidence that supports the use of the intervention strategies reviewed.

BEHAVIORAL APPROACHES

The main goal of most behavioral interventions in the treatment of anxiety is to alter habitual anxiety reactions to environmental events. *Systematic desensitization* (Wolpe 1958) is a procedure intended to alter habitual anxiety reactions by substituting an alternative, competing response, usually deep relaxation, for the anxiety response. The habit strength of the relaxation response is increased until it is the predominating response when the person encounters environmental events previously associated with anxiety. Procedurally, the client first learns to relax, a response generally considered to be incompatible with anxiety. While relaxation training is proceeding, a fear hierarchy (an ordered list of anxiety-evoking situations associated with the particular phobia or anxiety reaction) is prepared. Next, the client imagines him/herself in each situation described in the fear hierarchy, beginning with the situation that evokes the least anxiety and proceeding systematically through the list, while remaining relaxed. The criterion for progressing from one situation to the next is that the client can remain completely relaxed while visualizing a given scene. The procedure is completed when the person can imagine him/herself in the situation that initially generated the most anxiety while remaining completely relaxed. Transfer of the relaxation response into daily life is usually sufficient to enable the person to experience situations in the fear hierarchy *in vivo* without becoming overly anxious. (See Marquis, Morgan and Piaget 1971; Wolpe 1958, 1969, 1976 for more detailed discussions of the procedures involved in implementing a desensitization strategy.)

Systematic desensitization is perhaps the most widely researched anxiety-control procedure. Many excellent reviews of the literature in this area exist (cf. Davison and Wilson 1973; Franks and Wilson 1974; Kazdin and Wilcoxon 1976; Paul 1969). The results to date indicate that systematic desensitization is an effective procedure for reducing anxiety in over 80 percent of the empirical studies conducted (Kazdin and Wilcoxon 1976). However, recently the theoretical underpinnings of desensitization have been called into question (cf. Davison and Wilson 1973; Franks and Wilson 1974). The necessity of relaxation has been questioned (Borkovec 1972; Gillian and Rachman 1974; Walters, McDonald and Karesko 1972), the hierarchical ordering of anxiety-producing situations has been challenged (Richardson and Suinn 1973), the necessity for repeated pairing of relaxation with scenes from the hierarchy has been questioned (Aponte and Aponte 1971; Davison and Wilson 1973), and the facilitative role of expectancy in systematic desensitization has been emphasized (Kazdin and Wilcoxon 1976; Wilkins 1971). At this point, it seems safe to say that the mechanisms underlying desensitization may be different from those Wolpe (1958) originally postulated (Davison and Wilson 1973). However, one fact remains: systematic desensitization is an effective treatment procedure in a high proportion of cases. In the last ten years, several investigations have focused on using desensitization as a self-administered intervention (e.g., Denny and Rupert 1977; Gershman and Clauser 1974; Goldfried 1971; Goldfried and Goldfried 1977; Spiegler et al. 1976). To date, the results have been inconclusive (Barrios and Shigetomi 1979). However, one study (Denny and Rupert 1977) reported self-desensitization to be superior to traditional desensitization.

Covert modeling is a strategy to help people implement new skills or transfer what is learned in one situation to another (see Kazdin 1974). The procedure works by having a person relax and then imagine him/herself engaging in specific sequences of activities while remaining relaxed. The procedure is repeated several times to build a strong association between doing the activities and staying relaxed. After several practice trials, subjects typically report an increased tendency to stay relaxed while actually engaging in the visualized behavior sequence. (See Cormier and Cormier 1979; Kazdin 1973, 1974 for a more detailed methodological explanation.) Covert modeling has been used effectively

to reduce text anxiety (Gallagher and Arkowitz 1978), to reduce avoidance behavior (Kazdin 1973), and to reduce
anxiety when engaging in assertive behavior (Rosenthall and
Reese 1976).

General relaxation is another widely used personal coping strategy. Benson (1975) reported that people who regularly engaged
in some procedure for producing deep relaxation began to demonstrate lower physiological arousal after three to four weeks of
daily practice. When people become more relaxed, they have a
greater ability to enter into a variety of situations and not react
anxiously (Hamilton 1969; Mason 1980). Regular, daily use of
relaxation appears to be most effective when dealing with generalized, pervasive anxiety (i.e., stress). However, relaxation
training has been used effectively with specific anxiety reactions
such as test, public-speaking, and interview anxiety (Barrios and
Shigetomi 1979). Recently, relaxation training procedures have
been prepared within a self-instructional context (e.g., Bernstein
and Borkovec 1973; Hiebert 1980). The effectiveness of these self-
administered programs has yet to be determined.

Cue-controlled relaxation recently has received much research
attention. The procedure consists of three phases. First, clients
learn a relaxation procedure similar to that used in regular relaxation training. Second, a self-produced stimulus cue is desig-
nated (e.g., the word *calm* or *relax* or a deep breath with a slow
exhale) and repeated at the end of the relaxation sequence, thus
building a strong association between the cue and the relaxed
state. Finally, clients are told to use the cue each time they
perceive an increase in anxiety level. The perception of rising
anxiety becomes a signal to use the relaxation cue to arrest or
reduce the rising anxiety. When clients repeatedly use this procedure in specified situations, the process of using the relaxation
cue following a perceived increase in anxiety becomes habitual.
Barrios and Shigetomi (1979) report that seventeen out of eigh-
teen published investigations "reported substantial reductions
in anxiety among subjects receiving cue-controlled relaxation
(p. 507).

Successful use of cue-controlled relaxation requires the ability
to self-monitor anxiety levels. If a person is going to use the cue
she/he first of all has to be able to discriminate when anxiety

levels are increasing. The effects of this *self-monitoring* per se on anxiety level has been reported recently (Hiebert and Fox 1981). Subjects were taught to develop a "mental speedometer" to track anxiety level, using Wolpe's (1969) notion of Subjective Units of Disturbance (SUDS). Subjects who learned to self-monitor anxiety level demonstrated decreases in self-reported anxiety level and decreases in muscle tension (frontal EMG), even though no relaxation training was conducted. Thus, it would appear that teaching clients to self-monitor anxiety level in a systematic way can lead to anxiety reduction.

One further word on controlling the arousal component of anxiety would be appropriate at this point. Since the first reports appeared in 1969, there have been increasing numbers of reports attesting to the effectiveness of *biofeedback training* in teaching people to control directly many of the physiological components of an anxiety reaction. Procedurally, biofeedback utilizes electronic monitoring equipment to sense ongoing physiological activity and report it back to the client via a series of clicks, a variable tone, or a series of lights that vary according to the physiological function being monitored. Knowledge of the dynamic status of the biological function being monitored typically enables a person to gain some degree of voluntary control over that function (Paskewitz 1975). (See Blanchard and Epstein 1978; Brown 1974, 1976; Gaarder and Montgomery 1977, for a more detailed explanation.) Through biofeedback training, people have learned to gain voluntary control over such physiological functions as muscle tension (Budzynski and Stoyva 1972; Reinking and Kohl 1975), heart rate (Blanchard and Abel 1976; Gatchel et al. 1977; Wickramasehera 1974), peripheral skin temperature (Kewman and Roberts 1980; Taub and Emurian 1976), skin conductance (Shapiro et al. 1972), and brain wave activity (Benjamins 1976). After a person has learned voluntary control of the physiological responses accompanying an anxiety reaction, the next procedural step is to transfer this voluntary control to anxiety-evoking environmental situations. With repeated practice, the person builds a new habitual way of responding that includes reduced physiological reactions to situations that formerly produced anxiety (see Blanchard and Epstein 1978; Gatchel and Price 1979; Hiebert and Fitzsimmons 1981).

Above all, the behavioral strategies outlined utilize some form of behavior acquisition and repeated practice of the new behavior to form new ways of responding to anxiety-provoking situations. In most cases, some form of relaxation is used because of the natural anxiety-inhibiting qualities of deep relaxation. Relaxation may be used to lower arousal levels (as in *general relaxation*), thus altering a person's anxiety threshold and *reducing the perceived intensity* of the anxiety reaction. Relaxation also may be used in an active-coping manner (as in *cue-controlled relaxation* or *biofeedback training*) to assist clients in arresting or reversing rising anxiety levels (thereby *reducing the intensity* of anxiety reactions) and in reducing the time it takes to dispel the negative effects of an anxiety attack (Alexander 1972). Finally, relaxation may be used to *reduce the frequency* of stressors in a person's life. After *systematic desensitization*, situations that formerly elicited anxiety are accompanied by feelings of relaxation. Through *covert modeling*, clients acquire the ability to engage in new behaviors and remain relaxed, even though the same situation initially was anxiety producing. In one strategy (*self-monitoring*), relaxation was not used. Instead, the habit of objectively assessing anxiety level was developed. In this case, a *reduction in the intensity* of the anxiety reaction (both subjective report and muscle tension) also has been demonstrated.

Although the procedures outlined above all rely on developing some behavior or pattern of behaviors to inhibit anxiety, the controversy surrounding the mechanisms underlying systematic desensitization (cf. Franks and Wilson 1974; Kazdin and Wilcoxon 1976), debates over the operative factors involved in biofeedback training (cf. Lazarus 1975; Meichenbaum 1976), and questions concerning the nature of SUDS monitoring (cf. Hiebert and Fox 1981) indicate that the line between behavioral and cognitive interventions is somewhat fuzzy. Probably few, if any, interventions are purely behavioral or purely cognitive in the strict sense of the words. The above strategies were grouped together because of their common emphasis on habit formation. We next turn our attention to strategies that are relatively more cognitive in focus.

COGNITIVE APPROACHES

The main goal of most cognitive anxiety interventions is to alter the client's ongoing self-dialogue so as to interrupt self-denigrating subvocalizations or to realign dysfunctional cognitive appraisal mechanisms. Meichenbaum and his colleagues (Meichenbaum 1972; Meichenbaum and Cameron 1974; Meichenbaum and Turk 1976) pioneered a procedure called *cognitive stress-inoculation training*, which approaches anxiety reduction by training people to alter their self-denigrating internal dialogue, characteristic of anxiety reactions, and to replace it with a more self-supportive internal dialogue. The procedure typically has three phases: *education, rehearsal,* and *application*. In the educational phase, clients are told about the nature of stress and the role of one's ongoing self-dialogue in producing and sustaining an anxiety reaction. In the rehearsal phase, various direct action and cognitive coping skills are acquired. Typically, people learn some form of deep relaxation, some scheme for monitoring their ongoing self-dialogue, a system for identifying negative self-statements and changing them to more positive self-statements, and receive guided practice in the use of these skills in anxiety-producing situations. When clients have become proficient in the use of the direct action and cognitive coping skills, they move into the application phase where they implement their anxiety-control skills in real-life anxiety-producing situations. (See Cormier and Cormier 1979; Meichenbaum 1973; Meichenbaum and Turk 1976, for a more detailed explanation.)

Meichenbaum (1977) also has suggested a variation on the stress-inoculation procedure, commonly known as *self-instruction training* (Rudestam 1980). Self-instruction training makes use of coping self-statements to offset the negative impact of anxiety-producing self-talk. In self-instruction training, the monitoring of current client self-dialogue is often bypassed and relaxation training is not typically part of the procedure. Instead, the client is taught positive coping statements (e.g., "Just take it easy," "You can manage," "The anxiety might rise a little, that's to be expected, but just focus on what you're doing," "See, there, it's working") and is taught to use these coping statements in an active, ongoing manner to coach him/ herself through anxiety-producing situations. In this strategy, the client's perception of anxiety becomes a signal to begin the coping self-instructions.

Cognitive stress-inoculation and self-instruction training have been successful in alleviating a number of anxiety-related problems such as test anxiety (Meichenbaum 1972), speech anxiety (Trexler and Karsh 1972), interpersonal anxiety (Meichenbaum and Turk 1976), and anger control (Novaco 1977). Success rates are in the 80 percent range (Barrios and Shigetomi 1979), with some studies indicating a superiority of stress-inoculation training over such standard procedures as systematic desensitization (e.g., Holroyd 1976; Leal et al. 1981).

Cognitive restructuring approaches anxiety treatment from a slightly different perspective. Based on the work of Ellis (1962, 1974), the goal of cognitive restructuring is to alter the client's cognitive appraisal mechanisms in order to make them more in line with objective reality. Procedurally, the client is informed of the relationship between basic values and beliefs (against which all environmental interactions are evaluated) and emotional experience. Basic values and beliefs form the attitudes that influence the way in which environmental events are perceived. It is the perception of events (stemming from a person's attitudes, values, and beliefs) that decides the particular pattern of self-dialogue that gets initiated. Anxiety reactions occur when a person's basic beliefs become distorted or irrational. After the client is aware of the influence of basic beliefs on emotional experience, unproductive or irrational beliefs are confronted, and the client is encouraged to construct more rational alternative belief statements. These more rational belief statements then are rehearsed through role playing and modeling before being practiced *in vivo* in anxiety-producing situations (see Ellis 1962, 1974; Ellis and Harper 1976; Wessler and Wessler 1980). Cognitive restructuring procedures have been used successfully in helping clients cope with test anxiety (Goldfried, Linehan and Smith 1978), speech anxiety (Fremouw and Harmatz 1975; Fremouw and Zitter 1978), and interpersonal anxiety (Glogower, Fremouw and McCorskey 1978).

Sometimes a particular sequence of interfering self-statements or the iteration of a particular irrational belief statement starts to dominate a person's awareness—that is, the person spends an inordinate amount of time ruminating about a situation (e.g., "Oh, gee, I've got so much studying to do, I'll never get it done"), and this rumination becomes anxiety producing. *Thought stopping* (Wolpe 1969; Taylor 1963) has been used effectively in such cases to eliminate the rumination and reduce the accompanying anxiety. Procedurally, the counselor tells the client to "conjure up" the troublesome rumination and to indicate (usually with a finger signal) when the thought is "going around inside the person's head." When the client signals, the counselor yells "STOP" in a loud voice and then points out to the client that the rumination is no longer present. The procedure is repeated with the counselor fading out the "STOP" and the client taking control of the stopping, first by yelling "STOP" and ultimately by saying "STOP" subvocally. After a client has learned thought stopping, the awareness of ruminative thinking becomes a signal to use thought stopping to terminate the rumination and to avoid subsequent anxiety. Alternatively, thought stopping may be used in conjunction with stress inoculation, self-instruction training, or cognitive restructuring to terminate anxiety-producing self-statements or maladaptive belief statements before switching to more productive forms of internal dialogue. (See Mahoney and Thoreson 1974; Rimm and Masters 1974; Wolpe 1969 for a more detailed procedural elaboration.) Thought stopping has been used successfully to reduce a variety of compulsive ruminations (see Hackman and McLean 1975; Samaan 1975; Wisocki and Rooney 1974) and anxiety attacks (Anthony and Edelstein 1975).

The strategies discussed in this section all utilize some procedure for altering the client's internal dialogue in anxiety-producing situations. All the strategies operate in an active coping manner with the client monitoring his/her ongoing self-dialogue and using anxiety-producing self-statements as a signal to engage in cognitive control procedures. In this way, the use of these strategies serves to arrest or reverse rising levels of anxiety, thereby *reducing the intensity* of anxiety reactions. Further, some form of all of these strategies could be used following an anxious encounter to *reduce recovery time* (the time taken to return to normal following an anxiety attack).

Personal Coping in Instructional Counseling

At the present time, it would appear that there is widespread support for a conceptualization of anxiety as an unpleasant emotion having three components: (1) a behavioral component, (2) a cognitive component, and (3) a physiological component. Teaching people to respond with less anxiety should involve strategies aimed at one or more of these three components. Further, all the strategies discussed in this chapter work at one or more of three levels: (1) reducing the intensity of an anxiety reaction, (2) reducing the time taken to recover from an anxiety reaction, or (3) reducing the frequency with which a person encounters anxiety-producing situations in his/her daily life.

Personal coping as a focus in instructional counseling is aimed at reducing client anxiety. Anxiety might be the initial concern that led a client to counseling, or it might be a supplementary concern arising in a problem-solving or skills-acquisition context. In either case, instructional counseling for personal coping seeks to ensure that physiological arousal, maladaptive behavioral manifestations, and self-defeating cognitive activity all are reduced to levels that the client finds acceptable (Hiebert 1983). The final goal of personal coping training in instructional counseling is for clients to acquire a set of skills that they can use to reduce the anxiety they feel in certain situations. Personal coping skills provide clients with the tools they need to be able to answer the generic question "How can I reduce the anxiety associated with doing what I want to do?"

The following descriptions of personal coping training are drawn from the hypothetical case of Rosie, a young woman seeking relief from tension headaches that typically occur about three weeks before university examinations and last until exams conclude.

Goals

The goal-setting phase of personal coping training is procedurally similar to the goal-setting phase of other instructional counseling strategies. General client concerns in the area of anxiety reduction are explained within a general instructional context. It is important for both the counselor and the client to be aware that when people feel anxious in certain situations, there are only two alternative courses of action: (1) alter the situation or (2) alter one's reaction to the situation (Cox 1978). It is possible to alter the situation by directly changing the environment (e.g., enrolling in courses where there are no exams, changing jobs to find a less pressured work place) or by learning new ways of interacting with the environment (e.g., learning study skills to aid recall on exams, learning to manage time so as to provide more opportunities for studying, or learning new interpersonal skills to permit more effective interacting with a demanding job supervisor). Personal skills training is predicated on the assumption that the client cannot or does not wish to change the environment directly but can develop a reasonable repertoire of skills to handle the environmental situation. Only if direct or indirect environmental control is not possible (i.e., the person must continue in anxiety-evoking situations and has a reasonable repertoire of skills but still feels anxious) is counseling for personal coping indicated. ("If a man is troubled by pain from a thorn in his finger, sometimes it is easier to teach him how to remove the thorn than to teach him how to tolerate the pain.")

Once it is clear to both the counselor and the client that the client's goals are consistent with the assumptions underlying personal coping training, a specific orientation to instructional counseling for personal coping is undertaken. Client ownership of the anxious response and desire to change the anxiety reaction independently of any environmental change are verified. ("It seems like you're doing something around exam time that increases your anxiety level and triggers off these headaches.

You don't really see dropping out of university as a preferred choice, but you'd like to do something to curb the anxiety. Does that sum it up?") A plan for preassessment is outlined that includes some way for assessing the physiological, cognitive, and behavioral components of the anxiety reaction. The client's permission to consult with appropriate information sources (e.g., family physician, professors, etc.) is also obtained. Throughout the whole process, the general instructional nature of the counseling interaction is emphasized (i.e., "During counseling, you will learn skills that will help you control your anxiety response").

Preassessment

In the preassessment phase of personal coping training, the nature of the client's anxiety reaction is examined before, during, and after the client's experience of anxiety. Using the preassessment procedures outlined in chapter 1, the counselor, with the client's full involvement, systematically checks the physiological, behavioral, and cognitive symptoms of the anxiety experience. Typically, the counselor will investigate the existence of any somatic symptoms that might be indicative of sustained, heightened arousal. Excess muscle tension, either generalized or focused (e.g., in the jaw, shoulders, base of the neck), excessive sweating, butterflies in the stomach, headaches, and cold hands are but a few common physiological complaints (see Antonovsky 1980, for more elaboration). In the hypothetical case of Rosie, the client has recurring tension headaches beginning about a month before examinations and increasing in frequency until they become a daily occurrence about a week before exams. This same time period is also fraught with increasing "general nervousness" and frequent insomnia. The presence of such somatic symptoms usually indicates the advisability of some form of relaxation training.

The counselor also explores the basic beliefs, appraisal mechanisms, and ongoing self-dialogue that form the cognitive component of the anxiety experience. In this regard, it is especially important to trace the ongoing cognitive activity from the events leading up to the anxiety-producing situation, through the situation itself, and into the period immediately following the anxiety experience. In the case at hand, Rosie reports that during the month prior to an exam she is increasingly concerned that the headaches will reoccur and that she will be too nervous or too sick to write the exams. She will begin to worry that she will not be able to pay attention in class or concentrate on her studying, or that she might be too sick to attend class or do the assigned reading. She reports that the worrying seems to make the headaches worse but that she is so anxious about doing well that she just can't help it. Rosie also is concerned that if she learns how to control her headaches but the worrying persists, it will be only a matter of time until some other problem, maybe an ulcer, surfaces. (It is important to note that this concern over symptom substitution is a common one with anxious clients, but that there is little empirical evidence to justify this concern.)

Finally, the counselor will explore the behavioral components of the anxiety response. What does the client do in the situation? How does the client usually cope with the situation? What have been some past attempts to handle the situation more effectively? What is in the client's current repertoire of skills that might permit him/her to handle the situation with less anxiety? In the case at hand, Rosie usually adopts the "grin and bear it" strategy for controlling her headaches. She sometimes tries to do something else to take her mind off the headache. If the headache starts at the university, she will "get into" a lab project or an English novel. This strategy is usually effective until she has to switch to less absorbing work like studying or reading the economics text. Then her mind will start to wander and the headache will return. She has taken a "how to study" course and also seen her family physician to see if the problem has a medical basis. The doctor's report was negative. Although Rosie claims that she knows how to study and has good recall after studying, knowledge of these facts doesn't keep her from worrying.

In addition to assessing the physiological, cognitive, and behavioral components of the client's anxiety, it often is helpful to explore the way in which the client views the interaction between behaving, feeling, and thinking. Clients who view thinking as the central component (i.e., "I feel the way I think, and I act the way I think. The thinking comes first, the behavior and feelings follow") are likely candidates for a more cognitively based intervention. Clients who view behavior as the central component (i.e., "When I act in a positive, confident manner I think positively and I feel great. It really depends mostly on how I behave") are likely to be more receptive to behavioral interventions based on some form of relaxation training. Clients who view feelings as having the central and initiating role in emotional experience (i.e., "When I feel anxious, I start thinking negatively and I usually start acting all jittery and nervous. I can't help it. When I feel anxious the negative thinking and jittery behavior just appear") demonstrate a poor prognosis for change. The only way to change the anxiety is directly to change the anxious feelings. Medication is the primary way for effecting such direct changes. Most counselors are not qualified to administer medication, and although the use of medications in the treatment of anxiety and other stress-related disorders is extremely high (Albrecht 1979 estimates that 80 per cent of all physician case loads are emotionally based disorders that are treated with medications that do little or nothing to address the causes of the problem), many clients express a reluctance to take a medicative treatment. Typically, when instructional counselors encounter the view that feeling plays the central role, it is a signal that some kind of cognitive restructuring aimed at altering this basic belief should be included in the intervention program. Clients who view cognition, behavior, and affect as having reciprocal lines of influence have the greatest number of change alternatives at their disposal: if thinking changes, so do behavior and feeling; if behavior changes, so do thinking and feeling; and so forth. Of course, there is no "best or right way" to view the manner in which cognition, behavior, and affect interrelate. The point is that the client's view of the way in which these three variables interact is an important preassessment area to address when planning a personal coping program.

Finally, in instructional counseling for personal coping, it is important to set up some procedures for obtaining quantitative data about the relevant components of the anxiety reaction being addressed (see chapter 7). In this case, procedures for charting headache intensity and the nature of Rosie's ongoing self-dialogue are introduced. Data yielded by such procedures can be used to maintain client involvement in treatment (see chapter 6) and to evaluate client learning progress. The information obtained in the preassessment phase of personal coping training leads to the formulation of specific hypotheses for instructional intervention. In this case, it seems that some form of relaxation training to address the tension headache, coupled with a cognitive intervention to interrupt the worrying, would be an effective intervention. This hypothesis gives rise to a number of specific counseling objectives.

Objectives

In the third phase of instructional counseling for personal coping, specific counseling outcomes are delineated. These objectives are specific statements outlining what the client will be doing during counseling (e.g., "I will practice home relaxation each day and record my pulse rate, breathing rate, and finger temperature on the data sheet at the beginning and end of each practice session"), what personal coping skills the client will acquire as a result of counseling (e.g., "By rehearsing my relaxation cue at the end of each relaxation practice, I will develop a strong relaxation trigger"), and in what contexts the skills will be used to produce what effects (e.g., "When I catch myself tensing and starting a headache, instead of worrying, I will use my relaxation cue to get rid of the tension"). In the illustrative case, parallel objectives are established to address the self-instruction skills to be acquired and the procedure for using these in association with cue-controlled relaxation. It also is extremely important to have some objectives that directly address the client's general desire in seeking counseling (e.g., "I'll be happy if I have no more than one headache a week and if I can use the self-instruction in exams to keep myself from worrying about how I'm doing").

Activities

Instructional activities are the processes and procedures that the counselor and client undertake to teach personal coping skills to the client. These personal coping skills are taught first within the context of the particular anxiety-producing situation that led to counseling (e.g., exam anxiety) and later are generalized to other anxiety-producing situations (e.g., "I'd like to spend a bit of time outlining how these relaxation and self-instruction skills can be used in other everyday situations that you encounter"). In this way, the client becomes able to plan his/her own personal coping interventions for future anxiety-producing situations. For an example, see Martin and Martin (1983).

During the activities phase, the instructional counselor works to specify the nature and potential use of the skills to be learned, arranges for appropriate practice for the acquisition and implementation of personal coping skills, and provides informational and reinforcing feedback to the client concerning his/her practice attempts. The counselor might use any number of relaxation training procedures (e.g., progressive relaxation, self-hypnosis, autogenic training). There might be some demonstrating of appropriate posture or of common procedures for taking some self-monitored physiological data (e.g., heart rate, finger temperature, breathing rate) as indicators of how deeply the client is relaxing (see Hiebert 1980; Lamott 1976). There undoubtably will be some intersession practice activities for the client to do and some means for reviewing this home practice. There also might be some simulation activities to give the client an opportunity to practice implementing the personal coping skill (e.g., "Now I'm going to play a tape recording describing someone going into a statistics exam. I want you to listen to the description and try to stay relaxed"). In teaching self-instruction, it likely would be appropriate for the counselor to model coping self-dialogue and then to provide coached practice for the client—first having the client self-instruct aloud, then by whispering, and finally at a subvocal level. Through the whole process, the guiding principle should be to make the practice contexts as similar as possible to the contexts in which the skills are to be applied. *In vivo* practice of the coping skills will help to enhance the transfer of coping skills from the counseling setting to the client's real-life situations. (The suggestions provided by Hiebert [1983] might be helpful in planning such interventions.)

Evaluation

When the counselor is evaluating personal coping training, three questions must be answered. First, did the client follow the instructional program to an acceptable degree (e.g., was the home practice done, were the data collected, etc.)? Secondly, given that the client followed the instructional program, did she/he acquire the personal coping skills (e.g., can the client relax on cue, use the perception of rising anxiety as a signal to begin coping self-instruction, etc.)? Finally, given that the skills were acquired and used appropriately, did they have the desired effect (e.g., did using the relaxation cue result in the client remaining relaxed, were headaches reduced to one or less per week, did the use of coping self-instruction reduce the worrying to an acceptable level, etc.)? When the answer to all three questions is yes, it is time to terminate regular counseling interaction and enter the follow-up period. This follow-up period is especially important in personal coping interventions. Anxiety experiences, like other emotional experiences, tend to be cyclical in nature. Without long-term follow-up, a naive counselor is apt to attribute an effect to his/her intervention that is merely due to the client entering the "upswing portion" of the emotional cycle (see Miller 1978).

THE INSTRUCTIONAL SKILLS USED

The following section provides an illustration of some of the key counseling skills used by instructional counselors during each step of the counseling intervention just described. The specific examples are drawn from the case of Rosie discussed earlier and are intended to illustrate the different skills used during each step of the counseling program in order to provide a plausible example for counselors wishing to implement instructional counseling programs for personal coping training.

Goals

Major Counseling Skills	Illustrated Use
(Basic reacting skills such as Nonverbal Listening, Reflecting Meaning, Reflecting Affect, and	

Major Counseling Skills	Illustrated Use
Paraphrasing Verbal Content are used extensively thoughout this phase to establish rapport and to clarify the parameters of the client's anxiety.)	
Giving Overviews	"It appears that anxiety over exams and the resulting headaches have gone on long enough, and now you'd like to do something about them. But before we can begin any intervention, it is necessary for me to find out more about the anxiety you experience. What I'd like to do is to spend some time getting more specific information about the way in which you experience the anxiety and the kinds of situations that make you anxious."
Probing	"What are some of the ways in which you have tried to restructure your world so as to reduce exam pressure?" "Tell me about your study habits."
Paraphrasing Verbal Content	"At this point, it doesn't seem feasible to register only for courses that have no exams, and you'd rather

Major Counseling Skills	Illustrated Use
	not drop out of the university."
Using Markers of Importance and Promoting Ownership	*"The important point* is that exams (and perhaps other environmental situations as well) provide a certain amount of pressure, but the anxiety you experience comes from you—it's your reaction, not the situation, that gives you the anxiety and the headaches."
Summarizing and Stating Goals	"Right now it seems that you may be doing something around exam time to increase your anxiety level and bring on these headaches. You prepare well for exams and can remember the information when you're studying, but you blank out on exams. You don't really want to drop out of the university, but you don't want things to continue the way they are. What you really want is to be able to learn some ways for controlling the anxiety and getting rid of the headaches."

Preassessment

Major Counseling Skills	Illustrated Use
Stating Transitions	"Now I've got a better idea of the general way in which we might address this problem. Our focus will be on teaching you specific skills that you can use to control the anxiety and prevent the headaches from occurring. The first step toward that goal will be to get some more detailed information about the way in which you react when you see yourself becoming anxious and how you usually try to control the anxiety. That is where I'd like to head next."
Using Set Induction	"I'd like you to close your eyes and imagine yourself going into an exam. Make the picture as real as you can. Imagine the other people in the situation. What are they doing? What are they saying? Now focus on yourself. What kinds of things are you doing in the situation? What are you feeling? Where is the tension showing itself? What is going on inside your head? What are you

Major Counseling Skills	Illustrated Use
	thinking? What are you saying to yourself? O.K. Stop imagining that and describe your reaction."
Probing	"What are the physical symptoms that you feel in that situation?" "Describe what is going on inside your head, your thoughts and the things you're saying to yourself." "Tell me how it seems to you, Rosie. Do we feel the way we think or do we think the way we feel?"
(Paraphrasing Content, Reflecting Meaning, and Reflecting Affect also are used extensively in the preassessment phase to clarify the client's intended message and to check the counselor's perception.)	
Calling for Demonstration	
	"I'd like you to use this chart to keep track of your headaches. Stop every hour and chart the intensity of your headache on this five-point scale, then join the plot points to make a graph. You see there is enough space on the pamphlet for seven days worth of graphing."

Major Counseling Skills	Illustrated Use
Summarizing	"Just to recap, it seems that thinking plays a pretty important role in your anxiety reaction. You feel yourself getting anxious, and then you start to worry that you'll get another headache. This usually makes the anxiety worse and might in fact be creating the headache. Right now, it seems to you that any program we undertake would have to include some procedure for reducing the worrying in addition to addressing the anxiety and the tension headaches."

Objectives

Major Counseling Skills	Illustrated Use
Modeling	"Watch while I show you an easy way to take your pulse rate as an indicator of how much you relax. I'm wearing my watch on my left wrist so I take my pulse on my right wrist, counting each beat for thirty seconds and then doubling the number to get my pulse rate in beats per minute."

Major Counseling Skills	Illustrated Use
Calling for Demonstration and Giving Directions	"Now you try taking your own pulse rate." "O.K., then, we have agreed that you will practice relaxation every day. I want you to settle yourself in your recliner, wait about a minute, then take your pulse rate, respiration rate, and finger temperature and record them on the data sheet. Then go through the relaxation sequence. After the relaxation, take the three measures again and record them. That way you can see the effect of your relaxation training."
Stating Objectives	"During counseling you will learn two sets of skills: relaxation to control the tension headaches and self-instruction to get rid of the worrying. You also will learn how to use these skills to stay relaxed and remain thinking positively. If you learn how to use these skills in your daily living, they should reduce the headaches to one per week or less and keep you from worrying about exams."

Activities

Major Counseling Skills	Illustrated Use
Descriptive Praise	"Your skill in relaxation seems to be growing stronger. You've been practicing every day, your data indicate a nice decrease in headaches across the past three weeks, and you're starting to feel generally less jittery."
Promoting Ownership	"It must feel good knowing that you're doing this yourself. You're practicing, you're learning the skill, you're making it work."
Stating Transitions	"I think the relaxation is well established and that it's time to move on to some ways to interrupt the worrying."
Modeling	"So, I'm sitting in the library studying and I start to think about the exam and I start to worry—'Gee, I hope I don't get a headache I've got to do really well. I wonder if I can pull it off.' I catch myself saying that, and I yell 'STOP' and immediately switch to my coping statements: 'I'm studying hard, and I can remember this stuff. I'll do

Major Counseling Skills	Illustrated Use
	the best I can. I've got more skills now at keeping down the anxiety, and I'm using one of them right now. Hey, good for me!' "
Calling for Demonstration	"Now, I'd like you to verbalize the whole process, Rosie. Just talk out loud the way you would be talking to yourself if you were following the thought-stopping and self-instruction strategies."
Describing Inconsistency	"There's something that's not clear to me. On the one hand, you say you want to stop the worrying, and you have demonstrated how you would go about that here in my office. But last Tuesday, when you caught youself worrying, you just let it go on and on."
Using "I" messages	"While you're talking, I notice your voice starting to falter and your hands trembling. It seems to me that you're getting anxious right now.
and Suggesting Alternatives	What I'd like you to do is to use your relaxation cue right now and relax. When you're calmed down, we'll continue. If your anxiety

Major Counseling Skills	Illustrated Use
	starts to rise again, then use your cue again to calm down."
Using Markers of Importance	"The thing we're striving for, *and it's the key point*, is that a rising anxiety level is the signal to use relaxation. Worrying becomes the signal—*there it is again*. The worrying becomes the signal to use thought stopping followed by coping self-instruction."

Evaluation

Major Counseling Skills	Illustrated Use
Summarizing with Descriptive Praise	"Well, we've covered a lot of ground. You've learned how to relax deeply, and you've been using that skill every day to bring down your baseline arousal level and keep it low. You've developed a strong relaxation cue, and you can use it when you feel a headache coming on.
and Using Markers of Importance	You've actually aborted many headaches with that strategy. You've only had one headache in the last

Major Counseling Skills	Illustrated Use
	two weeks. That is better than your projected goal. You've developed a wide repertoire of coping self-statements, and you use them with thought stopping to interrupt the worrying. *And most important of all,* you now are habitually using the perception of anxiety increase as a signal to use your new personal coping skills."
Giving Informational Feedback	"There sometimes is a tendency to step back into your old habit of feeling sorry for yourself when you feel the anxiety rising and notice the worrying starting. That is normal."
Suggesting Alternatives	"But even that perception that you're feeling sorry for yourself can be the signal to use your personal coping skills."
Stating Transitions	"I think we're ready to phase out my role. I'd like you to continue taking all your data for the next three weeks and bring them with you three weeks from today. How does that sound to you?"

Personal Coping in Multifaceted Instructional Counseling

Several times in this chapter, it was mentioned that instructional counseling for personal coping may be undertaken with the primary intention of reducing debilitating anxiety or with the secondary intention of facilitating problem-solving or skill-acquisition interventions such as those described in chapters 3 and 4. If clients are not able to make decisions concerning their life circumstances and/or lack skills required to execute actions consistent with decisions they have made, decision-making/problem-solving and/or skill-training interventions clearly are indicated. However, if clients can make decisions and possess the skills required to implement their decisions, they still may be limited in their mastery of their own life situations because of dysfunctional anxiety and stress responses. In such cases, instructional counseling for personal coping may be particularly useful. This is the clearest case for appropriate application of the personal coping strategy outlined in this chapter.

However, instruction in personal coping often needs to be combined with decision-making or skill-training programs to form more multifaceted instructional counseling interventions. Many clients are indecisive, lack skills, and feel anxious, all at the same time. In such cases, it may be difficult to introduce decision-making or skill-training programs without some initial and perhaps interspersed personal coping counseling in the form of cognitive restructuring or relaxation training. It may be necessary simply to relax first and then to go about the hard work of systematically constructing decision-making strategies and skill repertoires.

Whether used in conjunction with other counseling strategies or alone, personal coping strategies are essential components in the professional repertoires of instructional counselors. "How can I reduce my anxiety?" is one of the most commonly encountered questions in counseling.

Chapter Summary

Personal coping strategies are aimed at reducing the anxiety that clients experience. In this chapter, we presented a conceptual framework for anxiety that included physiological, cognitive, and behavioral components. Reviewing the literature on anxiety and personal coping reveals that personal coping strategies have three main functions: (1) to reduce the intensity of an anxiety reaction, (2) to reduce the time taken to recover from an episode of anxiety, and (3) to reduce the frequency with which anxiety is encountered in an individual's environment. All the strategies reviewed fulfilled one or more of these three functions. An instructional approach to personal coping training was discussed, and vignettes from one hypothetical case study were presented to illustrate key skills in the instructional counseling approach to personal coping. The chapter concluded with a brief discussion of personal coping in multifaceted instructional counseling.

REFERENCES

Albrecht, K. 1979. *Stress and the Manager: Making It Work for You.* Englewood Cliffs, N.J.: Prentice-Hall.

Alexander, A. A. 1972. Psychophysiological concepts of psychopathology. *In*: N. S. Greenfield and R. A. Sternbach (eds.), *Handbook of Psychophysiology.* New York: Holt, Rinehart & Winston.

Anthony J., and Edelstein, B. 1975. Thought-stopping treatment of anxiety attacks due to seizure-related obsessive ruminations. *Journal of Behavior Therapy and Experimental Psychiatry* 6: 343–44.

Antonovsky, A. 1980. *Health, Stress, and Coping: New Perspectives on Mental and Physical Well-Being.* San Francisco: Jossey-Bass.

Aponte, J. P., and Aponte, C. E. 1971. Group preprogrammed systematic desensitization without the simultaneous presentation of aversive scenes with relaxation training. *Behaviour Research and Therapy 1971* 9: 337–46.

Barrios, B. A., and Shigetomi, C. C. 1979. Coping-skills training for the management of anxiety: A critical review. *Behavior Therapy* 10: 491–522.

Benjamins, J. 1976. The effectiveness of alpha feedback training and muscle relaxation procedures in systematic desensitization. *Biofeedback and Self-regulation* 1: 352. Abstract.

Benson, H. 1975. *The Relaxation Response.* New York: Morrow.

Bernstein, D. A., and Borkovec, T. D. 1973. *Progressive Relaxation Training: A Manual for the Helping Professions.* Campaign, Ill.: Research Press.

Blanchard, E. B., and Abel, G. G. 1976. An experimental case study of the biofeedback treatment of a rape-induced psychophysiological cardiovascular disorder. *Behavior Therapy* 1976, 7: 113–19.

————, and Epstein, L. H. 1978. *A Biofeedback Primer.* Reading, Mass.: Addison-Wesley.

Borkovec, T. D. 1972. Effects of expectancy on the outcome of systematic desensitization and implosive treatments for analogue fear. *Behavior Therapy* 3: 29–40.

Brown, B. B. 1974. *New Mind, New Body. Bio-Feedback: New Directions for the Mind.* Toronto: Bantam.

————. 1976. *Stress and the Art of Biofeedback.* New York: Harper & Row.

Buck, R. 1976. *Human Motivation and Emotion.* New York: Wiley.

Budzynski, T. H. & Stoyva, J. 1973. Biofeedback techniques in behavior therapy. *In*: D. Shapiro, X. T. Barber, L. V. DiCara, J. Kamiya, N. E. Miller, and Y. J. Stoyva (eds.), *Biofeedback and Self-Control*, 1972. Chicago: Aldine.

Cormier, W. H., and Cormier, L. S. 1979. *Interviewing Strategies for Helpers: A Guide to Assessment, Treatment, and Evaluation.* Monterey: Brooks/Cole.

Cox, T. *Stress.* 1978. New York: MacMillan.

Davison, G. G., and Wilson, G. T. 1973. Process of fear-reduction in systematic desensitization: Cognitive and social reinforcement factors in humans. *Behavior Therapy* 4: 1–21.

Denny, D. R., and Rupert, P. A. 1977. Desensitization and self-control in the treatment of test anxiety. *Journal of Counseling Psychology* 24: 272–80.

Dollard, J., and Miller, N. E. 1950. *Personality and Psychotherapy.* New York: McGraw-Hill.

Ellis, A. 1962. *Reason and Emotion in Psychotherapy.* New York: Lyle Stuart.

————. 1974. *Growth Through Reason.* Hollywood: Wilshire.

————, and Harper, R. A. 1976. *A New Guide to Rational Living.* Hollywood: Wilshire.

Eysenck, H. J. 1969. Psychological aspects of anxiety. *In*: M. H. Lader (ed.), *Studies in Anxiety*. Ashford, Kent: Headly Bros.

Fischer, W. F. 1970. *Theories of Anxiety*. New York: Harper & Row.

Franks, C. M., and Wilson, G. T. 1974. Flooding, modeling and behavior rehearsal. *In*: C. M. Franks and G. T. Wilson (eds.), *Annual Review of Behavior Therapy: Theory and Practice 1974*. New York: Brunner-Mazel.

Fremouw, W. J., and Harmatz, M. G. 1975. A helper model for behavioral treatment of speech anxiety. *Journal of Consulting and Clinical Psychology* 43: 652–60.

————, and Zitter, R. E. 1978. A comparison of skills training and cognitive restructuring-relaxation for the treatment of speech anxiety. *Behavior Therapy* 9: 248–59.

Freud, S. 1959. *Collected Papers of Sigmund Freud III*. New York: Basic Books.

Gaarder, K. R., and Montgomery, P. S. 1977. *Clinical Biofeedback: A Procedural Manual*. New York: Williams & Wilkins.

Gallagher, J. W., and Arkowitz, H. 1978. Weak effects of covert modeling treatment of test anxiety. *Journal of Behavior Therapy and Experimental Psychiatry* 9: 23–26.

Gatchel, R. J., Hutch, J. P., Watson, P. J., Smith, D., and Gaas, E. 1977. Comparative effectiveness of voluntary heart-rate control and muscular relaxation as active coping skills for reducing speech anxiety. *Journal of Consulting and Clinical Psychology*, 45: 1093–100.

————, and Price, K. P. 1979. *Clinical Applications of Biofeedback: Appraisal and Status*. New York: Pergamon.

Gershman, L., and Clauser, R. A. 1974. Treating insomnia with relaxation and desensitization in a group setting by an automated approach. *Journal of Behavior Therapy and Experimental Psychiatry* 5: 31–35.

Gillian, P., and Rachman, S. 1974. An experimental investigation of desensitization in phobic patients. *British Journal of Psychiatry* 124: 392–401.

Glogower, F. P., Fremouw, W. J., and McCorskey, J. C. 1978. A component analysis of cognitive restructuring. *Cognitive Therapy and Research* 2: 209–24.

Goldfried, M. R. 1971. Systematic desensitization as training in Self-control. *Journal of Consulting and Clinical Psychology* 37: 228–34.

————, and Goldfried, A. P. 1977. Importance of hierarchy content in the self-control of anxiety. *Journal of Consulting and Clinical Psychology* 45: 124–34.

————, Linehan, M. M., and Smith, J. L. 1978. The reduction of test anxiety through cognitive restructuring. *Journal of Consulting and Clinical Psychology* 46: 32–39.

Hackmann, A., and McLean, C. 1975. A comparison of flooding and thought stopping in the treatment of obsessional neurosis. *Behavior Research and Therapy* 13: 263–69.

Hall, K. 1954. *A Primer of Freudian Psychology*. New York: Menfor.

Hamilton, M. 1969. Diagnosis and rating of anxiety. *In*: M. H. Lader (ed.), *Studies in Anxiety*. Ashford, Kent, Headly Bros.

Hebb, D. O. 1955. Drevis and the C.N.S. (Conceptual Nervous System). *Psychological Review*, 62: 243–54.

_____. 1972. *Textbook of Psychology* (3 rd ed.). Philadelphia: W. B. Saunders.

Hiebert, B. A. 1980. *Self-Relaxation: Learn It, Do It*. Coquitlam, B. C.: Per Man Consultants.

_____. 1983. A framework for planning stress interventions. *Canadian Counsellor* 17: 51–61.

_____, and Fitzsimmons, G. W. 1981. The relative effectiveness of EMG training and alternative anxiety treatments. *Biofeedback and Self-Regulation* 6: 501–15.

_____, and Fox, E. E. 1981. The reactive effects of self-monitoring anxiety level. *Journal of Counseling Psychology* 28: 187–93.

Holroyd, K. A. 1976. Cognition and desensitization in the group treatment of text anxiety. *Journal of Consulting and Clinical Psychology* 44: 991–1001.

Jones, E. 1953. *The Life and Work of Sigmund Freud*. New York: Basic Books.

Kazdin, A. E. 1973. Covert modeling and the reduction of avoidance behavior. *Journal of Abnormal Psychology* 81: 89–95.

_____. 1974. Comparative effects of some variations of covert modeling. *Journal of Behavior Therapy and Experimental Psychiatry* 5: 225–31.

_____, and Wilcoxon, L. A. 1976. Systematic desensitization and nonspecific treatment effects: A methodological evaluation. *Psychological Bulletin* 83: 729:58.

Kewman, D., and Roberts, A. H. 1980. Skin temperature biofeedback and migraine headaches: A double-blind Study. *Biofeedback and Self Regulation* 5: 327–45.

Kutash, I. L., Schlesenger, L. B., and Associates. 1980. *Handbook on Stress and Anxiety: Contemporary Knowledge, Theory, and Treatment*. San Francisco: Jossey-Bass.

Lamott, K. 1976. *Escape from Stress*. New York: Putnam.

Lazarus, R. S. 1974. Cognitive and coping processes in emotion. *In*:

B. Weiner (ed.), *Cognitive View of Human Motivation*. New York: Academic.

————. 1975. A cognitively oriented psychologist looks at biofeedback. *American Psychologist* 30: 553–61.

————, and Averill, J. R. 1972. Emotion and cognition: With special reference to anxiety. *In*: C. D. Spielberger (ed.), *Anxiety: Current Trends in Theory and Research (vol. 2)*. New York: Academic.

Leal, L. L., Baxter, E. G., Martin, J., and Marx, R. W. 1981. Cognitive modification and systematic desensitization with test anxious high school students. *Journal of Counseling Psychology* 28: 525–28.

Leavitt, E. E. 1967. *The Psychology of Anxiety*. Indianapolis: Bobbs-Merrill.

Mahoney, M. J., and Thoresen, C. E. (eds.). 1974. *Self-Control: Power to the Person*. Monterey: Brooks/Cole.

Malmo, R. B. 1972. Overview. *In*: N. S. Greenfield and R. A. Sternbach (eds.), *Handbook of Psychophysiology*. New York: Holt, Rinehart & Winston.

Marquis, J. N., Morgan, W. B., and Piaget, G. W. 1971. *A Guidebook for Systematic Desensitization* (4th ed.). Palo Alto: Veterans Administration.

Martin, J., and Martin, W. 1983. *Personal Development: Self-Instruction for Personal Agency*. Calgary, Alta.: Detselig.

Mason, J. *Guide to Stress Reduction*. 1980. Cuber City, Calif.: Peace Press.

Meichenbaum, D. 1972. Cognitive modifications of text anxious college students. *Journal of Consulting and Clinical Psychology* 39: 370–80.

————. 1975. A self-instructional approach to stress management: A proposal for stress inoculation training. *In*: C. D. Spielberger and I. G. Sarason (eds.), *Stress and Anxiety*. New York: Wiley.

————. 1976. Cognitive factors in biofeedback therapy. *Biofeedback and Self-Regulation* 1: 201–16.

————. 1977. *Cognitive-behavior modification: An integrated approach*. New York: Plenum.

————, and Cameron, R. 1974. The clinical potential of modifying what clients say to themselves. *Psychotherapy: Theory, Research and Practice* 11: 103–17.

————, and Turk, D. 1976. The cognitive behavioral management of anxiety, anger and pain. *In*: P. O. Davidson (ed.), *The Behavioral Management of Anxiety, Depression and Pain*. New York: Brunner/Mazel.

Miller, N. E. 1978. Biofeedback and visceral learning. *Annual Review of Psychology* 29: 373–404.

Novaco, R. 1977. A stress inoculation approach to anger manɛgement in the training of law enforcement officers. *American Journal of Community Psychology* 5: 327–46.

Paskewitz, D. A. 1975. Biofeedback instrumentation: Soldering closed the feedback loop. *American Psychologist* 30: 371–78.

Paul, G. L. 1969. Outcome of systematic desensitization. In C. M. Franks (ed.), *Behavior Therapy: Appraisal and Status*. New York: Brunner-Mazel.

Reinking, R. H., and Kohl, M. L. 1975. Effects of various forms of relaxation training on physiological and self-report measures of relaxation. *Journal of Consulting and Clinical Psychology* 43: 595–600.

Richardson, F. C., and Suinn, R. M. 1973. A comparison of traditional systematic desensitization, accelerated massed desensitization, and anxiety management training in the treatment of mathematics anxiety. *Behavior Therapy* 4: 212–18.

Rimm, D. C., and Masters, J. C. 1974. *Behavior Therapy: Techniques and Empirical Findings*. New York: Academic.

Rosenthal, T. L., and Reese, S. L. 1976. The effects of covert and overt modeling on assertive behavior. *Behaviour Research and Therapy* 14: 463–69.

Rudestam, K. E. 1980. *Methods of Self-Change: An ABC Primer*. Monterey: Brooks/Cole.

Samaan, M. 1975. Thought-stopping and flooding in a case of hallucinations, obsessions and homicidal behavior. *Journal of Behavior Therapy and Experimental Psychiatry* 6: 65–67.

Schacter, S. 1966. The interaction of cognitive and physiological determinants of emotional state. *In*: C. P. Spielberger (ed.), *Anxiety and Behavior*. New York: Academic.

Selye, H. 1979. They all looked sick to me. *Executive Health* 16 (1): 1–4.

Shapiro, D., Schwartz, G. E., Shnidman, S., Nelson, S., and Silverman, S. 1972. Operant control of fear-related electrodermal responses in snake-phobic subjects. *Psychophysiology* 9: 271 Abstract.

Spanos, N. P., and Barber, T. X. 1974. Toward a convergence in hypnosis research. *American Psychologist* 29: 500–11.

Spiegler, M. D., Cooley, E. J., Marshall, G. J., Prince, H. T., Puckett, S. P., and Skenzzy, J. A. 1976. A self-control verus a counterconditioning paradigm for systematic desensitization: An experimental comparison. *Journal of Counseling Psychology* 23: 83–86.

Spielberger, C. P. 1975. Anxiety: State-trait process. *In:* C. P. Spielberger and I. G. Sarason (eds.), *Stress and Anxiety.* New York: Wiley.

Taub, E., and Emurian, C. S. 1976. Feedback-aided self-regulation of skin temperature with a single feedback locus: I. Acquisition and reversal training. *Biofeedback and Self-Regulation* 1: 147–68.

Taylor, J. G. 1963. A behavioral interpretation of obsessive-compulsive neurosis. *Behavior Research and Therapy* 1: 237–44.

Trexler, L. D., and Karsh, T. O. 1972. Rational-emotive therapy, placebo, and no treatment effects on public speaking anxiety. *Journal of Abnormal Psychology* 79: 60–67.

Valins, S. 1970. The perception and labeling of bodily changes as determinants of emotional behavior. *In:* P. Black (ed.), *Physiological Correlates of Emotion.* New York: Academic.

Walters, W. G., McDonald, D. G., and Karesko, R. L. 1972. Psychophysiological responses during analogue systematic desensitization and non-relaxation control procedures. *Behaviour Research and Therapy,* 10: 381–93.

Wessler, R. A., and Wessler, R. L. 1980. *The Principles and Practice of Rational-Emotive Therapy.* San Francisco: Jossy-Bass.

Wickramasehera, J. 1974. Heart rate feedback and the management of cardiac neurosis. *Journal of Abnormal Psychology* 83: 578–80.

Wilkins, W. 1971. Desensitization: Social and cognitive factors underlying the effectiveness of Wolpe's procedure. *Psychological Bulletin,* 76: 311–17.

Wisocki, P. A., and Rooney, E. J. 1974. A comparison of thought stopping and covert sensitization techniques in the treatment of smoking: A brief report. *Psychological Record* 24: 191–92.

Wolpe, J. 1958. *Psychotherapy by Reciprocal Inhibition.* Stanford: Stanford University Press.

―――. 1969. *The Practice of Behavior Therapy* (1st ed.). New York: Pergamon.

―――. 1970. Emotional conditioning: A rejoinder to Davison and Valins. *Behaviour Research and Therapy* 8: 103–04.

―――. 1973. *The Practice of Behavior Therapy* (2d ed.). New York: Pergamon.

―――. 1976. *Theme and Variations: A Behavior Therapy Casebook.* New York: Pergamon.

CHAPTER SIX

Self-Management

IT HAS BEEN said that the object of teaching a child is to enable the child to get along without his or her teacher. In a similar vein, an overall goal of any kind of instructional counseling is to enable the client to get along without the counselor. The idea of "looking after oneself," "controlling one's own destiny," "shifting for oneself," or "looking after number one" has been expressed in a great variety of forms throughout recorded history. Self-improvement and effective control of one's spiritual, physical, and social "selves" have been advocated for centuries by prominent thinkers including "Seneca, Pythagoras, Locke, Goethe, Carlyle, Milton, and Shakespeare, among many others" (Thoresen and Mahoney 1974, 1–2). The ability of people to manage themselves (their own thoughts, actions, and feelings) strikes at the very heart of what it means to be human.

This chapter begins with a brief review of major theories and research pertaining to *self-management*. The main body of the chapter is then devoted to a detailed description of the instructional/learning sequences, processes, and skills that define a generic self-management strategy within the framework of instructional counseling. A final section considers self-management in the context of multifaceted instructional counseling and presents a model for multifaceted counseling that combines specific strengths of the instructional strategies considered in chapters 3 to 6 inclusive.

While the ability to arrange one's own affairs may be, and has been, connoted with a variety of labels (e.g., *self-control, self-regulation, self-determination, willpower*), self-management is the term that is used in this book. The term self-managment implies a *systematic consideration and arrangement* of personal, environmental, and behavioral factors. Further, such management always occurs within the context of reciprocal influence among these three factors (Bandura 1978; Coates and Thoresen 1980). Self-management is not a matter of autonomous, personal agency (as implied by the term *willpower*), any more than it is a matter of strict, one-way environmental determinism. Rather, self-management results when an individual is able to recognize and to take advantage of behavioral, personal, and environmental influences on his/her life that are relevant to the attainment of personally desired life goals. The term self-management implies, and is intended to imply, the successful management of personal, behavioral, and environmental factors for the attainment of personal goals.

Instructional counseling is well suited to self-management since the basic five-step model (introduced in chapter 1) acts as a conceptual framework within which clients (learners) and counselors (instructors) can work together to accomplish each phase of the counseling process. Determining goals, preassessing current client capabilities in relation to these goals, establishing specific objectives for change, planning and executing series of activities intended to accomplish such change, and evaluating the extent to which the changes that occur are in line with the changes that are intended are all undertaken in a spirit of cooperation and mutual respect. The client is an active participant in all forms of instructional counseling. This active, participatory role allows a smooth transition from joint management of counseling programs by counselors and clients to self-managment of counseling programs by clients themselves.

Theories of Self-Management

While concepts of self-management have been discussed for centuries, formal theories of self-management are of very recent origin. Most of the recent theoretical work in self-management has occurred within the context of the cognitive-behavioral movement of the last decade. Consequently, any review of self-management theory, however, brief, must have a strong contemporary emphasis. However, while formal theories of self-management are relatively new, concepts of "self" and its hypothetical relationships to personal functioning have pervaded psychological and educational writings throughout the current century.

Prior to the 1970s, most views of self-management tended to be based upon some kind of unidirectional determinism that posited either personal factors (mostly in the sense of personality) or environmental factors as the primary causes of individual actions. Early psychoanalytic writers were among the first theorists to develop concepts of self as a personal variable capable of acting with a reasonable degree of autonomy. Jung (1954) saw the developing self as a midpoint in the personality of the individual, around which all other personality systems revolved. As such, the emergence of self in the life of an individual was accompanied by an increasing ability to manage one's life in all its facets. The work of Adler (1927) furthered this trend toward self. Unlike Freud's *ego*, whose functions were determined largely by inborn instincts, Adler's self was a highly subjective system that interpreted experiences and directed personal actions. To the growing tradition of *personal autonomy* (directed by the self) within psychoanalysis, Rank (1968) added his classic concept of *will*. Rank's thesis contained a mini-theory of self-management in the sense that it advocated that individuals learn to express their own personal wills and thereby take command of their own lives.

Phenomenological views of personality, therapy, and education put forth in the middle part of the twentieth century by Maslow (1954), Rogers (1951, 1969), Snygg and Combs (1949), and others extended the notion of one-way, self-direction of behavior that some of the early psychoanalysts had fostered. Rogers (1961) in particular was instrumental in popularizing the view that self-management or self-direction must be left to operate relatively independently of external social and environmental influences if individual growth and actualization are to be achieved. For the phenomenologists, as for many psychoanalysts, self-managment was primarily a one-way street, with the person exerting some kind of autonomous will (*willpower*) upon his or her surroundings to achieve desired personal ends.

Against this prevailing view, early behaviorists (e.g., Skinner 1953) were proposing a very different unidirectional pattern for self-control or self-managment. Skinner's classic conceptualization of behavior as a function of environmental forces (external stimuli) resulted in a unique view of self-control. For Skinner, self-control resulted when a person's actions led to environmental consequences that fostered future behavioral change in "desired" directions. In Skinner's conceptualization, self-control is possible only through a careful analysis of environmental factors leading to a kind of environmental engineering in which the individual plans and arranges environments that will support certain desired actions and changes. For Skinner, self-control is a special case of external behavior control in which an individual engineers his or her own influential environment. Autonomous agency of the sort advocated by phenomenologists and some psychoanalysts was clearly anathema to Skinner's environmentally determined model of self-management.

CONTEMPORARY THEORIES

Interestingly enough, when formal theories of self-management began to appear in the early 1970s, they tended to incorporate aspects of both unidirectional historical views. Among the most influential theories of self-management to be formulated were those of Kanfer (Kanfer 1970, 1977, 1980; Kanfer and Karoly 1972) and Bandura (1977a, 1978, 1980). Both of these theoretical formulations depend upon a framework of reciprocal determinism among behaviors, personal factors, and environments. Both eschew earlier attempts at unidirectional causal arguments with respect to self-management.

Kanfer's three-stage model for self-regulation or self-management discusses three psychological processes that, together with direct influences from external environment and physiological feedback factors, can determine intended behavior changes. These three self-management processes are: (1) *self-monitoring*, (2) *self-evaluation*, and (3) *positive self-reward*. Self-observation (or self-monitoring) and self-evaluation of previous actions lead an individual to establish a behavorial goal (e.g., a person may monitor a smoking rate of twenty-five cigarettes a day, evaluate this as being too many, and decide to cut his or her smoking down to ten cigarettes a day). In subsequent days and situations, the same individual self-monitors targeted actions (cigarette smoking) and self-evaluates these actions in relation to his or her behavior-change goals. When the self-evaluation indicates that goals for behavior change (10 cigarettes a day) have been met or exceeded, self-reward follows (e.g., upon self-evaluating a monitored rate of 5 cigarettes a day, the self-controlled smoker in our example treats himself or herself to a bit of self-praise and a dinner out).

Bandura's initial model of self-reinforcement (see Bandura 1976; Martin 1980) adds an explicit step of *self-prescription* of behavior-change goals to Kanfer's *self-monitoring, self-evaluation*, and *self-reward*. In Bandura's conceptualization of self-reinforcement, self-management of behavior is achieved through (1) self-prescription of behavior-change goals and standards, (2) self-monitoring of behavior in relation to these self-set goals and standards, (3) self-evaluation of behavior by matching the behavior monitored against the behavior intended, and (4) self-reward contingent upon self-evaluations that indicate that self-prescribed goals and standards have been met or surpassed.

In more recent years, Bandura (1978, 1980) has developed a theory of *reciprocal determinism* that provides an interactive model for self-management theories. Reciprocal determinism advocates a kind of *personal agency* that results from a triadic reciprocity among *behavioral, personal*, and *social environmental* factors. An example of the interplay among these three mutually interactive factors is provided by an obese individual who is attempting to reduce. Through counseling, this individual has learned some specific weight-loss skills (e.g., eating three meals a day at regular hours and in the same place, declining snacks, etc.),—*behavioral factors*. Whether or not these skills are used, however, will depend upon encouragement from friends, contact with the counselor, and occurrence of festive celebrations—*environmental factors*. Finally, not only do environmental and behavioral factors interact with each other to determine what the obese individual will do, but *personal factors* in the form of private cognitions (self-talk and beliefs) also enter into the equation in a manner that interacts with these other factors (e.g., "I'm good at doing what I want to do, so I know I can lose weight, too" versus "Oh, I'm just so weak; I can't stand it").

Bandura's formulation of a theoretical model that emphasizes cognitive as well as behavioral and environmental factors in the determination of behavior has been extremely influential. The field of self-management has been opened to a new wave of cognitive-behavioral psychologists and educators who have developed numerous strategies for self-management involving systematic, self-controlled alterations to both personal thoughts and actions (e.g., Meichenbaum 1977; Rudestam 1980; Stone 1980). Contemporary cognitive-behavorial frameworks posit that through cognitive self-instruction it theoretically is possible for individuals to direct their own behavioral, cognitive, and/or affective change programs without the direct, and often protracted, aid of external counselors, therapists, or teachers.

The model of instructional counseling advocated in this book is a good example of a systematic, cognitive-behavioral approach to client change through counseling. When operated by a client without assistance (or with minimal assistance) from a counselor, it is, in essence, a self-management strategy. Rudestam (1980) has shown that almost any instructional/ learning approach to behavorial, cognitive, and/or affective change can be used by clients with minimal counselor/therapist assistance. Clients can learn to (1) prescribe their own *goals*, (2) monitor their own performances in relation to these goals (*preassessment*), (3) set specific standards for change (*objectives*), (4) determine, plan, and excute a specific change strategy (*activities*), and (5) *evaluate* the success of their change program in relation to their goals and objectives. When they have acquired these skills, they have acquired a powerful self-management strategy that can be applied to a broad spectrum of human problems and situations.

Before we turn to a summary of the empirical evidence that is currently available in support of contemporary, cognitive-behavioral models of self-management, a very recent development in self-management should be mentioned. In the last few years, the increased attention given to cognitive factors in self-management theorizing has lead to specific speculation about the roles of self-talk and personal belief in self-management success. Early formulations of such cognitive factors tended to be in terms of *cognitive expectancies* and *cognitive attributions*. Cognitive expectancies are guesses about what will happen in the future—for example, "It doesn't matter what I do, it won't change" versus "If I get my act together, others will be forced to clean up their acts, and this situation will be much better." Cognitive attributions are personal beliefs about the causes of past events—for example, "I succeeded because I tried hard" versus "I failed because the teacher was out to get me." Generally speaking, cognitive expectancies that are realistic and positive and cognitive attributions that attribute occurrences to internally controllable and changeable phenomena (such as effort, good planning, etc.) are thought to be personal factors that can contribute to success at self-management (see Bandura 1977a). Bandura's theoretical construct of *self-efficacy* (Bandura 1977b) is a good example of a cognitive expectancy. Self-efficacy is a cognitive judgment of personal competence in relation to a specific task—for example, "I'm certain I can run a five-minute mile." versus "I'm almost sure that I couldn't possibly run a five-minute mile." Such cognitive judgments, as we shall see in the next section, are showing a strong likelihood of being influential with respect to attempts at self-management.

Empirical Studies of Self-Management

Empirical support for the effectiveness of many of the self-management components and practices just reviewed comes from a wide variety of sources. In this section, evidence for the utility of the four major components of Bandura's (1977a) model of self-management (i.e., self-prescription of goals and standards, self-monitoring, self-evaluation, and self-reward) will be considered. Further evidence will be presented that supports the central self-management notions of (1) total client involvement in the teaching/learning of self-management skills, (2) self-administration of many therapist- or counselor-administered intervention strategies and (3) the self-management benefits of positive cognitive expectancies (self-efficacy) and attributions.

A great deal of support has been amassed for the basic self-management process of self-prescription, self-monitoring, self-evaluation, and self-reward. Self prescription of goals and standards for anticipated (targeted) change is an obvious pre-requisite to systematic, personal efforts at altering behaviors or cognitions for personal benefit. Such self-prescription is in-dispensable for future evaluation of the occurrence and utility of self-management change programs. A great many studies by Kanfer, Bandura, and their colleagues (e.g., Bandura and Kupers 1964; Bandura, Grusec, and Menlove 1967; Kanfer and Marston 1963) have demonstrated that people faced with self-management tasks tend to adopt standards for performances based upon previously conditioned responding, standards modeled by others, and/or personal past performances. Re-search in counseling, instructional psychology, and personnel management also has demonstrated that such standards, and the goals they are associated with, are most useful for behavior change if they are explicit, specific, and proximal (i.e., within reach of the client given his or her current level of functioning) (Bandura and Simon 1977; Duell 1974; Latham and Yukl 1975; Tobias and DuChastel 1974).

Self-monitoring is logically indispensable for any self-manage-ment program. Personal implementation and evaluation of efforts to change performances, thoughts, or emotional reac-tions require that such phenomena be observed in some way by the self-manager. In addition, however, self-monitoring of tar-geted behaviors and cognitions often has been shown to pro-duce desired changes in such targets in and of itself (e.g., Nelson, Lipinski, and Black 1976; Richards 1975; Romanczyk 1974). According to McFall (1977), self-monitoring is most effec-tive in producing self-managed change when the monitoring is systematic and closely related to the change objectives and standards.

Self-evaluation and self-reward are difficult to separate opera-tionally, since a positive self-evalutaion automatically carries with it a certain amount of self-praise or congratulation (Martin 1979). Numerous studies exist that demonstrate that evaluation and reward components, when practiced by individuals in the context of self-management programs, produced changes in target responses (both cognitive and behavioral) of a similar magnitude to those produced through interactions with external teachers, counselors, and therapists (see Martin 1980; Thoresen and Mahoney 1974 for extensive reviews of such research).

When clients are taught specific skills of self-prescription, self-monitoring, self-evaluation, and self-reward, they are able to apply these skills to the self-management of a wide variety of instructional change strategies and interventions. Among others, each of the strategies discussed in chapters 3, 4, and 5 of this book has been executed successfully within the context of self-management programs (see Kanfer 1980; Stone 1980; Stuart 1977). Rudestam (1980) suggests that almost any systematic, instructional approach to therapy, teaching, or counseling can be operationalized within a self-management framework. Close, cooperative involvement between client and counselor within the context of well-structured, explicit counseling interventions can help to promote desired degress of self-management in many counseling programs.

Finally, positive correlations between client change and positive client attributions and cognitive expectancies (e.g., Bandura and Adams 1977; Bandura, Adams and Byer 1977) recently have suggested an increasing role for cognitive efficacy judgments ("I-can-do-it" beliefs) in successful self-management.

In summary, research on self-management phenomena tends to support the feasibility of increased client regulation and management of personal counseling programs. The desirability of client self-management is obvious with respect to client freedom and the maintenance/enhancement of client gains in natural client environments and at future points in clients' lives "Give a man a fish, and you feed him for a day; teach a man to fish, and you feed him for a lifetime." Counselors can help clients to acquire self-management capabilities by: (1) structuring counseling interventions in explicit, systematic ways (2) involving clients at each step in the instructional/learning process; (3) teaching explicit skills of self-prescription, self monitoring, self-evaluation, and self-reward; and (4) assisting clients to adopt positive cognitive expectations and self-attributions for performance successes. Each of these methods is incorporated into the following strategy for teaching self-management processes and skills within an instructional counseling framework.

Self-Management in Instructional Counseling

Self-management, as a single-purpose strategy within an instructional counseling framework, assists client learners in managing (extending, maintaining, and generalizing) their own learning. The strategy aims at imparting to clients specific skills of self-prescription (of both goals and standards), self-monitoring, self-evaluation, and self-reward. It also fosters an overall attitude of personal agency and self-control by promoting positive personal expectancies and attributions. Consistent with empirical findings on instruction for self-management, the client is fully involved as an active participant throughout each of the explicit instructional counseling steps that constitute the self-management counseling process.

Self-management skills and processes may be taught to clients in general terms. However, it is very often useful to work with a current client concern (or area for improvement) that can provide a specific, concrete focus for the acquisition of self-management capabilities. Whether this method is adopted or not, it is important to remember that self-management counseling always approaches the overall goal of preparing the client to manage his or her own affairs. It helps clients respond to concerns associated with the generic question "How can I continue to do the things I want to do?"

In the following descriptions of self-management counseling, examples and illustrations are drawn from a hypothetical instructional counseling program for a woman in her fifties who has just completed a course on dieting methods. She is now eager to employ some of these methods in controlling her habit of overeating.

THE STEPS

Goals

The goal-setting phase of self-management counseling parallels the goal-setting phase of other instructional counseling strategies. It deals with initial processes and procedures for determining general client desires for change and orients the client to the general instructional counseling approach. Once it is clear to both counselor and client that the client's goals are in the area of self-management, a specific orientation to instructional counseling for self-management is undertaken. Typically, self-management is indicated when the client knows what he or she wants to do, possesses the basic skills required to do it, is not overly anxious about pursuing his or her goal, but is unable to implement procedures for successfully accomplishing the goal. "I know what to do and how to do it, but I just can't make myself do it" is the cry of the client who desires self-management counseling.

The goal-setting phase continues with the client and counselor jointly clarifying the client's specific self-management goal (e.g., "I want to use the techniques I've learned for eliminating my overeating, and I want to use these techniques systematically and consistently to keep the pounds off"). The counselor then provides the client with a general overview of basic self-management skills and processes such as self-prescription, self-monitoring, self-evaluation, and self-reward. Throughout the initial orientation to self-management, the counselor continually stresses the basic notions that people can influence what happens to them through systematic effort and skilled performance.

Before the goal-setting stage of self-management counseling is terminated, the client and counselor also agree to work toward a more general goal of "acquiring basic self-management component skills." This more generic goal subsumes the more specifically focused goal (in this case the "management of overeating" goal). It helps to ensure that the client and counselor will attend to the essential processes and generic components of self-management throughout the counseling program.

Preassessment

In the preassessment phase of self-management counseling, the counselor and client reconstruct a detailed, concrete picture of the client's current actions, thoughts, and feelings associated with well-documented situations relevant to the client's overall goal. By using the preassessment methods described in previous chapters, the counselor, with the client's full involvement, systematically checks each of the assumptions upon which self-management counseling is based—that is, that the client does know what he or she wishes to do, does know how to do it, is not particularly anxious about doing it, but is unable to do it because of deficits in self-management skills. In the illustrative case of the client who wishes to manage her overeating, the counselor first would check the client's knowledge of overeating control techniques (e.g., eating all meals in one room without engaging in other activities such as reading or watching television, taking small bites and chewing and swallowing before taking more, making a list of activities other than eating and engaging in one of these rather than snacking, etc.). The counselor then would probe the client's perceptions of advantages and disadvantages associated with eating or not eating in a wide variety of eating situations.

When convinced that the client's concerns are appropriate to self-management counseling, the counselor engages the client in a detailed study of major self-management component skills or tasks—that is, self-setting of goals and/or objectives that are realistic, incremental, and specific; making personal commitments through written contracts; self-monitoring by means of charting and graphing target behaviors and cognitions; self-evaluating by systematically comparing monitored performances to self-determined goals and standards; self-rewarding successful accomplishment of management goals, and so on. Once this analysis of component self-management tasks is complete, the client and counselor negotiate procedures for assessing the client's current abilities to perform each of these self-management skills (tasks) in relation to his or her specific area of concern. Information gained from this preassessment of current client self-management abilities leads to the formulation of specific counseling objectives. Such objectives typically are targeted at the development of self-management skills that are not present or are underutilized in the client's current self-management repertoire.

Objectives

In the third phase of self-management counseling, client and counselor state and record specific objectives for acquiring and/or improving the self-management abilities that the preassessment procedures have selected for acquisition and/or improvement. In drafting these objectives, the counselor assists the client in stating the objectives in terms of performances that may be observed and evaluated readily (e.g., "I will write a contract that indicates the six specific eating practices I will follow and how I will monitor whether or not I do these things") and that are properly incremental and realistic (e.g., "I will reduce my caloric intake by one hundred calories a day for each of the next ten days.").

In addition to specific objectives in relation to a concrete self-management focus (such as dieting or reduction of overeating), the counselor and client should frame specific objectives in relation to the acquisition of generic self-management procedures and processes (e.g., "I will be able to apply the self-management components of self-prescription, self-monitoring, self-evaluation, and self-reward to a wide variety of personal self-management areas"). Such objectives help to ensure that the focus of counseling will be on the process of self-management per se. This generic focus should not be subordinated to the concrete self-management problem that is used as a convenient platform for the initial acquistion of self-management skills.

In the process of producing self-management objectives, the instructional counselor makes use of the obvious advantages that this task has for modeling the important self-management skills of self-prescription of goals and standards and for making commitments and contracts. The counselor engages the client in a careful analysis of the procedures they are employing together so that generic skills of self-management, in relation to the setting of personal goals and objectives, are understood and assimilated by the client.

Activities

In the activities phase of self-management in instructional counseling, the client actively practices each of the components of self-management. This practice first relates to the specific self-management problem being examined (i.e., dieting, in the case of our hypothetical client) and later to other self-management, or potential self-management, situations or events in the client's life (e.g., our client may generalize her learning of self-management components by applying them to create change in additional areas such as smoking, exercising, vocational development, etc.). During the activities phase, the counselor works to specify, arrange appropriate practice for, and provide informational and reinforcing feedback to the client's use of the various self-management subtasks of self-prescription, self-monitoring, self-evaluation, and self-reward. As already has been indicated, much of this training is done within the context of the specific self-management problem that has provided the focus for client/counselor collaboration during previous phases of goal setting, preassessment, and establishing objectives. However, it is essential that the counselor teach the client the generic components and processes of self-management independent of a specific problem focus. These generic aspects of self-management should be discussed and analyzed. By the end of the activities phase, the client should be capable of developing independent self-management programs in other areas of his or her life. Many of the instructional techniques described in previous chapters with respect to problem solving, skill training, and personal coping may be used to engage the client in appropriate practice of the basic self-management components of self-prescription, self-monitoring, self-evaluation, and self-reward.

Throughout the activities phase, the counselor also should teach the client the advantages of developing positive cognitive "sets" in support of self-management undertakings. Such "sets" consist of positive expectancies and judgments about one's ability to control and manage one's life and its various aspects. Positive cognitive attributions, by which successes or improvements are considered to result from one's own efforts and abilities, are fostered actively. Positive expectancies and attributions can create a powerful sense of self-efficacy and personal agency that can be instrumental in maintaining, motivating, and supporting self-management attempts (see Bandura 1977b, 1980). Meichenbaum's (1977) technique of self-instruction training can be a useful instructional technique for helping clients to acquire positive cognitive sets in support of self-management programs. In this approach, the client is taught to indoctrinate himself or herself with self-statements correlated with task accomplishments (e.g., "I can do this if I just take it one step at a time," "Just remember what my goal is now—what I'm trying to do," "I know that if I think positively I can do almost anything," "When I've approached problems like this in the past, I've been very successful," "I'm a competent, intelligent person who can handle these situations," etc.).

Evaluation

The evaluation phase of self-management counseling involves a final assessment to ensure that the client is capable of applying the basic components of self-management to a wide variety of life situations for which these components may be appropriate. A good way of doing this is to construct a representative sample of potential self-management situations and/or goals. Clients then can be required to develop detailed self-management programs in each of these areas. Such evaluations always should be added to a more straightforward final evaluation of the success of the specific self-management program that served as a focus for much of the counseling interactions (i.e., dieting or elimination of overeating, in the case of the client in our examples). The evaluation of self-management counseling must go beyond an assessment of specific self-management changes to an assessment of the client's knowledge and ability to apply the essential and basic components of self-management.

The evaluation phase of self-management counseling concludes with the usual summary of counseling objectives and activities, encouragement and reward (praise) for client progress, and negotiation of longer-term follow-up contracts between client and counselor.

THE INSTRUCTIONAL SKILLS USED

This section provides a detailed illustration of "key" counseling skills that are used by instructional counselors when working with clients in the area of self-management. The specific self-management program from which examples of counseling skills are drawn is a hypothetical program for teaching self-management skills to a female client troubled by her habit of overeating. The purposes of illustrating counseling skills in this manner are (1) to indicate the exact skills that are most important to the successful acquisition of self-management capabilities by clients, (2) to illustrate the use of these skills within the context of a realistic self-management program, and (3) to clarify the purposeful process of selecting and employing counseling skills to encourage predictable client learning in the area of self-management.

Goals

Major Counseling Skills	Illustrated Use
(Basic reacting skills such as Reflecting Meaning, Reflecting Affect, Paraphrasing Verbal Content, and Nonverbal Listening are employed extensively during the initial stages of goal setting to assist the client in clarifying her own wishes and desires.)	
Summarizing and Stating Goals	"You really know the kinds of things that you can do to

Major Counseling Skills	Illustrated Use
	prevent yourself from overeating. You also have had some training in how t do these things and are not all that worried about doing them. In fact, you are well aware of many of the advantages you would experience if you could stop your habit of eating too much and too often. Right now, the thing that you really want to do is to force yourself to use the techniques you've learned for eliminating your overeating—to use them systematically and consistently so that you wil overcome your poor eating habits."
Giving an Overview	"Over the next ten weeks, we can work together to help you acquire some basi skills of self-management that will help you to contro your habit of overeating by employing the techniques you've already learned. What we specifically will focus upon will be the self-management processes yo can use to help ensure that you will really do what yo know how to do. First of all, we will find out more

Major Counseling Skills	Illustrated Use
	about your current abilities at self-management, particularly in relation to some basic skills of self-management such as accurately observing your own use of your overeating control techniques. We'll then move on to learning about specific self-management skills, and you will practice these skills, with my assistance, until you are very good at performing them. In addition to helping you use good self-management procedures to control your habit of overeating, we will also examine self-management procedures in general. We'll discuss how you can use them in other areas of your life as well, should you wish to do so."
Stating Transitions	"Next time we get together, we'll start to determine your present use of self-management methods in relation to some of the things we know about effective self-management— that is, effective ways of making yourself do what you know how, and want, to do."

Preassessment

Major Counseling Skills	Illustrated Use
Probing	"I'd like you to tell me exactly what you do when you decide to use the techniques you've learned for controlling your overeating. What do you think and what do you do?"
Giving Examples and Illustrations	"Let me illustrate the basic tasks involved in self-management. If I decide to cut down on my television viewing, the first thing I do is to set myself a very precise objective in terms of exactly how much time I will spend watching television. I then determine how I will record the time I spend watch TV. After I've started my self-management program, I evaluate how well I did at the end of each day.
Using Markers of Importance	"In all of this, it is extremely important that you understand that it is possible for you, through your own hard work and effort, to exert some control over what happens to you."
Calling for Demonstration	"Now that we've broken down self-management into

Major Counseling Skills	Illustrated Use
	its various component tasks, let's see how you presently are doing in relation to each of these subtasks. Take a couple of minutes and write down some goals for changing your current pattern of overeating."
Giving Informational Feedback and Stating Transitions	"It seems pretty clear from our preassessment of your current self-management practices that you need to improve your skills at prescribing self-management goals, evaluating whether or not you are attaining your goals, and praising or rewarding yourself for any progress you make. You do seem to have a pretty good ability to observe your own actions accurately, so we probably won't need to work much on the self-monitoring business. At this stage, it's time to set some specific objectives for our work together that will act as guidelines for helping you to acquire better skills in some of the areas of self-management in which you currently are somewhat weak."

Objectives

Major Counseling Skills	Illustrated Use
Prompting	"O.K., now remember the concrete way in which we stated the first two objectives about making a contract and planning a specific meal schedule. How would you state this idea of engaging in activities that are incompatible with eating so that it would become an equally concrete objective?"
Stating Objectives	"Good. So, in addition to the specific objectives for your dieting, self-control program, you also will work toward more general self-management objectives such as 'I will apply my new skills of self-prescription and self-evaluation to at least two other personal change projects.'"

Activities

Major Counseling Skills	Illustrated Use
Giving Clear Instructions and Calling for Demonstration	"It is extremely important that you relate your self-monitoring records back to your objectives when you

Major Counseling Skills	Illustrated Use
	are self-evaluating your performance. Let's say you had this objective (*points*) and these self-monitoring records (*points*). Show me how you would evaluate whether or not you met the objective."
Descriptive Praise	"You've really come a long way. Not only are you meeting with success in your self-management program for controlling your overeating, but the descriptions of the general self-management processes, which you just gave me, were accurate and clear. You're becoming very skilled at this business of self-management."
Using Rhetorical Questions and Suggesting Alternatives	"What would happen if you reminded yourself that the only person who can help you in this regard is you— that whatever happens will happen as a result of your own efforts and ability to apply these self-management steps? I'd like you to try saying these things to yourself and see if they make a difference."

Major Counseling Skills	Illustrated Use
Giving Informational Feedback	"Your self-reward strategy made use of two of the three reward principles that we discussed last time. The reward you used was a good incentive for you, and it was a reward that was not incompatible with your dieting goals. It was, however, pretty delayed from the events that earned it and may have lost effectiveness through not being delivered immediately."
Stating Transitions	"Since we've done pretty much everything we agreed to work on, it's probably time to start doing a final evaluation of where you've come in relation to where you started. Since this is a self-management program, what do you think about this, and how can we proceed from here if you agree?"

Evaluation

Major Counseling Skills	Illustrated Use
Summarizing	"As you say, there's little question of the progress you've made with respect to acquiring the general skills of self-prescription, self-evaluation, and self-reward. When combined with your existing ability to self-monitor, these skills have equipped you to perform successful self-management programs. Your effective program for controlling overeating is a good illustration of your abilities at self-management."
Stating Transitions and Expressing Counselor Reactions with "I" Messages	"I agree that there is little more that I can help you do that you can't help yourself do. Let me know from time to time how your self-management programs are developing. I'd very much like to be kept informed of your progress. It has been very rewarding for me to have worked with you and to have seen you develop self-management skills so quickly and efficiently. I've enjoyed working with you."

Self-Management in Multifaceted Instructional Counseling

Chapters 3 through 6 should have made clear that instructional counseling (whether primarily for problem solving/decision making, skill training, personal coping, or some other general purpose) is inextricably associated with self-management. Although other forms of instructional counseling may not focus as long or as explicitly upon specific self-management procedures as does self-management counseling per se, the very nature of instructional counseling tends to foster self-management. The basic five-step model of instructional counseling acts as a conceptual framework within which clients (learners) and counselors (instructors) participate together in determining goals, preassessing current capabilities in relation to these goals, establishing specific objectives for change, planning and executing activities intended to accomplish such change, and evaluating the extent to which the changes that occur are in line with the changes that were intended. The client is an active participant at each of these steps and, during the final stages of instructional counseling, takes progressively more and more responsibility for conducting, monitoring, and evaluating his or her own progress. This active, participatory role allows the client to make a smooth transition from joint management of counseling programs with counselors to self-management of his/her own change programs.

Self-management also can be combined with problem solving, decision making, skill training, and personal coping to form a powerful multifaceted strategy for instructional counseling interventions appropriate to a very wide range of client difficulties and concerns. This combined strategy first was alluded to toward the end of chapter 3 and is shown schematically in figure 6:1. The multifaceted instructional counseling strategy in figure 6:1 employs many of the strengths of the four basic counseling strategies discussed in this book. Problem-solving/decision-making methods (particularly those associated with generating, prioritizing, and selecting alternatives for action) are employed to assist the client in setting general goals, preassessing current

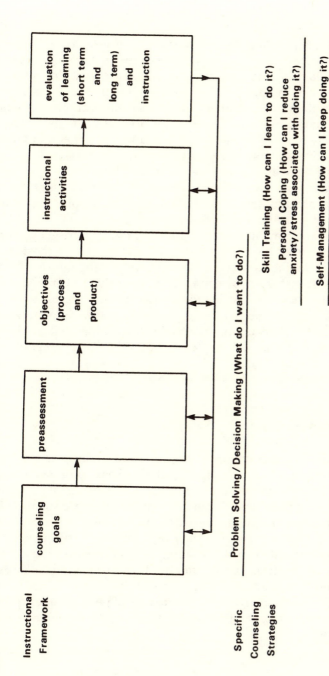

Figure 6:1 A multifaceted instructional counseling strategy

capabilities in relation to these goals, and establishing specific change objectives (i.e., elements of instructional counseling associated with the generic client concern "What do I want to do?"). Skill-training and personal-coping methods and procedures then are employed during the instructional activities phase of instructional counseling to help clients respond positively to the subsequent generic concerns "How can I learn to do it?" and "How can I reduce anxiety/stress associated with doing it?" Finally, the last step in instructional counseling (i.e., evalutaion) employs self-management methods to assist the client in evaluating, maintaining, and taking control of his or her own change program—"How can I keep doing it?"

Self-management is an integral part of all counseling. Total involvement of the client in counseling is one of the most basic premises of the approach. Without this open, informed participation, instructional counseling is deprived of much of its ability to specify client learning tasks in meaningful ways, to arrange appropriate practice of the skills associated with these tasks, and to provide instructional feedback that will maximize learning from this practice. As stated in the first chapter of this book, the overall goal of all instructional counseling is to assist clients to manage their own self-instruction.

Chapter Summary

A review of major theories and empirical findings in the area of self-management revealed that the basic process of self management involves the manipulation of personal, environmental, and behavioral factors in order to attain personal goals. Self-management in an instructional counseling framework assists clients in managing their own learning. The counseling strategy presented in this chapter aims at imparting to clients specific skills of self-prescription (of both goals and standards) self-monitoring, self-evaluation, and self-reward. It also is intended to foster an overall client attitude of personal agency and self-control by promoting positive personal expectancies and attributions.

The total involvement of the client-learner in the general

instructional counseling process makes instructional counseling very compatible with self-management. The final section in the chapter indicated how self-management can, and should, play an important role in a multifaceted instructional counseling model. This model (see figure 6:1) combines the general framework for instructional counseling first presented in chapter 1 with the specific counseling strategies for decision making/ problem solving, personal coping, and self-management discussed in chapters 3 to 6.

REFERENCES

Adler, A. *Practice and Theory of Individual Psychology*. New York: Harcourt, Brace & World, 1927.

Bandura, A. 1976. Self-reinforcement: Theoretical and methodological considerations. *Behaviorism* 4: 135–55.

————. 1977a. *Social Learning Theory*. Englewood Cliffs, N.J.: Prentice-Hall.

————. 1977b. Self-efficiency: Towards a unifying theory of behavior change. *Psychology Review* 84: 191–215.

————. 1978. The self system in reciprocal determinism. *American Psychologist* 33: 344–58.

————. 1980. The self and mechanisms of agency. *In*: J. Suls (ed.), *Social Psychological Perspectives on the Self*. Hillsdale, N.J.: Erlbaum.

————, and Adams, N. E. 1977. Analysis of self-efficacy theory of behavioral change. *Cognitive Therapy and Research* 1: 287–308.

————, ————, and Beyer, J. 1977. Cognitive processes mediating behavioral change. *Journal of Personality and Social Psychology* 35: 129–39.

————, Grusec J., and Menlove, F. 1967. Some social determinants of self-monitoring reinforcement systems. *Journal of Personality and Social Psychology* 5: 449–55.

————, and Kupers, C. 1964. Transmission of patterns of self-reinforcement through modeling. *Journal of Abnormal and Social Psychology* 69: 1–9.

————, and Simon, K. M. 1977. The role of proximal intentions in self-regulation of refractory behavior. *Cognitive Therapy and Research* 1: 177–93.

Coates, T. J. and Thoresen, C. E. 1980. Behavioral self-control and educational practice, or, Do we really need self-control? *Review of Research in Education* 7: 3–45.

Duell, O. K. 1974. Effect of type of objective, level test questions, and the judges importance of tensed materials upon posttest performance. *Journal of Educational Psychology* 66: 225–32.

Jung, C. G. 1954. *Collected works: Vol. 17, Development of Personality.* London: Routledge & Kegan Paul.

Kanfer, F. H. 1970. Self-regulation: Research, issues and speculations. *In:* C. Neuringer and J. L. Michael (eds.). *Behavior Modification in Clinical Psychology.* New York: Appleton-Century-Crofts.

Kanfer, F. H. 1977. The many faces of self-control, or behavior modification changes its focus. *In:* H. R. Stuart (eds.), *Behavioral Self-Management.* New York: Brunner-Mazel.

————. 1980. Self-management methods. *In:* F. H. Kanfer and A. P. Goldstein (eds.), *Helping People Change: A Textbook of Methods* (2d ed.). New York; Pergamon.

————, and Karoly, P. 1972. Self-control: A behaviorist's excursion into the lion's den. *Behavior Therapy* 3: 398–416.

————, Marston, A. 1963. Determinants of self-reinforcement in human learning. *Journal of Experimental Psychology* 66: 245–54.

Latham, G. D., and Yukl, G. A. 1975. A review of research on the application of goal setting in organizations. *Academy of Management Journal* 18: 824–45.

Martin, J. 1979. External versus self-reinforcement phenomena. *Journal of General Psychology* 101: 103–49.

————. 1980. External versus self-reinforcement: A review of methodological and theoretical issues. *Canadian Journal of Behavioral Science* 12: 111–25.

Maslow, A. H. 1954. *Motivation and Personality.* New York: Harper & Row.

McFall, R. M. 1977. Parameters of self-monitoring. *In:* R. B. Stuart (ed.), *Behavioral Self-Management: Strategies, Techniques, and Outcomes.* New York: Brunner-Mazel

Meichenbaum, D. H. 1977. *Cognitive Behavior Modification: An Integrated Approach.* New York: Plenum.

Nelson, R. O., Lipinski, D. P. and Black, J. L. 1976. The reactivity of adult retardates' self-monitoring: A comparison among behaviours of different valences, and a comparison with tokwn reinforcement *Psychological Record* 26: 789–801.

Rank, O. 1980. *Will Therapy and Truth and Reality.* New York: Knopf.

Richards, C. S. 1975. Behaviour modification of studying through study skills advice and self-control procedures. *Journal of Counseling Psychology* 22: 431–36.

Rogers, C. R. 1951. *Client-Centered Therapy.* Boston: Houghton Mifflin

————. 1961. *On Becoming a Person*. Boston: Houghton Mifflin.

————. 1969. *Freedom to Learn*. Columbus: Charles E. Merrill.

Romanczyk, R. G. 1974. Self-monitoring in the treatment of obesity: Parameters of reactivity. *Behavior Therapy* 5: 531–40.

Rudestam, K. E. 1980. *Methods of Self-Change: An ABC Primer*. Monterey: Brooks/Cole.

Skinner, B. F. 1953. *Science and Hunam Behavior*. New York: Macmillan.

Snygg, D., and Combs, A. W. 1949. *Individual Behavior: A New Frame of Reference for Psychology*. New York: Harper & Bros.

Stone, G. L. 1980. *A Cognitive-Behavioral Approach to Counseling Psychology: Implications for Practice, Research, and Training*. New York: Praeger.

Stuart, R. B. (Ed.) 1977. *Behavioral Self-Management: Strategies, Techniques, and Outcomes*. New York: Brunner-Mazel.

Thoresen, C. E., and Mahoney, M. J. 1974. *Behavioral Self-Control*. New York: Holt, Rinehart & Winston.

Tobias, S., and DuChastel, P. 1974. Behavioral objectives, sequences and anxiety in CAT. *Instructional Science* 3: 231–42.

CHAPTER SEVEN

Eclectic Uses of the Instructional Model

ESSENTIAL TO a sound eclectic approach to any undertaking is the belief that there is some truth in several of the major theoretical models and some utility to several of the major practical strategies that dominate the areas in which the undertaking is to occur. The task of the eclectic is to determine which theoretical approach, practical method, or combination of theoretical and practical elements works best with which type of situation or problem. In the case of counseling, the rational, purposeful development of effective eclectic programs has potential for working through an almost infinite variety of client learning problems. This is especially true when such resolution would be impossible by adherence to, or exclusive faith in, one favorite system or method to the virtual exclusion of all others.

What is missing for most would-be eclectics is an adequate integrative model that provides a framework for deciding among numerous theories and methods and for thinking and working across diverse perspectives. Eclecticism may involve the use of different theoretical and methodological approaches to counseling, depending upon the exact nature of the problem at hand. It may also involve an integration and combination of elements from different perspectives and approaches in dealing with a specific problem. Finally, it may involve both the problem-specific use of different approaches and the integration/combination of these approaches. Whatever the exact nature of the eclectic orientation and practice adopted, eclectic strategies must be planned systematically and implemented purposefully. Eclecticism does not result from indecisiveness and caprice. While eclectics often are accused of being "wishy-washy," unwilling to take a stand on fundamental issues in counseling, nothing could be further from the truth. The practice of eclecticism in counseling, properly understood, necessitates clear analyses of client situations and contexts and a decisive ability to make specific judgments concerning a host of factors that impinge on these situations—counselor characteristics, client situational variables, and intended learning/instructional outcomes. It may be true that some counselors who are unable, for whatever reasons, to formulate and operationalize systematic, purposeful counseling interventions with clients erroneously label themselves as eclectics. However, true eclecticism demands a careful and painstaking weighing/sifting of the multitude of variables operative in any human situation that has gone astray temporarily. The task of the eclectic counselor is very much as stated by Paul (1967, 111): to determine "what treatment, by whom, is most effective for this individual with that specific problem (or set of problems), and under which set of circumstances."

This chapter is organized in two main parts according to two principle aims. The first part of the chapter is intended to demonstrate the ways in which the instructional model described in this book may be employed as a general guide or heuristic to the development of effective eclectic strategies in counseling. To this end, a rather complex system of counseling processes and procedures gradually will be constructed using the information and concepts depicted in figure 1:1 (see chapter 1) as a point of departure. The second part of the chapter is devoted to a detailed description of how the instructional taxonomy of skills and strategies first presented in chapter 2 may be employed as a system for analyzing, organizing, and acquiring a broad range of counseling strategies described in the contemporary literature in counseling.

The Instructional Model as a Guide to Eclectic Practice

CYCLES AND LOOPS WITHIN PHASES

The five-phase instructional model upon which all the counseling conceptualizations (purposes, strategies, processes, decisions) advocated in this book are based is portrayed in figure 1:1 and was described initially in chapter 1. By this time, the phases or steps involving general goals, preassessment, objectives, instructional activities, and evaluation undoubtly are familiar to the reader. What the reader may not be as familiar with is the notion that these five processes can be used not only to map the overall counseling enterprise as it begins, evolves, and ends but also to describe individual sessions or series of counselor-client exchanges within each of the major phases depicted in figure 1:1. The second use of the five basic processes or steps of instructional counseling is essential to the eclectic use of the instructional system in counseling.

The use of the cycle of goal setting, preassessment, framing objectives, instructional activities, and evaluation within an individual counseling session or series of counselor-client transactions is best explained through the use of several illustrations. In the goal-setting phase of instructional counseling, a shared goal of both client and counselor in their initial contacts quite likely will be to get to know one another. The counselor and client preassess in relation to this goal as they process information about the other person's appearance, mannerisms, and tone/context of speech that results in the formation of general impressions and hypotheses concerning the other person. As these impressions and hypotheses are realized, specific objectives of determining the validity of such hypotheses emerge. Both client and counselor then proceed to act in ways intended to assist them to acquire additional information about each other (instructional activities). They then evaluate this information in order to affirm or dismiss their initial impressions.

A second illustration of the occurrence of the five-step cycle within a major phase of instructional counseling also may be drawn from the goal-setting phase. A common goal at this phase is to build a working relationship (a rapport) between counselor and client. Processing of information concerning body language, facial expressions, accuracy of each other's expressed perceptions, general attentiveness, and so forth assists in the preassessment of levels of trust and liking. Specific objectives concerned with building trust in the relationship to a level perceived as necessary to support effective counseling emerge from this assessment. The counselor, well versed in relationship enhancement methods and processes, then structures his/her selection of counseling skills and strategies and the activities pursued in subsequent counseling exchanges. By employing the reacting skills of paraphrasing content, reflecting meaning, reflecting affect, and self-disclosure, she/he helps the client explore issues and discover the levels of trust, acceptance, and support available in the counseling relationship. Monitoring of client and counselor reactions to these activities (e.g., subsequent ease of conversing over a broad range of relevant personal issues) can help to evaluate the success of this mini-strategy.

During the instructional activities phase of instructional counseling, it is common for many five-step cycles to define counseling purposes, structures, and functions. A general skill acquisition strategy might involve a number of five-step cycles— one for each discrete skill to be acquired. In a similar way, counseling done in association with a cognitive change strategy, such as that proposed by Meichenbaum (1977), may be operationalized during the instructional activities phase as a series of five-step cycles—one concerned with the goal of recognizing self-defeating self-talk, the next concerned with the goal of learning to interpret such self-talk, and so forth. In multifaceted interventions, series of five-step cycles may occur across behavior, thought, and feeling modalities and across issues associated with decision making, skill acquisition, personal coping, and self-management.

Use of the five steps of goals, preassessment, objectives, instructional activities, and evaluation—within each of the major phases of instructional counseling (also defined by these same terms) is thus a common, and probably essential, part of most counseling relationships. Through this means, it is possible for instructional counselors to act purposefully and to evaluate the effects of their actions on clients in an ongoing, dynamic manner throughout the entire course of counseling. By setting up a repetitive series of five-step cycles (goals, preassessment, objectives, activities, and evaluation), instructional counselors are able to maintain a concrete sense of direction and purpose in the short term that contributes significantly to the overall direction and purpose of the counseling enterprise. They also are able to operationalize and evaluate short-term counseling interventions in a way that contributes to, and is consistent with, the overall purposes and strategies of the entire counseling process. In short, they are able to see both the trees in the forest and the forest.

To ensure that the conditions essential for client learning are maintained continuously throughout the entire course of counseling, instructional counselors use combinations of structuring, soliciting, and reacting skills (see the taxonomy of such skills in chapter 2) to guarantee: (1) clear *specification* of what the client is learning, (2) opportunities for appropriate *practice* of what is being learned, and (3) effective *feedback* to the client's learning practice. Continuous looping among these three conditions (see figure 7:1) also is a main feature of instructional counseling.

When the series of five-step cycles and specification-practice-feedback loops described above are added to the basic five-phase model of instructional counseling portrayed in figure 1:1, a fuller picture of instructional counseling, as it actually occurs in practice, begins to emerge. Figure 7:2 attempts to capture this picture schematically. The large circles in this figure represent the five phases depicted originally in figure 1:1. The smaller

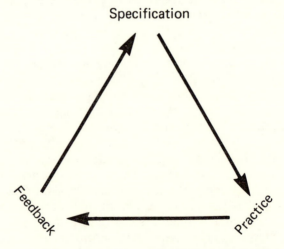

Figure 7:1. The specification-practice-feedback (Sp-Pr-Fb) loop

circle inserted in the middle of each of the larger circles represents the possibility of at least one (probably several) five-step
cycles within each major phase. Finally, the triangles intersect-
ing the smaller circles represent the continuous looping among
the learning conditions of specification, practice, and feedback
so essential to effective client learning and instructional counseling. The arrows in figure 1:1 that show the dynamic system of
information flow among the major phases of the instructional
counseling model have been omitted from figure 7:2 to permit a
focus on the five-step cycles and specification-practice-feedback
loops possible within each major phase of the model.

ECLECTIC SELECTION OF COUNSELING STRATEGIES

Figure 7:2 depicts instructional counseling as a dynamic, systematic series of five-step cycles and specification-practice-
feedback loops guided by an overall movement across the
phases of goals, preassessment, objectives, instructional activities, and evaluation. This conceptualization of instructional

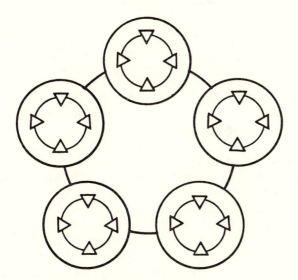

*Figure 7:2. Five-step cycles and Sp-Pr-Fb loops within
major phases of instructional counseling*

counseling is basic to its use as a heuristic and guideline for the purposeful, systematic determination of eclectic strategies that aim at facilitating desired client learning given specific client problems, counselor capabilities, and situational contexts. This use of the concepts and framework of instructional counseling is illustrated in this section with extended examples from the goal-setting and preassessment phases. It should be clear, however, that the same eclectic construction is possible at any phase of the instructional counseling enterprise.

The contemporary literature in counseling is a complex, rich source of numerous approaches to, and techniques for, conceptualizing and accomplishing any of the tasks implied by the five phases in the instructional counseling model. It is possible to do an effective job of goal setting, structuring and conducting instructional activities, evaluating client learning and counselor effectiveness, and so on in a great variety of ways. Many of these alternatives have some degree of theoretical and empirical support, and many of them may be appropriate given particular combinations of counselor and client characteristics and interactions, situational variables, and intended learning/instructional outcomes.

Figure 7:3 provides a graphic depiction of the possible selection of a limited number of counseling strategies during the goal-setting phase of instructional counseling. Many strategies in addition to those depicted are potentially available to counselors. However, the three strategies in figure 7:3 all may be used effectively in a wide variety of counseling contexts during the initial phase of counseling. Ultimately, the instructional counselor's selection of strategies at any phase in the instructional counseling process is limited only by his/her knowledge of and competence in implementing different strategies and by the appropriateness of these strategies to client concerns and desired learning outcomes.

During the goal-setting phase, the strategies of problem solving (especially initial phases in approaches such as the one described by D'Zurilla and Goldfried 1971), goal attainment scaling (Kiresuk and Sherman 1968), and active responding (the purposeful use of counselor attending, responding, and initiating skills, as developed by Carkhuff 1981 to foster client explo-

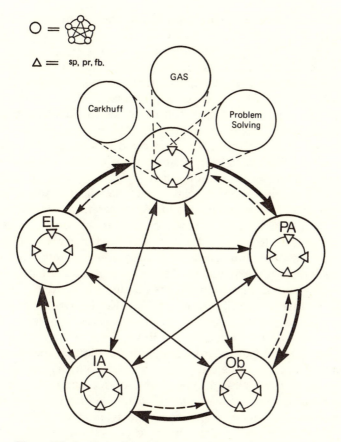

Figure 7:3 Some possible strategies for the goal-setting phase of instructional counseling

ration, understanding, and action) can be particularly useful and effective in helping clients to clarify their general goals for the counseling process. Each of these approaches has different advantages given particular client and counselor characteristics and interactions, client concerns, and situations. Goal-attainment scaling (see chapter 8 for a fuller description) can furnish a clear, personalized statement of client goals when clients come to counseling with well-developed ideas about their own learning needs. Problem solving can help clients who pre-fer a structured, rational approach to their current difficulties. Carkhuff's systematic but somewhat more open-ended strategy can be particularly effective for clients who initially are uncertain as to the nature of their concerns and desires. Each of these strategies and others like them may be employed separately or in combination to help counselors and clients work through the phase of goal setting in instructional counseling.

A second illustration of the eclectic use of the instructional counseling framework is drawn from the preassessment phase. Figure 7:4 illustrates the possible use of at least three different strategies for the acquisition, during preassessment, of data concerning client variables relevant to overall counseling goals. From such data, counselors and clients can frame specific counseling objectives and make decisions about what counseling interventions to employ during the instructional activities phase of instructional counseling. The three preassessment strategies depicted are not exhaustive of such strategies but are commonly used by a great many counselors (alone or in combination with other strategies). Self-monitoring (see Kanfer 1980; Stuart 1977) typically involves training the client to observe his/her feelings, behaviors, and/or thoughts and to use an appropriate and convenient method of recording this information so that it can be employed as baseline data against which to measure the effectiveness of counseling and as a basis for decision making during the preassessment phase. Often, such data may be summarized conveniently using some form of feelings-thoughts-actions (F-T-A) matrix in which client responses, in each of these modalities, that are associated with problem situations are summarized. Typically, the F-T-A matrix technique is used to probe and summarize client feelings, thoughts, and behaviors before during, and after problem-related occurrences or the encountering of problem situations (see Meichenbaum 1977). While the F-T-A matrix often is employed with self-monitoring strategies it can be used as a convenient method of representing and organizing client data derived from any source. A third preassessment method, depicted in figure 7:4, is formal testing. This is a time-honored method of gathering reliable and valid information in counseling. A wide variety of formal, standardized tests (mostly paper and pencil) are available for assessing client

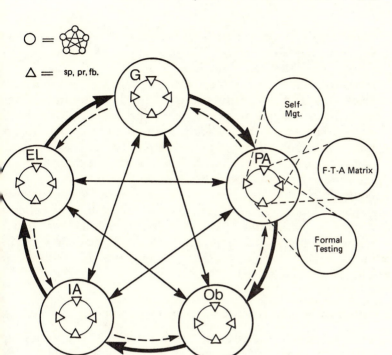

Figure 7:4. Some possible strategies for the preassessment
phase of instructional counseling

attitudes, aptitudes, interests, desires, and capabilities in areas
such as intelligence, creativity, interpersonal relationships,
vocational choices, and so forth (see, for example, Shertzer and
Linden 1979). Many of these instruments have been developed
as a result of extensive sampling, testing, psychometric calcula-
tions, and norming procedures—all intended to create standardized tests that yield valid and reliable information. The
Buros Mental Measurement Yearbooks (e.g., Buros 1972) are comprehensive sources of information about formal test instruments
and their psychometric properties.

A number of different counseling strategies and methods can
be employed, singly or in combination, to assist the eclectic
counselor and his/her client(s) during the goal-setting and
preassessment phases of instructional counseling. Many differ-

ent strategies and methods also may be employed during sub sequent phases of instructional counseling. Depending on the nature of client/counselor characteristics and interactions client concerns and goals, and important situational vari ables, any or many of the counseling techniques and change inducing strategies reviewed in chapters 3 to 6 might be appropriate means of fostering desired client change during the instructional activities phase. A number of possible meth ods from which eclectic counselors can construct appropriate relevant evaluation procedures is examined in chapter 8 of this book. In the final analysis, the employment of various tech niques, strategies, and methods appropriate to particula phases of the instructional counseling model and matched to client situations, problems, and goals is limited only by the imagination, knowledge, and competence of instructiona counselors themselves.

SHARED INITIATION AND DYNAMIC FLOW

Two essential properties of the instructional counseling ap proach that have been implied by and discussed briefly in pre vious chapters are the focus of this section of chapter 7. Each of these properties is indispensable to effective instructional coun seling, whether or not such counseling is done from an eclecti perspective. However, since instructional counseling is basicall an eclectic approach to counseling from an instructional per spective, it makes sense to discuss these properties in som detail in this chapter.

The first property to be discussed relates to the initiation of activity throughout the instructional counseling process and within each of the major phases in this process. In instructiona counseling, such initiation is a shared responsibility of client and counselors. Figure 7:5 depicts the general manner in which this sharing occurs across the five major phases of instructiona counseling. In keeping with the client-centered focus of instruc tional counseling, initiation during the goal-setting phase is the client's responsibility. The counselor may facilitate, support, or create an interpersonal environment in which the client explore his/her concerns and arrives at general desires and goals. The

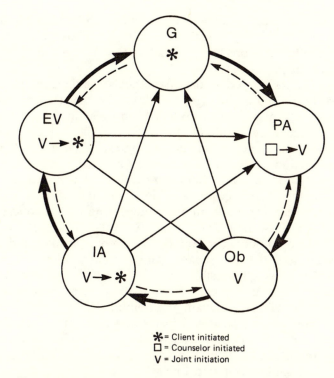

* = Client initiated
□ = Counselor initiated
V = Joint initiation

Figure 7:5 Initiation of activity in instructional counseling

counselor also may assist the client in forming goals in as precise and descriptive a manner as possible. However, goals in instructional counseling always must come from the client. If the client is to work hard in the joint venture of instructional counseling, he/she must "own" the goals that fuel the entire process. Even though counselors may believe that goals other than those selected by the client would be most beneficial for the client to pursue, they should be prepared (within the limits of their own ethical frameworks) to assist clients in pursuing goals that clients perceive as being the most important and desirable. It is, of course, the counselor's responsibility to ensure that the client has examined and explored significant issues surrounding his/her concerns in a reasonably thorough manner before goals are framed as guides for subsequent phases in the instructional counseling process. Clients should be helped to articulate their goals and the likely input that pursuing such goals might have on their life situations before deciding to work systematically to achieve them.

The client-centered initiation of goals may mean that the instructional counseling process is repeated several times with the same client as goals different from those initially pursued arise (often as a result of previous instructional counseling cycles). It also may mean that, at times, initial goals will be abandoned in favor of others after the acquisition of additional information in preassessment or instructional activities phases. Both of these, and other possible eventualities, must be expected to occur at times in any undertaking that is concerned with human learning. There is no guarantee that similar eventualities would not occur under a system of counselor initiation of goals, and the advantages gained from client initiation of goals far outweigh possible liabilities. By taking responsibility for the initial setting of goals in counseling, clients tend to experience counseling as relevant and helpful. These positive views often translate into positive expectancies and enthusiasm, both of which can be important factors in successful client change. Most important, in setting their own counseling goals, clients take an essential first step toward the overall goal of instructional counseling—that is, becoming effective, efficient self-instructors.

Initiation of the preassessment process in the second phase of instructional counseling usually begins as the responsibility of the counselor, since it is the counselor who possesses experience and expertise in structuring the acquisition/collection of information vital to the counseling enterprise and in considering the utility of different intervention strategies in light of this information. However, instructional counselors, as good teachers, explain each step in the preassessment phase to clients and encourage clients gradually to take a greater and greater part in important decisions and tasks that define the preassessment phase. By the end of preassessment, a joint initiation of decisions and tasks between counselors and clients should emerge. No phase of instructional counseling should terminate until the counselor is satisfied that the client understands the nature of the tasks and decisions that define the phase and can apply this understanding in systematic future attempts to resolve similar difficulties or to approach similar goals.

The framing of specific objectives for instructional counseling is a joint undertaking in which client-initiated goals are translated (with the counselor's technical expertise and assistance) into specific statements of intended learning outcomes that can be used to evaluate the effectiveness of instructional counseling. As in the preassessment phase, counselors should satisfy themselves that the skills and strategies necessary for executing the tasks and making the decisions required to complete this phase successfully have been acquired by clients before proceeding to the next phase. In each phase of instructional counseling, clients should be helped to accomplish the specific purposes of that phase in relation to the counseling goals that have been set. In doing so, they also should acquire some functional expertise in the tasks and decision-making skills that define the instructional work in each phase.

In the instructional activities and evaluation phases of instructional counseling, joint counselor-client initiation of tasks and decisions gives way to client self-initiation. Because of the number of five-step cycles that typically are involved in these final phases of instructional counseling, these phases may be used to ensure that clients have acquired facility with the tasks and decision-making skills necessary to complete previous phases. Clients and counselors might work together to pursue and evaluate activities intended to promote client learning in relation to a few initial objectives. Gradually, however, clients increasingly work single-handedly (under the watchful eye of the counselor) to design, implement, and evaluate activities intended to promote learning in relation to other objectives. Before instructional counseling has been completed, clients should be functioning as self-instructors, at least in the general areas in which counseling goals were pursued.

Figure 7:5 (see the arrows in the figure) also protrays the dynamic flow of information that can occur among the various phases of instructional counseling. This dynamic flow is the second essential property of instructional counseling to be clarified in this section of chapter 7. The instructional counseling process proceeds logically and pragmatically from goals to pre-assessment and on to objectives, instructional activities, and evaluation. However, within this overall direction, instructional counseling is far from a linear process. At any phase in this process, it may be necessary to refer back to information generated in previous phases or to anticipate the requirements of forthcoming phases. At other times it may be necessary to return to previous phases to supplement, correct, or redo tasks and decisions that subsequently have been shown to be less than optimal or simply dysfunctional in promoting client change.

The experienced instructional counselor is aware of the dynamic, interactive nature of instructional counseling and uses the five-phase system as a guideline or a map to know where counselor-client interactions have been, where they are, and where they still must go. The instructional counselor does not employ the system as a linear straightjacket that prohibits spontaneity, creativity, or (at times and if necessary) simple trial and error when little guidance is available from other sources. Within its overall, purposeful, systematic structure, instructional counseling is a dynamic process concerned with the design of personal, interpersonal, and social/environmental conditions necessary to support client learning and self-instruction.

Using the Instructional Taxonomy to Analyze and Acquire Counseling Strategies

The taxonomy of counseling skills and strategies presented in chapter 2 and devised from contemporary work in instructional psychology (Bellack et al. 1966; Clark et al. 1979) may be employed as an eclectic system for analyzing, organizing, and acquiring a broad range of counseling intervention strategies that are described in the contemporary literature in counseling. The major advantage of incorporating this taxonomy into a system for the acquisition of counseling intervention strategies is that the use of the taxonomy in this regard makes it possible to specify (in a precise, meaningful way) the sequences of counseling skills that typically comprise the intervention strategies. Use of the taxonomy by counselors concerned with their own learning of counseling strategies also is valuable in that it helps guarantee the provision of specific, descriptive feedback to counselors' practice of these intervention strategies. In other words, the instructional taxonomy of counseling skills/strategies helps counselors acquire competence in the skill sequences that define different intervention strategies by ensuring that their practice of these skill sequences will be preceded by a meaningful specification of the sequence to be practiced and followed by precise feedback to that practice. The essential learning conditions of specification, practice, and feedback (see chapter 2) apply to the learning of counselors as well as to the learning of clients. Use of the instructional taxonomy thus can help counselors learn new intervention strategies because it helps supply essential conditions of learning to counselor's efforts at strategy acquisition.

The precision and meaningfulness that the instructional taxonomy brings to counselor's strategy acquisition derives from its properties as a professional language system specific to instructional undertakings in counseling. Through learning this specialized language, counselors are helped to discriminate, and to develop concepts and labels for, a wide array of actions performed by counselors in their instructional roles. This enhanced ability to perceive, discriminate, and attend to specific elements of counselor activity in an exacting manner is the inevitable result of learning this language. We tend to see what we discriminate in our language, and language often is essential to our functioning (e.g., Eskimos have many words for snow while Australian aborigines have no words for this concept). Our ordinary language systems do not supply references for words and phrases that are specific to narrow professional contexts. Taxonomies such as the one in chapter 2, if learned thoroughly, can provide a language key that unlocks counselors' perception, conceptualization, and awareness about what they do.

Use of the instructional taxonomy in counselor strategy acquisition begins with a thorough analysis of the various skills and skill sequences that comprise the strategy of interest. To illustrate this process of analysis, the counseling intervention strategies of participant modeling (Bandura 1969; Cormier and Cormier 1979) and problem solving (as conceptualized by

D'Zurilla and Goldfried 1971) will be dissected into their respective skill components.

Figure 7:6 provides a key to the most important instructional skills that are employed in each of the five major phases of participant modeling. During the initial phase of verbal description, the counselor provides an overview of the counseling intervention, emphasizing (with markers of importance) the most important aspects of, or elements in, the skill to be acquired. The counselor also explains the level and extent of skill acquisition to which counseling will be directed in terms of what the client should be able to do as a result of successful skill training. This statement of objectives may be accompanied by verbal examples to provide a concrete impression of the desired level of skill attainment.

When the client has indicated an understanding of the skill to be acquired and the counseling procedures to be employed, the counselor makes a transition to the modeling/demonstration phase of participant modeling. Immediately prior to modeling the skill for the client (either directly by the counselor or through presentation by a modeling assistant or videotape recording), the counselor uses clear instructions and markers of importance to direct the client's attention to critical aspects of the modeling performances he/she is about to witness. These counselor statements serve as cues to alert and channel the client's attentional or observational learning capabilities.

Once modeling/demonstration has been completed, the counselor makes a transition to providing an opportunity for the client to practice the modeled skill. A likely "skill use" situation is described and imagined in detail (set induction), clear directions are given about the most important aspects of the desired skill performance, and the client is encouraged to make an attempt to perform the skill (calling for demonstration).

Once the client has practiced the skill, a transition is made to a feedback phase in which the counselor proffers instructionally useful feedback to the client's skill practice. The counseling skills of descriptive praise, informational feedback, and suggesting alternatives are used extensively during this phase. In most instances, participant modeling will involve numerous cycles of

1. Verbal Description
   —overview
   —markers of importance
   —statement of objectives
   —examples (optional)

2. Modeling/Demonstration
   —statement of transition
   —clear instructions (identify skill elements)
   —markers of importance
   —alerting cues
   —modeling

3. Skill Practice
   —statement of transition
   —set induction
   —clear instructions/directions
   —calling for demonstration

4. Feedback
   —statement of transition
   —descriptive praise
   —informational feedback
   —suggesting an alternative

5. Coaching for Transfer
   —statement of transition
   —markers of importance
   —clear instructions/directions
   —probing
   —paraphrasing content
   —reflecting meaning and affect
   —summarizing

Figure 7:6. Analysis of participant modeling

skill practice and feedback as the information from the feedback phase is channeled into further skill practice to help the client refine and improve his/her skill use.

In the final phase of participant modeling, the counselor uses a wide variety of counseling skills to help ensure that the client will be able to transfer his/her newly acquired expertise from the training situation to those real-life situations in which the client wishes to employ the skill. This transfer should already have been considered in the preceding phases of skill practice and feedback. As repetitive cycling through these phases continues, the training situations and demands progressively should resemble real-life contexts and demands to a greater and greater extent (see Bandura 1969). In the final phase of participant modeling, the counselor emphasizes important considerations pertaining to the transfer of the skill to real situations without the counselor's presence (markers of importance and clear instructions/directions). The counselor also probes the client's understanding of the skill and explores the client's attitudes and feelings concerning the skill-transfer process (paraphrasing content, reflecting meaning and affect) to make sure that the client's emotional and attitudinal responses to the skill transfer will support the process. Finally, the participant modeling process and the client's progress in skill acquisition are summarized to encourage the client and to provide still more information with the intention of promoting generalizable client learning of the skill-acquisition strategy itself.

A second illustration of the way in which the instructional taxonomy may be employed to provide detailed specifications of counseling intervention strategies appears in figure 7:7. This figure provides an analysis of counseling skills often employed in the conduct of the *problem-solving* strategy proposed by D'Zurilla and Goldfried (1971). In the initial, orientation phase of this intervention strategy, the counselor provides an overview of the strategy, its phases, and the client/counselor work involved in executing it. Objectives are stated and important attitudes relating to successful problem solving are emphasized with markers of importance (e.g., "Problems are a normal part of living. We all have them and it is possible to learr effective ways of dealing with them").

In the problem-definition phase, the counselor helps the client explore, understand, and provide information about the problem situation and his/her responses (thoughts, feelings and behaviors) to it. The typical skills used here are those

1. Orientation
   —giving overview
   —stating objectives
   —stating markers of
      importance

2. Problem Definition
   —providing statement of
      transition
   —paraphrasing content
   —reflecting meaning and
      affect
   —probing
   —using set induction
   —summarizing

3. Generation of Alternatives
   —providing statement of
      transition
   —giving clear instructions/
      directions
   —using set induction
   —summarizing

4. Decision Making
   a) Consequenting
      —providing statement of
         transition
      —probing
      —summarizing
   b) Prioritizing
      —providing statement of
         transition
      —giving clear instructions/
         directions

   c) Selection
      —providing statement of
         transition
      —reflecting affect and
         meaning
      —summarizing

5. Verification
   a) Planning actions and
      evaluations
      —providing statement of
         transition
      —giving overview
      —probing
      —giving clear instructions/
         directions
      —summarizing

   b) Evaluation
      —probing
      —paraphrasing content
      —reflecting affect and
         meaning
      —describing discrepancies
      —suggesting alternatives
      —giving descriptive praise
      —giving informational
         feedback
      —summarizing

*Figure 7:7 Analysis of D'Zurilla and Goldfried's (1971)
problem-solving strategy*

common to most initial interviews during the goal-setting phase of instructional counseling—that is, paraphrasing content, reflecting meaning and affect, probing and summarizing. Set induction also may be used to help the client imagine responding to the problem situation.

After making a transition to the third phase (generation of alternatives) of the D'Zurilla and Goldfried strategy, the counselor employs clear instructions/directions and set induction to encourage the client to brainstorm possible alternative responses to the problem situation. Once such alternatives have been generated and summarized, a transition to the decision making phase is made.

The decision-making phase in the D'Zurilla and Goldfried strategy may be conceptualized in three subphases. The first task for the client in this phase is to imagine likely consequences of engaging each of the alternatives generated in the previous phase. The counselor assists this process by probing and summarizing the client's work in "consequenting" each alternative. On the basis of their likely consequences, alternatives then are ranked in a priority list. Clear instructions/directions from the counselor help the client perform this task. Finally with the assistance of the counselor's reflection of meaning affect and summarizing, the client selects an alternative for implementation in his/her problem-solving efforts. While other counseling skills may be employed in the fourth phase of problem solving (as conceptualized by D'Zurilla and Goldfried) the skills listed in figure 7:7 are essential to facilitation of the problem-solving process.

The final, or verification, phase of the D'Zurilla and Goldfried strategy may be viewed as consisting of two subphases. In the first subphase, the client is helped to plan the implementation and evaluation of the action alternative she/he has selected Counselor overviews, probes, instructions/directions, and summaries assist this process. Once the chosen alternative for action actually is implemented, the counselor helps the client to evaluate its effectiveness in resolving the problem. A wide variety of counseling skills may be employed in this regard. Figure 7:7 highlights some of the most important of these.

Through the use of the instructional taxonomy presented in

chapter 2, it is possible to specify the essential counseling skills that make up almost any counseling strategy that is intended to promote client learning, whatever the nature of that learning. Such specification is an essential ingredient in any attempt by counselors to acquire competence in using different counseling strategies. It prepares the way for practice in using the strategies and helps to guarantee that feedback to this practice whether from one's own or another's observations, audio or videotape recordings, or some other means) will be focused, specific, descriptive, and relevant. In short, the instructional taxonomy, if used wisely, can help make skill/strategy acquisition by counselors highly efficient, purposeful, and relatively painless. Counselors, like clients, learn better when what is to be learned is clearly specified, rigorously practiced, and has the advantage of precise, informational feedback. Through use of the instructional taxonomy, counselors can structure, plan, and consistently monitor their ongoing attempts at expanding their own professional repertoires. As a result, they can become better eclectic practitioners, capable of making decisions to implement, and actually implementing, a wide variety of counseling intervention strategies in a purposeful way as required by different client characteristics, concerns, and problem situations.

Chapter Summary

The practice of eclecticism in counseling necessitates rational, informed decision making with respect to matching counseling strategies to counselor/client characteristics and interactions, situational variables, and intended learning/instructional outcomes. This, in turn, necessitates performative competence in a wide variety of counseling intervention strategies. The first part of this chapter demonstrated the use of the instructional counseling framework as a general guide or heuristic to the development of effective eclectic strategies in counseling. The second part of the chapter explained how the taxonomy of instructional skills/strategies described in chapter 2 could be used to help counselors analyze, organize, and acquire competence in exe-

cuting a broad range of counseling intervention strategie
described in the contemporary literature in counseling. In pu
suing these purposes, the conceptualization of the basic five
phase instructional model, first presented in chapter 1, wa
expanded: (1) to encompass the possibility of a variety of five
step cycles and specification-practice-feedback loops withi
each of the five major phases in the instructional counselin
model, and (2) to clarify the dynamic and cooperative (in th
sense of shared initiation on the part of counselor and clien
nature of instructional counseling. Use of the taxonomy c
instructional skills and strategies to analyze counseling inte
vention strategies so that these might be specified clearly an
learned more efficiently was illustrated with reference to th
strategies of participant modeling (Bandura 1969) and proble
solving (as developed by D'Zurilla and Goldfried 1971).

REFERENCES

Bandura, A. 1969. *Principles of Behavior Modification*. Englewood Cliff
N.J.: Prentice-Hall.
Bellack, A. A., Kliebard, H. M., Hyman, R. T., and Smith, F. L.
1966. *The Language of the Classroom*. New York: Teachers College
Press.
Buros, O. 1972. *The Seventh Mental Measurement Yearbook*. Highland
Park, N.J.: Gryphon Press.
Carkhuff, R. R. 1981.*The Art of Helping IV*. Amherst, Mass.: Human
Resources Development Press.
Clark, C. M., Gage, N. L., Marx, R. W., Peterson, P. L., Stayook,
N. G., and Winne, P. H. 1979. A factorial experiment on teacher
structuring, soliciting, and reacting. *Journal of Educational Psycholog*
71: 534–52.
Cormier, W. H., and Cormier, S. C. 1979. *Interviewing Strategies for
Helpers*. Monterey: Brooks/Cole.
D'Zurilla, T. J., and Goldfried, M. R. 1971. Problem-solving and
behavior modification. *Journal of Abnormal Psychology* 78: 107–26.
Kanfer, F. H. 1980. Self-management methods. *In*: F. H. Kanfer and
A. P. Goldstein (eds.), *Helping People Change: A Textbook of Method*
(2d ed.). New York: Pergamon.
Kiresuk, T. J. and Sherman, R. E. 1980. Goal attainment scaling: A
general method for evaluating community mental health program
Community Mental Health Journal 4: 443–53.

Meichenbaum, D. 1977. *Cognitive Behavior Modification: An Integrated Approach.* New York: Plenum.

Paul, G. L. 1967. Strategy of outcome research in psychotherapy. *Journal of Consulting Psychology,* 1: 109–19.

Shertzer, B. and Linden, J. D. 1979. *Fundamentals of Individual Appraisal: Assessment Techniques for Counselors.* Boston: Houghton Mifflin.

Stuart, R. B. (ed.). 1977. *Behavorial Self-Management: Strategies, Techniques, and Outcomes.* New York: Brunner-Mazel.

CHAPTER EIGHT

Evaluating Instructional Counseling

WHEN PEOPLE TALK about counseling and evaluation, they typically are talking about one of two things: (1) *research* into counseling effects and counselor effectiveness or (2) *evaluation* of the outcomes of a particular counseling intervention plan. Research into counselor effects is concerned usually with investigating the effectiveness of different approaches to counseling (e.g., Rogerian counseling, behavior counseling, instructional counseling, and so on) or of different counseling strategies (e.g., self-instruction, role playing, relaxation training, goal setting, and the like). Evaluating the outcome of a particular counseling intervention usually involves taking some measure(s) of client change during the counseling interaction, upon termination, and/or at some later, follow-up time. We previously have summarized the implications of the instructional counseling model for research on counseling (see Hiebert, Martin, and Marx 1981). This chapter is devoted entirely to a discussion of the evaluation of specific counseling interventions.

In the instructional counseling model discussed in chapter 1, evaluation was depicted as the fifth step in the instructional sequence. However, what happens during the evaluation phase of instructional counseling must be interfaced tightly with the entire counseling process from beginning to end. With the three-fold emphasis on intention, structure, and function in instructional counseling (see chapter 1), counselors must be continuously vigilant about what they are doing during counseling ("Am I doing what I think I'm doing?") and about client responses to these counselor actions ("Is the client following the program we agreed upon?" and "Is the program we agreed upon having the effect we thought it would have?"). The referent for scrutinizing counselor behavior and client responses always lies in the counseling objectives that have been mutually agreed to by the counselor and the client. When evaluation is seen as an ongoing process occurring during counseling interactions, at the end of counseling (i.e., upon termination), and at follow-up times, the counselor can use evaluation to indicate the effectiveness of a particular intervention plan. Such constant monitoring of counselor actions and client responses also can "catch" difficulties as these arise and permit quick, efficient remediation. The specific procedures and considerations involved in evaluating instructional counseling endeavors are the foci of this chapter.

In instructional counseling, evaluation always occurs at three levels, one level focusing on counselor behavior and two levels focusing on client behavior. At the first level, it is necessary to examine the counselor's purposeful use of counseling skills, the degree to which the counseling skills are appropriate for the instructional objectives, and the prowess with which the counselor uses the skills. Second, it also is necessary to evaluate how the client is responding to the counselor. The counselor must have some means for assessing whether or not the client is responding as the counselor intended and whether or not the intervention plan is being followed. Third, it is necessary to have some assessment of the degree to which the counseling objectives have been met, whether or not the intervention plan worked as anticipated, and the impact of the intervention plan on the client's life. In practice, these three factors are closely interrelated. However, it is possible conceptually to separate these three components for purposes of discussion and specification.

Evaluating Counselor Behavior

Instructional counseling is purposeful activity on the part of a counselor that results in client learning consistent with intended counseling outcomes. To say that instructional counseling has taken place (i.e., that client changes are not the result of acciden-

tal learning) requires some demonstration of purposeful coun
selor activity. Typically, this area of evaluation is concerned
with how well the counselor "executes the moves" or "uses
skills" and whether or not the counselor's use of skills has been
undertaken with a definite purpose in mind. Instructional coun
seling skills should not be employed in a capricious manner
(e.g., "winging it," "playing it by ear," "flying by the seat of
your pants").

There is growing research evidence suggesting that students
learn more when teachers have a clear understanding of which
instructional skills they are using (Anderson, Everston and
Brophy 1979). Large repertoires of instructional skills and quali
tative competence in the use of those skills (Good and Grows
1979) also are associated with positive learner gains. Intentional
use of instructional skills and active monitoring of instructional
behavior are clearly major contributors to instructional success
(Good 1979; Rosenshine 1979). Therefore, it would seem to be
important when evaluating instructional counseling to have
some procedure for assessing what counselors do, how well
they do it, and whether or not counselor actions are executed in
a purposeful manner. When such procedures are in place, coun
selors are in a position systematically to evaluate their own
performance and improve their use of counseling skills. The
procedures outlined for supervising counselors in training in the
next chapter are also appropriate for counselors to use in assess
ing their own performance. The important point is that it i
necessary to assess both the quality and purpose with which
counseling skills are used when evaluating instructional coun
seling. It is true that the ultimate goal in instructional counseling
is to produce client change. However, if we wish to attribute
that change to instruction, it is necessary to ascertain that appro
priate counseling skills have been employed in a purposeful
manner.

Evaluating Client Behavior

When evaluating client behavior in instructional counseling, it i
necessary to monitor both the extent to which the intervention

plan was implemented and the amount of client change that took place. Most counselors would agree to the importance of assessing client change during counseling. Even when formal assessment procedures are not used, counselors invariably form an impression of "how things are going." This impression tells the counselor that counseling is drawing to a close, that resistance is being encountered, that it is time to seek another opinion as to what might work, or any number of other progress-related evaluative conclusions. It is likely that some form of outcome-related evaluation almost always takes place at an explicit, implicit, or an inadvertant level. However, if we want to draw conclusions that a specific counseling intervention plan is responsible for client change, it is necessary to determine that a reasonable approximation of the intervention plan was being followed by the client. If we fail to do this, we are likely to be living under what Horan (1980) calls the "Treatment Deployment Myth." Just because a client in counseling is receiving a particular intervention does not necessarily mean that the client is actually performing in the way directed by the counselor (e.g., a client receiving self-instruction training may or may not self-instruct).

A client may feel "rotten" because she is having difficulty deciding to work at her current job or to return to school and pursue her lifelong dream of becoming an interior decorator. After some exploration and clarification, the counselor and client may embark on a decision-making intervention. Appropriate preassessment information is obtained, objectives are set, the client is well into the fourth phase of a decision-making plan (see chapter 3), and only three weeks have passed since the initial contact. The client reports that she is feeling better and that things seem to be working out well. She now thinks that the counseling has been helpful and that it is probably no longer necessary. This seems to be a testament to the powerfulness of following a systematic treatment plan until the client mentions how much help both you (the counselor) and Aunt Harriette have been. Upon probing a bit further, the counselor discovers that it was Aunt Harriette who suggested that she quit her job and go back to school because it would be more and more difficult to do this the longer she put it off. Aunt Harriette further explained that if she didn't do it now, she would always feel like she had robbed herself of an opportunity. Further probing reveals that the brainstorming and prioritizing that was done in the counseling session was not followed up—the consequences of enacting the high-priority alternatives were not checked out. In short, the counseling plan was not translated into actual client action.

Clearly, the client in this example feels better and has made a decision. However, it was Aunt Harriette's influential position in the client's eyes and not the counseling intervention plan that was responsible for the client's decision. In this example, it would be a mistake to conclude that decision-making counseling was responsible for the client's resolution to return to school. Such a conclusion is unwarranted because the client never followed the intervention plan.

Miller (1978) points out that client problems are typically cyclical in nature. The severity of symptoms fluctuates over time. Sometimes problems (indecision, lack of assertiveness, anxiety, unfulfilled goals) are handled quite adequately; at other times the impact of these problems on clients' lives is very great. Things will seem to be going well for a time, then will slowly deteriorate, will level off at some low point, and after a while will begin to get better again. Clients invariably seek counseling at the low point in the cycle. Therefore, even if counselors did nothing at all in counseling sessions, the simple passage of time would see these cycles swing up again, and many clients would start to feel better. Unless there is some procedure for monitoring the degree to which the client follows a negotiated counseling intervention plan, there is considerable risk of making an inappropriate link between client change and counseling intervention.

As previously stated, it is necessary to evaluate client behavior in instructional counseling for two reasons: first, to determine the degree to which the counseling intervention strategies are being followed in an appropriate manner; and second, to determine the degree of client change that takes place as a direct result of counseling per se.

MONITORING TREATMENT IMPLEMENTATION

The purpose of monitoring treatment implementation is to assess the degree to which counseling intervention strategies are being followed appropriately by clients. In most cases, this will necessitate establishing some procedure for monitoring client behaviors *between* counseling sessions in addition to monitoring client practice and performance *during* counseling sessions. This monitoring may take such forms as making a check mark on a cigarette package each time a cigarette is lit, recording SUDS levels in a pocket notebook, charting weight each morning before breakfast, clipping out certain categories of job advertisements from the newspaper for a two-week period, listing and prioritizing post-secondary institutions within commuting distance, recording heart rate and finger temperature before and after daily relaxation practice, and so on. In most cases, it also will be important to have some procedure for obtaining estimates of the reliability and validity of client self-monitored data. This may involve some third-party observation system (e.g., having a spouse also make a check mark for each cigarette smoked) or some "objective" assessment procedure (e.g., having the client self-monitor pulse rate while hooked up to a heart-rate monitoring device). In both kinds of situations, the two recordings can be compared for consistency. Taking reliability checks is an excellent way of ensuring that the changes we observe in counseling are not the result of subtle self-delusion or inaccurate self-monitoring on the part of clients.

When monitoring treatment implementation, it is sometimes sufficient to ask clients to give a verbal account of how they used their intervention strategy since the last session. When soliciting these verbal accounts, it is better to ask the client to relate the specific activities that were engaged in rather than to indicate whether or not the program was being followed in a general sense. Clients often feel they are following directions, but for various reasons (perhaps the directions were misunderstood or two people's notions of "close enough to the directions" are different) the end product is different from what was anticipated by the counselor. When counselors ask their clients to relate what they did, the counselor is in a position to determine the extent to which a given intervention plan has been followed.

Most often, procedures for monitoring treatment implementation will involve some record keeping on the part of clients. Clients' monitoring, recording, or charting of their progress tends to have a motivating effect in addition to fulfilling essential record-keeping functions (Nelson 1977; Rudestam 1980). Clients often report that seeing their chart and having some visual representation of how they are doing help them to stick to their change program.

When procedures for monitoring treatment implementation are established and used during counseling, the counselor and client have some assurance that a specific intervention plan is being followed and that client changes are not the result of serendipitous events. Further, the monitoring process itself can have a motivating and reinforcing effect on client adherence to the counseling program. Visual records of progress also have been known to sustain counselor enthusiasm.

MONITORING TREATMENT EFFECTS

Once we have determined that counselors purposefully have deployed appropriate instructional skills and that clients are following specific intervention strategies as intended, outcome effects can be investigated meaningfully. In instructional counseling, outcomes are always evaluated in relation to counseling objectives. Counseling objectives are framed in terms of who will do what, under what circumstances, and to what extent. Having established what was done, the counselor and client may turn their attention to examining the degree of change that took place. Establishing targeted change levels in advance helps to ensure that outcome expectations do not shift. Counseling effects should not be measured with subjective rubber rulers. All too often, client change is viewed as a "wait and see" phenomenon—"we'll try 'it' and see what happens." Such imprecision makes it difficult to draw purposeful and clear links between counseling process and outcome. Setting explicit and relevant criteria in advance and using these criteria as standards against which to evaluate counseling make possible the process of drawing connections among counseling intentions, processes, and outcomes.

When outcomes in instructional counseling are being evaluated, it is not enough merely to determine whether change took place. Changes must be consistent with the goals and objectives previously established. According to the definition of instruction given in chapter 1, change that is consistent with objectives must occur if one is to claim that instruction has taken place. It is true that unexpected events occur in counseling. It also is true that unexpected client changes sometimes occur and that some of these changes can be congruent with client desires and wishes. It is even the case that the whole interactional counseling process might have acted as a catalyst for, or even precipitated directly, these incidental changes. However, if the changes were not initially specified, and the counselor was not attempting to initiate such changes, it cannot be claimed that the changes, however dramatic and beneficial to client functioning, are the result of instruction. There can be accidental learning. There cannot be accidental instruction.

Monitoring Techniques

Recently there has been an increasing move toward establishing measurable criteria for the evaluation of counseling endeavors (cf. Henjum 1982; Hiebert 1982), and several procedures for collecting such data have been developed. The first consideration when evaluating counseling effects is to obtain some adequate baseline data against which to compare client change. Unless some baseline data are collected, the only indication of client change will be the subjective testimonial of the counselor or client that change has occurred or that the client feels better. Such subjective testimonials have their place, but data that depict client change across time are likely to be more convincing to clients as well as program evaluators.

At this point, it is appropriate to acknowledge some of the problems associated with collecting baseline data. Frequently the presenting problem is difficult to define in measurable terms. Also, the collecting of systematic data might seem incompatible with the theoretical orientation of the counselor. Another objection that clinicians sometimes raise is that clients come to counseling expecting some action and will object to an initial pretreatment baseline period. Probably the first step that counselors must take is to help clients come to a position where they see the utility of collecting baseline data. The next task is to define the problem in a measurable way. Often it is sufficient simply to ask the client to describe the symptoms that indicate that the problem exists or what sorts of signs would indicate that the problem no longer existed. In other cases it might be helpful to do a task analysis of the proposed intervention or a component analysis of the problem as a means of identifying some measurable indicators of treatment success. Once the problem has been defined in a measurable way, data collection can begin. If baseline measures are initiated early in counseling, data can easily be gathered during the initial preassessment interviews, with the result that baseline data are complete when the interventions are ready to be implemented. Thus, collecting baseline data need not delay unduly the commencement of an intervention strategy. For example, a client could use one or more of the procedures discussed later in this section to collect data on such things as headache intensity or frequency, mood swings, types or frequencies of activities engaged in, or general satisfaction with life. If the process was begun in an initial interview, it could continue while the counselor and client clarified counseling goals and while relevant preassessment data were obtained. When the counselor and client were ready to plan an intervention, there would be some baseline data against which to compare progress.

Some authors (e.g., Tracey 1983) recently have suggested the use of *single-case designs* to evaluate counseling effects. The practicing counselor is in a position to make every interview applicable to counseling research. When procedures for differential diagnosis are systematic (e.g., Hutchins 1982) and treatment is well documented, it is possible to approximate a multiple baseline design (see Hersen and Barlow 1976) across subjects with similar presenting problems. If client changes occur in similar patterns across similar cases that utilize similar interventions, then a strong argument can be made for a causal influence of the counseling interaction in producing the change.

Another procedure that permits the collecting of systematic

data that are comparable across clients is *Goal Attainment Scaling* (cf. Kiresuk and Sherman 1968; Paritzky and Magoon 1982). Briefly, Goal Attainment Scaling is a procedure whereby clients identify specific counseling outcomes (objectives) and criterion descriptors that would be evidence of varying degrees of outcome expectation. These descriptors typically range from *much better than expected* ($+2$) to *as expected* (0), to *much worse than expected* (-2). Clients rate their current level of behavior at the beginning of treatment and also at the end of treatment (and sometimes at selected evaluation points during treatment). Using this procedure, it is possible to have some measure of counseling effectiveness that is comparable across different clients with different problems.

In collecting data on counselor or client behavior, some form of *self-monitoring* likely will result in useful data. This might take the form of self-monitoring physical gestures in a social-skills training program (Trower, 1979), physiological data in a home relaxation program (Hiebert et al. 1984), analogue cognitive estimates of anxiety level (Hiebert and Fox 1981), or a variety of interpersonal skills (Sherman and Cormier 1974). In most cases, these self-monitored data demonstrate adequate reliability and provide discrete evidence that a treatment procedure has been followed or that client skills have been acquired. This evidence provides a valuable link when the claim is being made that client change is the result of the therapeutic intervention. Such self-monitoring data can be a useful supplement to data from counselor observations, objective measures of client change when these are available (e.g., weight loss where a client's goal is to become more physically fit), and more standardized psychometric instruments (e.g., personality, aptitude, or performance tests). These latter forms of data are thoroughly and competently discussed in texts such as those by Ciminero, Calhoun, and Adams (1977) and Shertzer and Linden (1979).

Additional Considerations

Evaluation of instructional counseling should go beyond the determination of whether or not any progress has been made toward the attainment of counseling objectives. This involves

consideration of variables other than simple changes in targete
behaviors, cognitions, or emotional reactions.

It is difficult to specify all of these variables because the sc
ence of instruction is so young. As research in instruction cor
tinues to flourish, the appropriate variables by which t
measure instructional effects will be identified more explicitly
However, an initial list of appropriate variables with which t
measure instructional effects likely would include such facton
as speed of change, durability of change, efficiency of th
change process, and transferability of learning changes outsid
instructional situations.

When the focus of counseling is only on whether or not th
client is changing at all, factors like *speed of change* typicall
receive little attention. However, such a factor can be of tremen
dous practical importance. When collecting speed-of-chang
data, it is important to be able to identify when the attempt t
produce change was initiated. Usually, this will be after gener.
counseling goals have been established, preassessment ha
been completed, and precise counseling objectives have bee
set; in short, when the instructional activities phase (i.e., th
specific intervention strategy) is begun. The counselor's pu
poseful activity in the initial phases of counseling likely wi
have a strong modeling effect that may be instructional. Cour
selors who collect preassessment data in a systematic, logic.
way, informing the client of the rationale for each area assesse
in order to prepare the client for assessing consequences an
prioritizing alternatives in a problem-solving intervention, ai
surely engaging in instruction. However, the specific attempt t
produce client change does not get underway until an interver
tion strategy begins to be implemented. When counselors ider
tify temporal markers at each phase of the instruction.
counseling process and record the elapsed time between whe
an intervention strategy is initiated and when the counselin
objectives are met, they are in a position to better self-manag
their own time commitments and to provide the kind of infor
mation to clients that will promote wise "consumerism" whe
purchasing counseling services. [Note. The authors support i
principle the position advanced by Smith (1975) and othen
(Albrecht 1979; Antonovsky 1979) that the same kind of wis

consumer attitudes that apply to purchasing appliances, car repairs, and other consumer items also apply to the purchase of professional services, including counseling services. Therefore, it becomes legitimate for prospective clients to request estimates of items like dollar costs, time costs in terms of number of sessions, amount of home practice required, total treatment time, probability of success, and durability of effect before counseling is begun. In instructional counseling, where the ultimate goal is to help clients to self-instruct, it is important that clients acquire the notion that it is just as important to be a wise consumer when purchasing health care services as it is when shopping for a color television. This is no longer a radical position (see Albrecht 1979; Antonovsky 1979), and counselors who are prepared to record data from their own case loads, base their intervention plans on research-based methodologies, and engage in a demystified approach to counseling likely will respond to this type of accountability in a positive way.]

Assessing *durability of change* emphasizes the importance of follow-up assessments of counseling effects. It is necessary to conduct follow-up assessments if counselors want assurance that any client change is the result of specific counseling interventions and not of the cyclical nature of most client problems discussed earlier in this chapter. This follow-up assessment may be conducted by mail-out questionnaires, a return visit to the counselor, or a telephoned report of self-monitored data. Regardless of the specific procedures used, the criteria for success at follow-up should be the same as those specified in the original counseling objectives. Often, the follow-up procedures can be included in an initial treatment contract. When clients are presented with the rationale for conducting follow-up assessment, they usually agree that such follow-ups are important and are more than willing to participate in follow-up procedures. When counseling intervention is followed up, the client's perception of treatment gains is reinforced, and the counselor obtains data as to the long-term effects of the intervention strategies used.

Efficiency of treatment is assessed by investigating such factors as time involved in treatment, special equipment required, cost of expendables (if required), whether or not the treatment could be conducted in a group setting, and numbers of ancillary people involved in implementing the treatment program. For example, electromyographic (EMG) biofeedback has been demonstrated to be a powerful treatment for tension headaches (Budzynski, Stoyva and Adler 1970; Cox, Freundlich and Meyer 1975). However, the equipment costs involved are such that many counselors elect to use alternative procedures such as differential relaxation for tension headache patients. Some intervention strategies (e.g., systematic desensitization) can be implemented in a group setting (cf. Richardson and Suinn 1974), thereby reducing the per client cost while increasing the amount of service that the counselor can provide. Efficacy of treatment can be a potentially useful variable in choosing an intervention strategy, but only if data pertaining to treatment efficiency are collected and made available.

A final goal in most counseling interventions is for some *transfer of training* to occur. Most counseling objectives will be framed so that they include transfer of training from the counseling setting to some real-life situation in which the client is involved. Sometimes the client will be able to use new skills in situations that differ from the target situation initially addressed. For example, a client may use a self-instruction strategy to slow down food consumption and self-reinforce adherence to a plan to alter eating behavior. The same client may deduce that a similar self-instruction plan also could be used to make afternoon jogging more enjoyable and may begin to focus self-talk (while jogging) on the fresh air, the trees in the park, and the distance already traversed and to make reinforcing self-statements about the effect that jogging is having on weight reduction. The transfer of self-instruction and self-reinforcement skills from eating behavior to jogging may result in the client, in this example, having skills to handle two situations more effectively, even though only one situation (eating behavior) was the target of formal counseling. Instructional counselors attempt to instruct their clients in ways that promote transfer of training. It is important to assess how much transfer has occurred in order to evaluate the total impact of instructional counseling on the client's life. Methods of performing such evaluations must be actively pursued and researched.

Some procedure for evaluating treatment effects is probably an element of most counseling interventions. The instructional counselor engages in an ongoing monitoring of client progress toward counseling objectives so as to determine whether instruction is in fact taking place. In addition to this ongoing monitoring, and in those cases where instruction has occurred, the counselor shifts his/her focus to other variables when evaluating the success of the counseling intervention. An initial list of appropriate variables to consider might include the speed and durability of counseling effects, treatment efficiency, and transfer of training. When these variables are assessed, the real impact of the counseling intervention can be evaluated more appropriately.

Chapter Summary

Evaluation in instructional counseling is an ongoing process occurring during counseling, upon termination, and at follow-up. The counseling objectives, jointly established by counselor and client, serve as the primary reference points against which success is measured. Instructional counselors typically will evaluate their counseling endeavors on three levels—assessing their own use of counseling skills and strategies, the degree to which counseling intervention plans are followed by clients, and the impact of these intervention plans on clients' lives. When counselor behavior is being evaluated, the focus is on the counselor's appropriate and purposeful use of the basic counseling skills and strategies discussed in chapters 2 through 6. Monitoring treatment implementation involves establishing procedures for ascertaining clients' intersession practice of the skills being taught during the counseling session. Assessing treatment effects involves monitoring client progress toward counseling objectives in order to verify that instruction is occurring. Once this has been determined, such factors as the speed and durability of client change, treatment efficiency, and transfer of training should be assessed in order to determine the total impact of counseling interventions on clients' lives.

REFERENCES

Albrecht, K. 1979. *Stress and The Manager: Making It Work for You.* Englewood Cliffs, N.J.: Prentice-Hall.

Anderson, L., Evertson, C., and Brophy, J. 1979. An experimental study of effective teaching in first-grade reading groups. *Elementary School Journal* 79: 193–223.

Antonovsky, A. 1979. *Health, Stress and Coping: New Perspectives on Mental and Physical Well-Being.* San Francisco: Jossey-Bass.

Budzynski, T., Stoyva, J., and Adler, C. 1970. Feedback-induced muscle relaxation: Application to tension headache. *Journal of Behavior Therapy and Experimental Psychiatry* 1: 205–11.

Ciminero, A. R., Calhoun, K. S., and Adams, H. E. 1977. *Handbook of Behavioral Assessment.* New York: Wiley.

Cox, D. J., Freundlich, A., and Meyer, R. G. 1975. Differential effectiveness of electromyograph feedback, verbal relaxation instructions, and medication placebo with tension headaches. *Journal of Consulting and Clinical Psychology* 43: 892–98.

Diamond, S., Diamond-Falk, J., and DeVeno, T. 1978. Biofeedback in the treatment of vascular headache. *Biofeedback and Self-Regulation* 3: 385–408.

Good, T. L. 1979. Teacher effectiveness in the elementary school. *Journal of Teacher Education* 30: 52–64.

_____, and Grouws, D. 1979. The Missouri Mathematics effectiveness project: An experimental study in fourth-grade classrooms. *Journal of Educational Psychology* 71: 355–62.

Henjum, R. 1982. The criterion problem in the evaluation of guidance. *School Guidance Worker* 38: 5–10.

Hersen, M., and Barlow, D. H. 1976. *Single Case Experimental Designs: Strategies for Studying Behavior Change.* New York: Pergamon.

Hiebert, B. A. 1982. *Preparing Vocational Counsellors. NATCON2.* Ottawa: Employment and Immigration Canada.

_____, Cardinal, J., Dumka, L., and Marx, R. W. 1984. Self-instructed relaxation: A therapeutic alternative. *Biofeedback and Self Regulation.* In press.

_____, and Fox, E. E. 1981. Reactive effects of self-monitoring anxiety. *Journal of Counseling Psychology* 28: 187–93.

_____, Martin, J., and Marx, R. W. 1981. Instructional counselling: The counsellor as teacher. *Canadian Counsellor* 15: 107–14.

Horan, J. J. 1980. Experimentation in counseling and psychotherapy, Part I: New myths about old realities. *Educational Researcher* 18: 5–10.

Hutchins, D. D. 1982. Ranking major counseling strategies with the TFA/Matrix System. *Personnel and Guidance Journal* 60: 427–30.

Johnson, W. G., and Turen, A. 1975. Biofeedback treatment of migraine headache: A systematic case study. *Behavior Therapy* 6: 394–97.

Kiresuk, J. J., and Sherman, R. E. 1968. Goal attainment scaling: A general method for evaluating community mental health programs. *Community Mental Health Journal* 4: 443–53.

Miller, N. E. 1978. Biofeedback and visceral learning. *Annual Review of Psychology* 29: 373–404.

Nelson, R. O. 1977. Assessment and therapeutic functions of self-monitoring. *In*: M. M. Hersen, R. M. Eister, and P. M. Miller (eds.), *Progress in Behavior Modification* (vol. 5). New York: Academic Press.

Paritzky, R. S., and Magoon, T. M. 1982. Goal attainment scaling models for assessing group counseling. *Personnel and Guidance Journal* 60: 381–84.

Richardson, F. C., and Suinn, R.M. 1974. Effects of two short-term desensitization methods in the treatment of text anxiety. *Journal of Counseling Psychology* 21: 457–58.

Rosenshine, B. 1979. Content, time, and direct instruction. *In*: M. P. Peterson and H. Walberg (eds.), *Research on Teaching: Concepts, Findings and Implications*. Berkeley: McCutchan.

Rudestam, K. E. 1980. *Methods of Self-Change: An ABC Primer*. Monterey: Brooks/Cole.

Sherman, T. M., and Cormier, W. H. 1974. An investigation of the influence of student behavior on teacher behavior. *Journal of Applied Behavior Analysis* 7: 11–21.

Shertzer, B., and Linden, J. D. 1979. *Fundamentals of Individual Appraisal: Assessment Techniques for Counselors*. Boston: Houghton Mifflin.

Smith, N. J. 1975. *When I Say No I Feel Guilty*. New York: Bantam.

Tracey, T. J. 1983. Single case research: An added tool for counselors and supervisors. *Counselor Education and Supervision* 22: 185–96.

Trower, P. 1979. Fundamentals of interpersonal behavior: A social-psychological perspective. *In*: A. S. Bellack and M. Hersen (eds.), *Research and Practice in Social Skills Training*. New York: Plenum.

CHAPTER NINE

Counselor Training and Professional Conduct

IN THIS CHAPTER we examine the implications of instructional counseling for counselor training and professional conduct. When counseling is viewed as an instructional process, it is crucial that practicing counselors be well versed in a wide array of instructional theories, perspectives, and actions. Further, such substantive knowledge must manifest itself in the ability to perform specific counseling skills and strategies in a purposeful way that results in desired client learning.

Training Instructional Counselors

When counseling is viewed as instructional in nature, it becomes appropriate to view counselor training from the same instructional perspective. This is to say that the same attitudes, approaches, and manners that counselors (or counseling students) demonstrate in their interactions with their clients should be evident in the interaction between the counselor educator and the counseling student. To put it another way, the counselor training program should model an instructional orientation to counseling. When the task of the counselor is to instruct the client, the task of the counselor educator is to instruct the counseling student in how to instruct the client (see figure 9:1).

All the information discussed in the first eight chapters of this book should be embodied in the counseling training program. If the general goal of a counselor training program is to train instructional counselors, the underlying orientation of the program and the interrelation of the component parts of the program (e.g., courses, clinical observation, practica, assignments) must be delineated clearly. It is important to *preassess* the entry skills of counseling students and to create program objectives that specify expected terminal performances and competencies. Training activities should be arranged that provide ample opportunity for the specification and practice (with feedback) of instructional performances stated in training objectives. Just as instructional counselors look to client change as a measure of counseling effectiveness, counselor educators must look to changes in the counseling knowledge and skill repertoires of their students as a measure of the effectiveness of the counselor training program.

Employing an instructional model as a basis for counselor training programs represents a departure from traditional approaches to counselor education. Traditionally, counselor training programs have embodied two broad foci. They have focused on the development of, or in some cases preselection of, certain counselor characteristics (e.g., warmth, congruence, empathy, understanding) and/or on the development of certain counseling skills (e.g., questioning techniques, verbal and affective reflections, confrontation skills). A clear implication of both these approaches is that counseling can be defined in terms of counselor behavior alone. Recently, there has been a move toward competency-based counselor training models where the behavioral components of counselor characteristics and discrete counseling skills are identified and established as criteria for effective counseling (cf. Conklin, Altmann, and Boak 1976; Duncan, Korb, and Loesch 1979; Menne 1975; Springer and Brammer

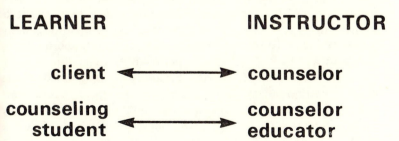

LEARNER   **INSTRUCTOR**

client ⟷ counselor

counseling student ⟷ counselor educator

Figure 9:1. Parallel learner-instructor roles

1971; Winborn, Hinds, and Steward 1971). This move has made the task of observing counselor behavior easier and has facili tated the establishment of specific objectives for counselor train ing programs (cf. Winborn, Hinds, and Stewart 1971). However the central assumption remains the same. Counseling is seen to comprise a set of counselor characteristics or behaviors, and counselor effectiveness is the degree to which counselors dem onstrate these characteristics or make appropriate use of these counseling skills. From the perspective of instructional counsel ing, this structural emphasis, while important, is not sufficien to ensure the training of effective counselors. It must be com bined with intentional and functional elements (see discussion in chapter 1). Counseling students must not only learn to per form specific counseling actions, they must learn to perform these actions in purposeful ways that result in client learning consistent with counseling objectives.

A MODEL FOR TRAINING INSTRUCTIONAL COUNSELORS

The five-component instructional framework of goals, pre assessment, objectives, instructional activities, and evaluation is at once an appropriate model for both counseling and counselo training.

Goals

It will be recalled from chapter 2 that there are three necessary conditions that must be met in order for learning to occur: what is to be learned needs to be specified meaningfully, appropriate learning practice must be arranged, and the learner must receive feedback about his/her practice. The instructional counterparts of these three conditions are structuring, soliciting, and reacting (see figure 2:2). To provide specification, practice, and feedback for client learning, the instructional counselor structures, solic its, and reacts to client activity. Similarly, counselor educators must structure, solicit, and react to provide specification, prac tice, and feedback to student counselors learning counseling skills and strategies. One general goal of the counselor training program is to ensure that these conditions are met. The coun selor educator's initial task is to identify subject matter content and general program goals. These usually are related to the theoretical orientations of the instructors involved in the counseling program (e.g., Adlerian, behavioral, cognitive, Rogerian, and so on). Specifying content and program goals helps to add meaning to the universe of possible inclusions in a counselor training program, affects the practice experiences utilized in the counseling program, and affects the type and manner of feedback the counseling student receives. Of course, the overriding general goal is to have counselor trainees learn how to do instructional counseling. From our perspective this will be accomplished most readily if the three necessary elements for learning and their instructional counterparts are modeled consistently within the counselor-educator–counseling student interaction.

Preassessment
A fundamental aspect of sound instruction is the tailoring of instructional experience to the needs and abilities of the learner. This is possible only when an instructor ascertains the learner's present repertoire of content-related skills and knowledge. This task is no less important when the instructor-learner dyad consists of counselor-educator–counseling student than when the dyad consists of counselor-client (see figure 9:1). Traditionally, attempts to determine student entering behavior typically have included such things as personal interviews with prospective students, written papers on counseling orientation, submission of tapes depicting counseling style, references from supervisors, written examinations, and undergraduate grade point average. The attempt is to screen out unsuitable candidates rather than to match program activities to levels of student expertise. Once admitted to a program, all students typically receive the same input regardless of differing levels of entering behavior.

From the vantage point of instructional counseling, counselor-educators probably should pay more attention to using preassessment data as a basis for tailoring counselor training experiences to student entry capabilities. This probably will increase the probability that counselor-educators will be effective in promoting desired student learning. It simply makes sense to start counselor training from where students currently are. To do this requires a solid preassessment of relevent stu-

dent entering capabilities (skills and knowledge) upon admis
sion to the training program.

Objectives

After program goals have been established and learner enter
ing behavior has been determined, specific instructional objec
tives can be set. In counselor education, it is helpful to conside
two types of objectives: objectives that focus on what th
instructor and the learner are doing and objectives that focus o
the projected effect that these activities will have on learne
behavior. These objectives determine the instructional activitie
contained in classes, seminars, and practica experiences. All c
these activities are designed and chosen with specific outcome
in mind. The counseling student engages in activities designe
to teach both process skills (e.g., skills in communications, rela
tionship building, specific intervention strategies) and evalua
tion skills (e.g., skill in observation, monitoring, recording
charting). Further, the counseling student must be able to trans
fer these skills into clinical settings for the purpose of promotin
client change. For example, counseling students may engage i
role-play activities, with counselor educator feedback, for th
purpose of developing the ability to perceive and reflect verba
content. Such objectives concern the degree to which th
counselor-educator is able to engage students in meaningfu
activities and provide specific and supportive feedback and th
degree to which the students are able to demonstrate accurat
verbal reflection. On a second level, if these objectives hav
been met, the counseling student should be able to demonstrat
an appropriate use of these specific skills when working wit
clients. Finally, the use of these skills should be accompanied b
targeted client change. The ultimate test of whether or not th
counselor-educator's objectives have been met lies in the abilit
of the counseling students to use the skills they have learned t
produce client change.

Instructional activities

The instructional skills and activities outlined in this book ar
applicable both to counseling and counselor training. The in
structional skills used by the counselor educator are the sam

skills as those used by the counselor. The subject matter may differ from instructing an individual client in problem solving to instructing a group of counseling students in preassessment procedures. The specific skills used at any one time may differ, depending on whether the instruction is taking place in a group context or with an individual, and may vary according to the subject matter being taught. However, the specific skills used are still a subset of the structuring, soliciting, and reacting skills discussed in chapter 2. Moreover, the same intentional, structural, and functional elements that earmark instructional counseling should be present in those counselor-educator-counseling student interchanges in which instruction is intended to take place. (There are many interactions in which instruction is not the focal purpose—e.g., interactions during lunch or around the coffee machine, informal discussions, or debates. Our comments in this section have been intended only for those interchanges in which instruction is the goal.) Some examples of key instructional activities are discussed later in this chapter under the heading "Program Content."

Evaluation

Within an instructional framework, evaluation is always carried out in the manner specified in the objectives. When objectives contain both a statement of intended outcome and a statement of the procedure for determining whether the outcome has been achieved, evaluation procedures are decided before intervention begins. This puts the instructor in the position of being able to evaluate counseling or training on an ongoing basis. The goal of counseling, i.e., the purpose of the specific instructional activities utilized, remains constant. Ellis (1977) points out that teaching skills to clients without maintaining a clear notion of the purpose for acquiring such skills is likely to result in rapid but superficial changes in client functioning, client self-deception, and ultimate retrogression. The statement is probably equally true when the words *counseling students* are substituted for *clients*. Counseling from an instructional perspective and structuring counselor training programs according to proper instructional criteria promote a goal-oriented approach in which such problems are less likely to occur.

PROGRAM CONTENT

The specific content of any counselor training program will be
function, in part, of the program's foci (e.g., school counseling
family counseling, adolescent corrections, etc.) and the thec
retical orientation of the people working in the program (e.g
Adlerian, cognitive, behavioral, Gestalt, Rogerian, etc.). How
ever, two broad content categories likely will be present in th
training of instructional counselors: (1) a substantive componer
and (2) a practical component.

Substantive component
It follows that if one accepts the proposition that counseling
instructional in nature, acquiring a sound theoretical base i
learning and instruction must be an integral part of any cour
selor training program. If counselors hope to foster client learr
ing, they must have a good idea of how people learn. Further,
counselors wish that learning to be purposeful, rather than hap
hazard or incidental, they must know what kinds of activities c
their part are likely to produce client learning. Therefore, a goo
foundation in theories of learning and instruction is essential. I
noncounseling instructional settings, it has been found tha
increasing substantive background in learning theory and ir
structional methodology also has increased student learnir
(Good 1979). Because of the functional emphasis on clien
change in instructional counseling, some preparation in obse
vation, assessment, and evaluation procedures also will be a ke
part of a counselor training program with an instructional focu
In most cases, it would be advisable to augment these two sul
stantive areas with the usual "core courses" found in most cour
selor training programs—theories of counseling, personalit
developmental psychology, research and design, and so on. Th
specific courses offered in any one program will reflect the focu
of the program and the theoretical biases of the faculty; how
ever, the foregoing substantive preparation is likely to be con
mon to most instructional counseling programs.

Practical component
The practical component of an instructional counselor trainir
program should contain three central elements: (1) some pr

cedure by which students can acquire basic instructional counseling skills and strategies, (2) a plan for practicing these skills in a clinical setting (practicum), and (3) some procedure for supervising the practicum work. In our own counseling training programs, we have found that massed practice of generic counseling skills, followed by spaced practice in combining these skills into basic intervention strategies, is a useful procedure for acquiring initial facility in the use of basic *instructional counseling skills and strategies.* The generic skills discussed in chapter 2 are presented within the threefold context of structuring, soliciting, and reacting, together with the corresponding learning conditions to which these skills relate—meaningful specification, practice, and feedback. Thus, the student's focus in the practical component of the training program is on the use of skills with some functional intent. Typically, we begin with structuring or soliciting skills because these skills already are most well developed with our students (preassessment procedures are used to determine the most appropriate place to begin, the guiding rule of thumb being to "begin in areas of strength and to add to an existing skill repertoire").

In peer *microcounseling* situations, students are given opportunities to practice specified instructional skills and to receive specific, descriptive feedback about their skill practice. Once an acceptable repetoire of generic instructional counseling skills has been established, the focus shifts to combining these skills into counseling strategies. Typically, the theoretical bases for the strategies are discussed, practice guidelines are specified, and simulated practice of the component parts of the strategies is undertaken. This instructional procedure provides opportunities for trainers to model appropriate uses of given intervention strategies, to coach appropriate student behavior, and to provide reinforcing feedback to successful student performances.

As students successfully demonstrate their facility with basic counseling skills in simulated settings, it becomes appropriate for them to begin to practice the same skills in actual clinical settings. This is usually accomplished via some *practicum* arrangement where the student spends a specified amount of time in a real clinical setting, working on real problems, with real clients, under the tutelage of an on-site supervisor. The counseling practicum is perhaps the most central component of most counselor training programs. However, within an instructional framework, certain levels of expertise are required prior to engaging in direct counseling practice. The instructional counselor must have a knowledge of learning theory, instructional methodology, and counseling theory and must have attained a repertoire of basic counseling skills and strategies. These are all necessary preconditions if the counselor is to know what to teach the client, how to teach it, and how to tell when learning has occurred. Once these preconditions have been attained, the counseling student is ready to interact with clients in a supervised practicum. Again, if the practicum is to be a learning experience for the student, it must provide the opportunity for careful skill specification, focused practice, and precise feedback.

To facilitate meaningfulness in skill practice, most practicum settings make some provision for the counseling student to observe and/or participate in the ongoing casework of the on-site supervisor and/or other counselors working in the practicum setting. In addition, an experienced counselor (usually the on-site supervisor) observes the student counselor's *in vivo* practice and offers instructionally useful feedback immediately after the student's counseling sessions. This observation may be via video- or audiotape or may involve the supervisor sitting in on a counseling session, either as a participant-observer or as a silent observer, depending on the arrangements made among the student, the supervisor, and the client(s). If such observations are to be instructional for the student, it is important that observation guidelines be specified clearly and that some systematic procedure for recording observations be agreed upon so that feedback to the student is specific and descriptive (Martin 1983).

Emphasis on the purposeful behavior of instructional counselors necessitates one additional requirement not found in most practicum observation procedures. Some interaction between the student and the supervisor must take place before the counseling student's session is observed. If the supervisor is going to offer specific feedback concerning the counseling student's purposeful use of counseling skills to foster client change, the supervisor must know in advance what the student proposes to do. With this information, the supervisor can observe the counseling session from a more meaningful perspective, and the feedback he/she gives to the student can be given within the context of what the student counselor intended. One procedure that we have found particularly useful in structuring practicum supervision is the *instructional supervision cycle* (based upon earlier work by Cogan 1973 and Goldhammer 1969) shown in figure 9:2. This cycle consists of four distinct steps: (1) precounseling conference, (2) counseling and observation, (3) descriptive analysis of counseling, and (4) postcounseling conference (see Martin, Hiebert, and Marx 1981).

The instructional supervision cycle can be enacted by two individuals (a supervisor and a counselor) or by a single counselor skilled in systematic self-observation, perhaps with video- or audiotape to assist in the observation component of the cycle.

The *precounseling conference* is perhaps the most important step in the instructional supervision cycle. In the precounseling conference, the session objectives are outlined, the counseling skills used to meet these objectives are identified, and observation and recording procedures are spelled out. The counselor specifies the session objectives in terms of observable client actions that will be demonstrated during, or at the conclusion of, the session. The main counseling skills to be used are then outlined along with the rationale for the use of those particular skills and their intended effects on the client. Usually this includes some indication of whether or not the skills being used are having the desired effect; that is, whether they are fostering the attainment of session objectives. During this discussion, the supervisor engages in as much clarification as is necessary to ensure that the counselor and supervisor share common perceptions of what is going to happen. When there is agreement between counselor and supervisor over the session objectives and skills to be used, the observation and recording procedures are discussed. The supervisor may make anecdotal recordings of the counselor's use of the skills to be observed, along with client reactions before and after the skill is used, or may devise some more elaborate way for coding frequency of occurrence and functional effects of the skills to be observed. In any case, the

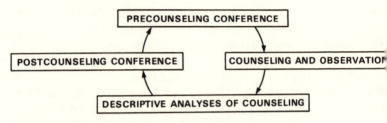

Figure 9:2. The instructional supervision cycle

counselor and supervisor decide together how the observation will be done. At the conclusion of the precounseling conference both the counselor and supervisor should have a clear and shared understanding of specific counseling objectives, the interactive skills to be focused on, and the precise methods to be used in observing and recording the use and effects of those skills. This shared understanding is crucial to the entire supervisory process for it helps to ensure that postcounseling feedback will be perceived by the counselor to be both fair and relevant.

The precounseling conference is followed by *direct observation of the counseling session*. During the counseling session, the supervisor monitors the focal counseling skills using the procedures agreed upon in the preconference. In addition, client learning in relation to session objectives, and client cues used as indicators of that learning, also must be monitored.

This is not to suggest that session objectives must be pursued regardless of client reaction. Unanticipated events encountered in counseling sessions can sometimes make the counseling game plan inappropriate. This fact does not negate the worthwhileness of counselor planning, since the process and skills involved in purposeful planning for counseling are valuable and important in their own right. In situations where unanticipated events suggest abandoning or altering the precounseling plan, the student counselor should be able to formulate new objectives and identify the subset of skills she/he will use to achieve those objectives and work according to the new game plan. In some cases, it may not be possible to inform the supervisor of the change in objectives or of the different skills involved. In such cases, the supervisor's observations might lack some of the specificity and appropriateness to the new objectives that make for optimal student learning. However, such cases typically represent a small proportion of the student counselor's total practice sessions. If the observation is being conducted using videotape, it is possible for the counselor to inform the supervisor about changes in plan, counseling skills, and objectives prior to joint observation of the videotape. In most cases involving direct observation of the counseling session, it is possible for the student simply to turn to the supervisor and inform him/her of the change and then continue. Such informing can be of benefit to the client as well, helping to put subsequent counselor-client interactions in a more meaningful context.

Following the counseling session, the counselor and supervisor both should spend a brief interval alone so that they can organize their observations into precise and specific accounts of what transpired. This is referred to as the *descriptive analysis* of counseling. The emphasis here is on a *descriptive* account of what happened. Were the counseling objectives met? Were the focal skills used by the counselor? How often? In what context? Did the use of focal skills help the client meet the objectives? All of these questions should be answerable with descriptive statements. Both counselor and supervisor should be careful to avoid making inferences and value judgments about the use of counseling skills or about the events that took place. Most counselors in training tend to be unduly critical about their performance. This self-criticism tends to interfere with their ability to be descriptive and objective about what transpired in the counseling session. It is only when counselors can make descriptive statements about their own performances in counseling interactions that they are in a position to give themselves the kind of specific feedback that will allow them to self-instruct.

After the observations and perceptions of both counselor and supervisor are formed into descriptive accounts, they are ready to be shared in a *postcounseling conference*. The postcounseling conference should incorporate the characteristics of feedback that enhance learning, that is, the feedback should be immediate, descriptive, specific, positive, and encouraging (Martin

1983). Vague comments, casual speculations, and formalistic value judgments should be avoided. The discussion in the post-counseling conference should be confined largely to the areas outlined in the precounseling conference. This practice helps to alleviate student-counselor anxiety about being supervised. The counselor and supervisor decided together on the focus of observation and methods for observing. When this agenda is adhered to in the postcounseling conference, the counselor learns that the supervisor can be trusted to stick to an agreement, and potentially threatening surprises are kept to a minimum. When obvious difficulties are observed, informational feedback accompanied by suggested (or modeled) alternatives reduces the likelihood of defensive student-counselor reactions and seems to enhance learning. It is usually best to address such suggestions at the end of the postcounseling period, after discussion of the descriptive accounts of the current session has concluded and plans for future sessions are being formulated. In this way, one postcounseling conference leads naturally to the next precounseling conference.

The structure of the postcounseling conference should encourage, as much as possible, the counselor to observe and evaluate his/her own performance. It is usually a good practice for the supervisor to begin the postcounseling conference by allowing the counselor to share his/her descriptive analysis of what happened and then to augment and elaborate the counselor's account with descriptive comments from the supervisor's observational record. Thus, the entire instructional supervision cycle can become, with practice, a means for counselors to learn to observe and evaluate their own counseling performance. The following instructions to counseling students illustrate and summarize the whole procedure.

> Before each counseling session, you and your supervisor (either on-site supervisor or faculty supervisor) should sit down during a *precounseling conference* and discuss what you plan to do in the next counseling session. Generally speaking, the goals for counseling should be clear to both you and your client. Further, you should be able to specify your objectives for a particular counseling session,

the skills you intend to use to achieve those objectives, and the client and process cues that will tell you whether the objectives are being met or whether some alternative plans (objectives and strategies) are more appropriate. After specific objectives and appropriate counseling skills have been determined, you also should decide how the supervisor will observe and record your performance during the counseling session. You probably will find it advantageous to record (videotape or audiotape) your counseling session or to invite your supervisor to sit in on, or to participate in, your counseling session with you (*counseling and observation*). This process allows both you and the supervisor to zero in on specific elements of your counseling behavior. Following the counseling session, both you and the supervisor should take a few minutes alone to analyze and draw together your observations of the session in general and of your own performance in particular (*descriptive analysis*). Were the goals of the session attained? Did you make use of the specific counseling skills selected as appropriate during the precounseling conference? Was your use of these skills timely, appropriate, and powerful? How did the use of the skills contribute to the goals of the session? How did the client(s) react to the use of each skill? How did the skills selected match up with your own counseling style? Are there some skills that need to be practiced further? Are there other skills that would have worked better than those selected? What would you do differently next time? What skill areas would you select for immediate improvement? These same questions then should be pursued in dialogue between yourself and your supervisor during a *postcounseling conference*. Remember that during the postcounseling conference, it is your responsibility openly to accept feedback (positive or negative) about your skill practice so long as it is specific and oriented toward future skill development. It is the supervisor's responsibility to ensure that his/her comments are directed toward the goals and skills agreed upon during the precounseling conference; that these comments are tied to careful observations of the actual counseling session; and that his/her feedback is constructive and, in the final analysis, understood by you. Only with careful skill specification, focused practice, and precise feedback is it possible to build up an extensive repertoire of counseling skills and strategies. We find that when supervisors and students follow this instructional cycle it helps to ease the anxiety that is sometimes associated with being observed, helps to make formative supervision a learning experience, and gives good practice in developing a procedure that you can use to self-monitor your own clinical practice and to continue to develop as a professional counselor.

Professional Conduct

PREPARATION

Few professional issues are as relevant to practicing counselors as standards for counselor training. The cry for more qualified counselors is heard almost continuously in public schools government agencies, and business/industrial establishments In-house training programs often are mounted to upgrade pro fessional qualifications and skill repertoires of practicing coun selors (cf. Bezanson and DeCoff 1981; Roessler and Rubin 1980 Rosove 1981). Few would deny that the attitudes, mannerisms and methods attained during counselor training have a grea impact on the way in which counselors function after gradua tion. Throughout this chapter, we have emphasized the im portance of acquiring a solid theoretical background and a reasonable repertoire of counseling skills before counselor trainees begin interacting with clients. We believe that adequate preparation prior to initiating counseling interventions with other people is an ethical responsibility of training programs and counselor educators. When the focus of training is on the development of purposeful behavior that counselors can employ to produce change in clients, there is no substitute for such conceptual, theoretical preparation.

CLIENT CONSENT

In instructional counseling, care must be taken to avoid other areas of potential ethical concern. When using the instructional supervision cycle or other procedures involving any kind of intrusion into normal client-counselor interactions, assurances must be given to protect client confidentiality. Client permission must be obtained before audio- or videotape recordings are made and before direct observation by a supervisor is undertaken. Usually this is most easily accomplished via standard release forms that counselor and client both sign. Such forms specify safeguards for client confidentiality and outline the uses to which any record of the proceedings will be put. Clients are assisted in comprehending the forms thoroughly before they sign them.

Similar contractual procedures should be used by counselors to specify individual treatment programs, objectives, and evaluation procedures whenever instructional counseling is undertaken (see relevant discussion in chapter 2). Clients always have the right to be informed about counseling procedures and plans.

CLIENT INVOLVEMENT

We have emphasized throughout this book that counselor and client should work together to develop skills that the client can use to resolve, or to cope more effectively with, currently troublesome situations. We have underlined the necessity for obtaining client permission before consulting with medical, family, or other relevant persons. We repeatedly have stated that the client is involved fully in setting counseling objectives and evaluating counseling success. The ultimate goal of instructional counseling is for the client to demonstrate the ability to self-instruct. In order for this to happen, the client must be part of the intervention process from its very inception. Keeping clients informed of the systematic, purposeful nature of instructional counseling helps to demystify the counseling process. Such open sharing of counseling process revolves around the notions that people encounter difficulties when they are in situations for which they lack skills and that learning requisite skills helps to resolve most difficulties. Developing these client attitudes helps to promote client independence and helps the counselor avoid the moral and ethical double bind resulting from client dependency. The instructional counseling process is an active process, with the counselor taking the initiative to provide supportive structure for the counseling interactions. The process is not an autocratic one. The counselor engages clients at each step, informing them of the component parts of the counseling intervention and securing their permission before proceeding to the next step. We feel that this kind of professional conduct is fundamentally important to continued client well-being.

COUNSELOR AFFILIATIONS

Counseling is a broad label used to describe a wide range of people and occupational settings. Counselors work as social workers, corrections workers, parole officers, rehabilitation counselors, school counselors, family counselors, employment counselors, occupational therapists, psychiatric nurses, and psychologists. While the nature of one's counseling context will determine professional reference groups, it is important for practicing counselors to have some professional affiliation if they wish to remain current in their knowledge of counseling skills and practices. Most counselors acknowledge benefit from membership in such large national organizations as the American Association for Counseling and Development (AACD), Canadian Guidance and Counselling Association (CGCA), and appropriate divisions of the Canadian Psychological Association (CPA), the American Psychological Association (APA), and the American Educational Research Association (AERA). In addition, membership in more highly specialized associations (e.g., the Registered Psychiatric Nursing Association—RPNA) and in local state/provincial associations can be useful with respect to special counseling concerns and immediate resources. Professional publications, conferences, and newsletters sponsored by such organizations inform counselors about their occupational fields, new intervention strategies, the comparative effectiveness of alternative counseling approaches, professional training opportunities, job possibilities, and ethical standards for professional conduct.

Membership in professional organizations and the necessity to "remain current" are probably best considered to be individual professional responsibilities at this time. In most states and provinces, legislation governing the certification, licencing, and continuing education of counselors is at a developmental stage. Most states and provinces have some legislation governing the certification, licencing, and continuing education of professionals such as physicians and psychologists. Such legislation helps to ensure that professionals will be qualified to practice, will continue to learn after they are working in the field, and will not let their knowledge atrophy. In the field of counseling, there are few external pressures to "remain current," but the need is no less important. At this time, the most the committed counselor can do is to make sure his/her own professional house is in order. It is hoped that, many of the discussions and descriptions of counseling theory and practice presented in this book will help many counselors to do just that.

Chapter Summary

In this chapter we have described a training program for instructional counselors. This model for counselor training followed the same five-step model for instruction that has been a constant theme throughout this book. The training program, as described, had two main components: (1) a substantive component with emphasis on theories of learning, instruction, counseling, and evaluation and (2) a practical component emphasizing the gradual acquisition of counseling skills and strategies. The chapter concluded with some comments on professional standards and professional affiliations, highlighting some ethical concerns and emphasizing the need for continuing professional development.

REFERENCES

Bezanson, L., DeCoff, C. 1981. Competency-based inservice program of the Canada Employment and Immigration Commission. *In*: G. G. Ross (ed.), *Workshop Presentations of the World Seminar on*

Employment Counselling. Ottawa: Employment and Immigration Canada.

Cogan, M. L. 1973. *Clinical Supervision*. Boston: Houghton Mifflin.

Conklin, R. C., Altmann, H. A., and Boak, T. 1976. The effect of a six-week program of systematic training on counsellors. *Canadian Counsellor* 10: 78–82.

Duncan, M. V., Korb, M. P., and Loesch, L. C. 1979. Competency counselor training for paraprofessionals. *Counselor Education and Supervision* 18: 223–31.

Ellis, A. Skill Training in Counselling and Psychotherapy. *Canadian Counsellor*, 1977, 12: 30–35.

Goldhammer, R. 1969. *Clinical Supervision*. New York: Holt, Rinehart & Winston.

Good, T. L. 1979. Teacher effectiveness in the elementary school. *Journal of Teacher Education* 30: 52–64.

Martin, J. 1983. *Mastering Instruction*. Boston: Allyn and Bacon.

————, Hiebert, B. A., and Marx, R. W. 1981. Instructional supervision in counselor training. *Counselor Education and Supervision* 20: 193–202.

Menne, J. M. 1975. A comprehensive set of counselor competencies. *Journal of Counseling Psychology* 22: 547–53.

Roessler, R. T., and Rubin, S. E. 1980. Advanced facilitative case management series: Training package. Unpublished manuscript. Arkansas Rehabilitation and Research and Training Center, College of Education, University of Arkansas, Fayetteville, Arkansas.

Rosove, B. 1981. Place: Guided steps to employment readiness. In G. G. Ross (ed.), *Workshop Presentations of the World Seminar on Employment Counselling*. Ottawa: Employment and Immigration Canada.

Springer, H. C., and Brammer, L. M. 1971. A tentative model to identify elements of the counseling process and parameters of counselor behavior. *Counselor Education and Supervision* 11: 8–16.

Winborn, B. C., Hinds, W. C., and Stewart, N. R. 1971. Instructional objectives for the professional preparation of counselors. *Counselor Education and Supervision* 10: 133–37.

Recapitulation

INSTRUCTIONAL COUNSELING is a comprehensive, conceptual framework for counseling within which it is possible to relate specific counseling practices to a general model of instruction in a direct, nondogmatic manner. Clear comprehension of the five-step instructional model that forms the basis of instructional counseling can assist counselors in clarifying counseling roles, processes, and actions. The model helps counselors to make decisions about what to do when confronted by different clients with different problems, desires, and abilities.

Counseling interventions conceptualized within an instructional framework should have a clear instructional purpose, should encompass discrete skills and strategies consistent with this purpose, and should result in the attainment of relevant client learning. These basic elements of intention, structure, and function should be evident in counseling programs in areas such as decision making/problem solving, skill training, personal coping, and self-management. The same elements should be considered with respect to counselor training and the evaluation of counseling.

This book has attempted to show how a basic instructional process consisting of five steps (goals, preassessment, objectives, activities, and evaluation) provides an adequate basis for the consideration of counseling purposes (intentions), processes (structures), and products (functions) in a number of basic counseling areas. It provides an instructional framework for counseling that differs significantly from prevailing models of counseling that are cast predominantly within medical, psychological, or broad humanistic frames of reference.

Index

Contemporary Community Health Series

A Mad People's History of Madness
Dale Peterson, Editor

A Mind That Found Itself
Clifford W. Beers

The Psychiatric Halfway House: A Handbook of Theory and Practice
Richard D. Budson

Racism and Mental Health: Essays
Charles V. Willie, Bernard M. Kramer, and Bertram S. Brown,
    Editors

The Sociology of Physical Disability and Rehabilitation
Gary L. Albrecht, Editor

In cooperation with the Institute on Human Values in Medicine:

Medicine and Religion: Strategies of Care
Donald W. Shriver, Editor

*Nourishing the Humanistic in Medicine: Interactions with the Social
    Sciences*
William R. Rogers and David Barnard, Editors